Bahá'í Faith

BLOOMSBURY GUIDES FOR THE PERPLEXED

Bloomsbury's Guides for the Perplexed are clear, concise and accessible introductions to thinkers, writers and subjects that students and readers can find especially challenging. Concentrating specifically on what it is that makes the subject difficult to grasp, these books explain and explore key themes and ideas, guiding the reader towards a thorough understanding of demanding material.

Bahá'í Faith

ROBERT H. STOCKMAN

BLOOMSBURY

LONDON · NEW DELHI · NEW YORK · SYDNEY

Bloomsbury Academic
An imprint of Bloomsbury Publishing Plc

50 Bedford Square	175 Fifth Avenue
London	New York
WC1B 3DP	NY 10010
UK	USA

www.bloomsbury.com

First published 2013

© Robert H. Stockman, 2013

British Library Cataloguing-in-Publication Data
A catalogue record for this book is available from the British Library.

ISBN: HB: 978-1-4411-3396-0
PB: 978-1-4411-9201-1
ePDF: 978-1-4411-0447-2
ePub: 978-1-4411-8781-9

Library of Congress Cataloging-in-Publication Data
Stockman, Robert H., 1953–
Bahá'í faith : a guide for the perplexed / Robert H. Stockman. – First [edition].
pages cm – (Guides for the perplexed)
Summary: 'Founded by Bah'u'llah in Iran in the 19th century, the Bahá'í Faith is one of the youngest of the world's major religions. Though it has over 5 million followers worldwide, it is still little understood outside of its own community. The Bahá'í Faith: A Guide for the Perplexed explores the utopian vision of the Bahá'í Faith including its principles for personal spiritual transformation and for the construction of spiritualized marriages, families, Bahá'í communities, and, ultimately, a spiritual world civilization.
Aimed at students seeking a thorough understanding of this increasingly studied religion, this book is the ideal companion to studying and understanding the Bahá'í Faith, its teachings and the history of its development.' – Provided by publisher.
Includes bibliographical references and index.
ISBN 978-1-4411-3396-0 (hardback) – ISBN 978-1-4411-9201-1 (paperback) – ISBN 978-1-4411-8781-9 (ebookepub)
1. Bahai Faith. I. Title.
BP365.S77 2012
297.9'3 – dc23
2012011034

Typeset by Newgen Imaging Systems Pvt Ltd, Chennai, India
Printed and bound in India

To Nabil

CONTENTS

ACKNOWLEDGEMENTS

This book would have been impossible without the encouragement, wise advice and mentoring I have received from many
Bahá'ís over 38 years, my doctoral studies at Harvard Divinity
School, my 23 years of service at the Bahá'í National Centre in the
United States and my 22 years of part time instruction in religious
studies at DePaul University. My colleagues on the Tarikh listserv
for Bahá'í history, who collectively generate over 5,000 emails per
year on a wide variety of subjects, have been encouraging and have
provided critical comments on the text as it went through various
drafts. Particularly helpful have been comments by Loni Bramson,
Christopher Buck, Marleen Chase, Steve Cooney, Mark Foster,
Omid Ghaemmaghami, Daniel Grolin, Jan Jasion, Anthony Lee,
Susan Maneck, Sen McGlinn, Moojan Momen, Brent Poirier, Julio
Savi, Peter Smith, Peter Terry, Phillip Tussing and Ismael Velasco.
Some of my colleagues on the Board of the United Religious
Community of Saint Joseph County, Indiana – the interfaith organ-
ization for the region – have read the manuscript and provided
very helpful suggestions: Bradley Bohrer, Leonard Jepson, Carol
Mayernick and John Pinter. Iraj Ayman, Manuchehr Derakhshani
and Roland Faber provided essential advice about specific aspects
of the project. Hugh McNamara carefully read through the entire
manuscript and caught many typos and grammatical errors.

I am thankful to my wife, Mana, my daughter, Lua, and my
son, Nabil, for their endurance and support for the project as it has
taken me from them. Having dedicated books to Mana and Lua,
Nabil, who is named for the famous historian of the Bábí Faith,
gets the honour this time.

CHAPTER ONE

A religion of the word

The Bahá'í Faith* started in Iran a century and a half ago and soon became an independent religion that spread around the globe. Arising out of the matrix of Shi'ite Islam, within half a century its membership had expanded to include Sunni Muslims, Jews, Zoroastrians, Burmese Buddhists, Orthodox Christians, Catholics, Protestants and Hindus. Parts of its sacred scripture have been translated into over 800 languages. Its teachings of world unity, equality of all peoples and a life of prayer and service have, at this writing (2012), attracted some five or six million followers, residing in almost every nation and significant territory in the world.

Any study of the Bahá'í Faith must begin with its founding figures and the prodigious writings they produced in order to express their teachings. There are three of them: the Báb, Bahá'u'lláh and 'Abdu'l-Bahá (their birth names and the details of their lives and ministries will be covered in later chapters). The Báb (1819–50) started a religion, the Bábí Faith, in 1844. He claimed to be a Manifestation (messenger) of God, succeeding Muhammad, Jesus and a series of earlier divine teachers. His claim was extremely controversial and resulted in his execution. Many of his writings were lost but 2,000 unique works – in Arabic and Persian – many of

---

*Bahá'ís use *Bahá'í Faith* (with a capital F) as the proper name of their religion. The term Bahá'í is pronounced ba-HA-ee or ba-HIGH. Academics increasingly have adopted it. Bahá'ís dislike the term Bahaism as demeaning.

The Bahá'í Faith adopted an official system for transliterating Persian and Arabic words into the Roman alphabet in 1923. It was based on a system adopted by an Orientalist Congress in the late 1890s. Tens of thousands of books, pamphlets, periodicals and other documents have been published in it, the Worldwide Web has spread it and it is gradually becoming universal.

which are lengthy treatises, have survived, comprising at least five million words. They are considered scripture by Bahá'ís. Because many of his teachings were intended to be replaced or modified by *He whom God shall make manifest* (the Promised One of the Bábí Faith, whom Bahá'u'lláh claimed to be), relatively few of his writings have been translated into English. The Báb's remarkable life, his short and dramatic ministry, the surprising events surrounding his execution by firing squad and the turbulent movement he started, constitute one of the most remarkable chapters in the history of the nineteenth century.** The vast majority of his followers, if they survived the pogroms against them, accepted Bahá'u'lláh and became Bahá'ís in the 1860s and 1870s.

Bahá'u'lláh*** (1817–92) became a follower of the Báb in 1844 and was the founder of the Bahá'í Faith. His life was one of exile and great suffering for his teachings. The Bahá'í World Centre in Haifa, Israel, has some 18,000 unique works by him, in Arabic and Persian, comprising over six million words. Approximately 8 per cent has been translated into English.[1] The texts as a whole identify themselves as divine revelation and the Word of God. Bahá'u'lláh used many genres: poetry, the treatise, the book and the epistle. The bulk of his writings are letters, some private missives to individuals, some public ones to rulers or enemies of the Faith. His teachings, elaborated in writing over a 40-year period (1853–92), focused initially on the mystic relation of the individual with God and on the nature of God and religion, then expanded to include the laws and ordinances for creating a religious community (the Bahá'í community) and principles for constructing a unified world civilization.

'Abdu'l-Bahá (1844–1921) was Bahá'u'lláh's son and chief assistant, and succeeded him as head of the Faith in 1892, upon Bahá'u'lláh's passing. He was also remarkably prolific; 30,000 unique works by him are extant, in Arabic, Persian and Ottoman Turkish, comprising over five million words. All but four are letters. Since 'Abdu'l-Bahá was not a Manifestation, his writings are not considered the Word of God, but as the 'Mystery of God'

**The Báb and the Bábís are the subject of Chapter Six.

***Pronounced ba-HA-oo-LA. His life and literary corpus will be described in Chapter Seven. The process of revelation that he experienced is described in Chapter Three.

(as Bahá'u'lláh called him) they are considered a part of Bahá'í scripture. 'Abdu'l-Bahá oversaw the expansion of the Bahá'í Faith beyond the Middle East, North Africa and Central and South Asia, to North America, Europe, Latin America, East Asia and Australia. His travels to Europe and North America (1911–13) brought the Bahá'í Faith to western audiences.****

The Bahá'í authoritative texts also include the writings of Shoghi Effendi Rabbani (1897–1957), 'Abdu'l-Bahá's grandson, whom 'Abdu'l-Bahá designated as his successor and *Guardian of the Cause of God*. Shoghi Effendi mastered English and French and studied for a time at Oxford University. He wrote over 34,000 unique works – in Arabic, Persian, English and French – comprising over five million words. All are letters, some of book length, except one, a history. Shoghi Effendi's station is less than 'Abdu'l-Bahá's; his writings are considered authoritative interpretation of the Word, but are not referred to as 'revealed', nor are they are part of Bahá'í scripture. During his 36 year ministry (1921–57) he built the Bahá'í organizational system – the Administrative Order – elaborated the principles on which it was to function, oversaw its establishment across the globe and laid the foundation for the election of the Universal House of Justice, the current coordinating institution for the Bahá'í Faith. He also translated Bahá'u'lláh's most important works into elegant English, began to build up the world centre of the Faith in Palestine (now Israel) and coordinated the expansion of the Bahá'í community to Latin America, sub-Saharan Africa and the Pacific islands.*****

The nine-member Universal House of Justice, whose authority and mode of election were defined in detail in the writings of Bahá'u'lláh, 'Abdu'l-Bahá and Shoghi Effendi, was first elected in 1963. It is re-elected every 5 years and is the head of the Bahá'í Faith today. It has an extensive staff to answer questions, which are often reviewed and approved by part or all of the House's membership, and as a body it produces various messages, some of considerable length. 'Abdu'l-Bahá and Shoghi Effendi described it to be infallible in matters of protecting the Bahá'í Faith, ensuring

---

****Chapter Eight will explore 'Abdu'l-Bahá's accomplishments in detail.
*****Chapter Nine will consider Shoghi Effendi's contributions to the Faith.

its unity and in legislating on matters not previously covered in Bahá'í authoritative texts. Its writings are thus authoritative as well, though they are not scripture. In the nearly 50 years since its establishment, it has overseen a 10 to 15-fold increase in the number of Bahá'ís worldwide (from about 400,000 to 5–6 million) and a huge expansion of Bahá'í efforts in external relations, use of the media, social and economic development, translation of Bahá'í scripture, scholarship and the arts.******

The chain of authority and the requirement of declared Bahá'ís to accept it is an aspect of the Bahá'í Covenant, about which more will be said later. No writings by a theologian or prominent Bahá'í can ever become a part of the authoritative texts; the texts themselves preclude this. Even oral transmissions of words attributed to the Báb, Bahá'u'lláh, 'Abdu'l-Bahá and Shoghi Effendi can never be added to the authoritative texts, unless they were approved by one of them (e.g. 'Abdu'l-Bahá read and corrected transcripts of many talks he had given, and Shoghi Effendi quoted words attributed to Bahá'u'lláh by an English scholar, Edward Granville Browne).

The extensive body of authoritative texts – excluding the output of the Universal House of Justice, 84,000 documents comprising at least 21 million words – has profound implications for the development of the Bahá'í community. One might say that the Bahá'í Faith is not a 'Religion of the Book', but a Religion of the Books (and increasingly of the scripture website and the app). One can find an authoritative statement on almost anything, from the nature of God to the raising of children, from the importance of music to the setting of interest rates, from the study of languages to the use of birth control. Because the Universal House of Justice is authorized to legislate, new problems and issues may eventually be the subject of authoritative guidance as well. Lest this slip into a detailed body of law, like the Islamic shari'ah, the texts also stress consulting ones conscience and relevant experts, leaving the final decision on many matters to the person or persons concerned. When individuals write to the head of the Faith seeking guidance about a specific issue, sometimes they are told they should resolve the matter personally after prayer, meditation and study of the texts.

******The results of the endeavours of the Universal House of Justice are the subjects of Chapters Ten and Eleven.

In spite of the detailed nature of the Bahá'í teachings, however, they demonstrate a logic of their own with an internal unity and consistency, as Part 1 of this work strives to show. 'One might liken Bahá'u'lláh's teachings to a sphere', noted a secretary of Shoghi Effendi, writing on his behalf. 'There are points poles apart, and in between the thoughts and doctrines that unite them'.[2] Central to understanding the Bahá'í teachings are the related concepts of oneness and unity. The oneness of humankind and the achievement of human unity is the subject of the next chapter. The unity and oneness of God, the nature of divine revelation and the world religions are the collective focus of Chapter Three. Chapters Four and Five explore the relationship of the individual with God and human beings, the latter in progressively larger circles: marriage, family and society. Part 2 of the book explores the history of the development of the worldwide Bahá'í community, starting with the ministry of the Báb, continuing through the ministries of Bahá'u'lláh, 'Abdu'l-Bahá and Shoghi Effendi, and culminating in the current era of the Universal House of Justice. The book concludes with a survey of the worldwide Bahá'í community today and its prospects for the future.

PART ONE

The Bahá'í teachings

CHAPTER TWO

The watchword: Unity

The concepts of *oneness* and *unity* are important starting points in understanding the Bahá'í Faith. The Faith has often been summarized as teaching three onenesses: the oneness of God, of religion and of humanity. The oneness of humanity is an ancient teaching; the statement that humans have been created in God's image (Gen. 1.26) is a statement of the oneness of humanity, for it describes an essence common to all. It powerfully unites humans in spite of race or gender and distinguishes them from lesser forms of life. Bahá'u'lláh describes the distinction between humans and other creatures thus: 'Upon the inmost reality of each and every created thing', God has 'shed the light of one of His* names, and made it a recipient of the glory of one of His attributes'. On the reality of human beings, however, God has 'focused the radiance of all of His names and attributes, and made it a mirror of His own Self'. He adds that 'alone of all created things', humanity has 'been singled out for so great a favor, so enduring a bounty'.[1]

To a spiritual definition of human oneness can be added a genetic definition. The Bahá'í authoritative texts note that all human beings come from the same stock[2] and are members of the same race. Such a concept can also be found in the Bible, which states that all humans are descended from Adam and Eve, ancestors (literally or metaphorically, depending on one's perspective) of all humanity.

For Bahá'u'lláh, the oneness of humanity has crucial ethical implications:

---

*Bahá'u'lláh's writings have been translated into English using male pronouns for God, even though those writings make it clear that God utterly transcends gender. I have retained the language as is, though I will not use male pronouns for the Divinity in my own writing.

Know ye not why We created you all from the same dust? That no one should exalt himself over the other. Ponder at all times in your hearts how ye were created. Since We have created you all from one same substance it is incumbent on you to be even as one soul, to walk with the same feet, eat with the same mouth and dwell in the same land, that from your inmost being, by your deeds and actions, the signs of oneness and the essence of detachment may be made manifest. Such is My counsel to you, O concourse of light![3]

In short, the oneness of humanity implies the need for the unity of all human beings. Shoghi Effendi describes the oneness of humankind as the 'pivot round which all the teachings of Bahá'u'lláh revolve'.[4] He refers to the Faith's 'watchword' alternately as 'unity' and 'unity in diversity'.[5] 'Abdu'l-Bahá added that the purpose of Bahá'u'lláh's life and the reason he endured enormous hardships – for Bahá'u'lláh was severely persecuted for his teachings – was to ensure that 'the oneness of humankind become a reality, strife and warfare cease and peace and tranquility be realized by all'.[6] A study of the Bahá'í notion of unity is a study of the central principle underlying the Bahá'í teachings. Unity is the backbone, to which the other teachings serve as lesser bones, muscles and nerves making up the body of Bahá'í teachings.

Unity as process

The Bahá'í concept of unity is described as an ongoing process with various levels or stages. The idealized form of unity is expressed in the metaphor that the Bahá'ís should be 'one soul in many bodies'.[7] This form of spiritual unity is rarely achieved in practice. 'Abdu'l-Bahá describes it in these words:

Another unity is the spiritual unity which emanates from the breaths of the Holy Spirit. . . . Human unity or solidarity may be likened to the body, whereas unity from the breaths of the Holy Spirit is the spirit animating the body. This is a perfect unity. It creates such a condition in mankind that each one will make sacrifices for the other, and the utmost desire will be to forfeit life and all that pertains to it in behalf of another's good. This is the unity which existed among the disciples of Jesus Christ and bound together the Prophets and holy Souls of the past. It is the unity which through the influence of the divine spirit is permeating the Bahá'ís so that each offers his life for the other and strives with all sincerity to attain his good pleasure.[8]

Spiritual unity is a goal behind many efforts of Bahá'ís. Almost every Bahá'í event starts with prayers from the Bahá'í scriptures in order to establish a spiritual atmosphere and invoke a spiritual dynamic that allows the gathering to achieve its true purpose.** The creation of spiritual unity is a principal purpose of the *Nineteen Day Feast,* the monthly Bahá'í community gathering for worship, consultation and socializing.[9] 'Abdu'l-Bahá composed a prayer to use at the start of meetings of *Spiritual Assemblies* (local or national Bahá'í coordinating councils) that asks that 'our thoughts, our views, our feelings may become as one reality, manifesting the spirit of union throughout the world';[10] a prayer designed to foster spiritual unity. Spiritual unity is also a goal of Bahá'í conventions, where spiritual assemblies are elected. Many Bahá'í prayer books contain a section titled 'meetings' filled with prayers that seek, in their poetic language and the divine power they invoke, to create spiritual unity.

'Abdu'l-Bahá contrasted 'spiritual unity' with a lesser form, 'human unity', a practical and collaborative unity. Bahá'u'lláh offers a pragmatic metaphor for it: 'be ye as the fingers of one hand, the members of one body.'[11] A hand needs fingers in order to function; a body depends on the complementary efforts of its organs. Spiritual unity, however, need not be achieved for unity in action to be possible. While spiritual unity is the ideal, a lower level of unity is adequate to work together and may be a stage in the path to creating spiritual unity. Efforts to work together are emphasized and highly praised in the Bahá'í authoritative texts, which state 'verily, God loveth those who are working in His path in groups, for they are a solid foundation'.[12]

** When Bahá'ís pray they almost always use written prayers revealed by Bahá'u'lláh and 'Abdu'l-Bahá, not prayers composed by themselves or by other Bahá'ís. In this way Bahá'í prayer is an act of reconnection to God's revelation.

The importance of education

Spiritual unity requires more than prayer and collaboration to be achieved. Issues of inequality and injustice must also be resolved. Education is one key need. Bahá'u'lláh says that human beings are 'a mine rich in gems of inestimable value. Education can, alone, cause it to reveal its treasures, and enable mankind to benefit therefrom'.[13] Education requires literacy, both to read the Word of God and to acquire the sciences, arts and cultural knowledge. He calls on his followers to 'be busied in whatever may be conducive to the betterment of the world and the education of its peoples'.[14] In his book of laws (1873), Bahá'u'lláh obligates parents to educate their children and even advocates that teachers be included in one's will. The Bahá'í authoritative texts describe aspects of a universal curriculum that should include science, the arts, the humanities and world religion. A key theme of education should be the oneness of humanity.

In Iran, the Bahá'í community achieved near-universal literacy over a half century ago in a country that still had high levels of illiteracy, and made important contributions to the development of Iranian education.[15] For decades, Bahá'í communities in less-developed parts of the world have organized special literacy classes for all adults or for women, and have set up schools to educate local children. In the last decade, study circles for adults and classes for children, junior youth (ages 12–14) and youth (ages 15–20) have become standard features of Bahá'í community life everywhere. Such classes do not focus primarily on imparting knowledge of Bahá'í scripture, but on developing skills that strengthen community life or on understanding and expressing virtues. They include exercises to help participants learn how to read and understand texts and to provide opportunities to use the arts. Quoting the Qur'án (39:12; 13:17), 'Abdu'l-Bahá rhetorically asks 'Are they equal, those who know, and those who do not know? . . . Or is the darkness equal with the light?'[16] The unity of humankind is dependent on the universal dissemination of education.

Unity in diversity

Education alone, however, cannot wipe out inequality between people based on race, gender and class. Bahá'u'lláh proclaimed that

'God hath . . . as a bounty from His presence, abolished the concept of "uncleanness", whereby divers things and peoples have been held to be impure'.[17] This refers to a traditional Muslim practice of refusing to associate closely with non-believers on the grounds that they were unclean, and that their use of eating and drinking utensils made the utensils unclean. Bahá'u'lláh forbade slavery, something neither the Bible nor the Qur'án attempted. He encouraged the Bahá'ís in the Middle East and South Asia (which constituted virtually all the Bahá'ís in the world in his day) to reach out to minorities, with the result that in the late nineteenth-century Iranian Zoroastrians and Jews, Sunni Muslims, Syrian and Egyptian Christians and Burmese Buddhists joined and diversified a religious community that was otherwise primarily of Shi'ite Muslim background. He also stated that 'it is incumbent upon each one of you to engage in some occupation – such as a craft, a trade or the like' because 'we have exalted your engagement in such work to the rank of worship of the one true God' and he made no exception for women, thereby implying the right of women to pursue an occupation.[18]

'Abdu'l-Bahá oversaw the spread of the Bahá'í Faith to the west, starting in 1894. The American Bahá'í community attracted African Americans as early as 1898. In 1899, Robert Turner, an African American butler, went on pilgrimage to Acre,*** Palestine, to meet 'Abdu'l-Bahá. In 1910 Louis Gregory, an African American Bahá'í who was a Washington, DC attorney, took a pilgrimage to meet 'Abdu'l-Bahá, and they discussed the nature of American racism extensively. 'Abdu'l-Bahá commanded that racially segregated Bahá'í meetings should not be held in Washington, DC, a sharply segregated city at the time. When he came to the United States in 1912, 'Abdu'l-Bahá spoke at Howard University, Metropolitan African Episcopal Church in Washington, DC, to the fourth annual convention of the National Association for the Advancement of Colored People and to many predominantly white audiences about the oneness of humanity and its implications for race unity. He gently encouraged Louisa Mathew, a British Bahá'í, and Louis Gregory, to consider marriage; when they married in September 1912, their interracial union was illegal in more than half of the 48 states then making up the United States.

*** Acre, twenty kilometres north of Haifa, Israel, is called Akko in Hebrew and 'Akká in Arabic.

'Abdu'l-Bahá also critiqued discrimination against Japanese Americans in California by adding a Japanese Bahá'í to his entourage and speaking at the Japanese Independent Church in Oakland. Subsequently, 'Abdu'l-Bahá encouraged a series of Race Amity Conferences. The commitment to racial inclusion has remained strong in the American Bahá'í community; the nine-member National Spiritual Assembly, the national coordinating Bahá'í body, currently (2012–13) has two African American members, and African Americans have served as Secretary (the executive position on the Assembly) for 37 of the Assembly's 87 years. The current chair of the National Spiritual Assembly is an African American man.

'Abdu'l-Bahá also spoke out strongly in favour of equality of women during his western tour. He advocated votes for women and said that in the future women would fill all occupations, even as presidents of nations. 'But be it known that if womankind had been trained according to military tactics, I believe that they could kill as many [as men] too. But God forbid womankind to learn military tactics! May they never make up their minds to take up the gun. Because that is not a glory. Home-making and joy-creating and comfort-making are truly glories of man! Man should not glory in this, that he can kill people. Man should glory in this, that he can love'.[19] Of the nine members of the National Spiritual Assembly of the Bahá'ís of the United States, currently five are women. Bahá'ís would not claim that they have achieved the vision of the oneness of humanity that is enshrined in their scriptures, but they have striven to actualize the principle in their communities, and have made progress.

Consultation

The Bahá'í authoritative texts contain a mechanism for fostering unity called *consultation*. The basic concept (*shúrá* in Arabic) is Qur'ánic (42:38), but Bahá'u'lláh emphasized it ('in all things it is necessary to consult'),[20] and 'Abdu'l-Bahá and Shoghi Effendi elaborated on it. Consultation is a process based on the expression of virtues: 'the prime requisites for them that take counsel together are purity of motive, radiance of spirit, detachment from all else save God, attraction to His Divine Fragrances, humility and lowliness amongst His loved ones, patience and long-suffering in difficulties and servitude to His exalted Threshold.'[21] Some of them – such as purity of motive, detachment and humility – have obvious value in a decision-making context. Others, such as servitude to God, are relevant when one remembers that the ultimate purpose of consultation is to create spiritual unity, not just a practical level of unity. For this reason Bahá'ís often pray before they begin consulting, or stop to pray if the atmosphere in the room has become unfavourable to proper consultation. Bahá'ís will also interrupt their consultation to research the Bahá'í authoritative texts, to insure that their decisions are guided by principle.

Consultation cannot succeed without 'absolute freedom' to express one's opinions. It must be based on respect for and trust in the participants. Although 'no occasion for ill-feeling and discord' should arise, and one should 'on no account feel hurt', disagreement is not prohibited; indeed, 'the shining spark of truth cometh forth only after the clash of differing opinions'.[22] Consultation thus calls on individuals to express themselves freely and frankly, and to offer differing views without giving or taking offense, a combination that requires great maturity and tact. Consultation also includes detachment from one's views, so that once one offers an idea to the group, it belongs to them and is not an extension of one's ego.

Since consultation is a process for arriving at truth that involves human beings, it often may be imperfect and opposing views may not be reconciled: 'if, after discussion, a decision be carried unanimously, well and good; but if, the Lord forbid, differences of opinion should arise, a majority of voices must prevail.'[23] Thus, unlike the Quakers, the Bahá'ís do not require unanimity for decision making (though sometimes decisions are postponed until it can be achieved). Once a decision has been reached, however, the Bahá'í authoritative texts emphasize that all should support the decision, whether they previously had agreed with it or not:

> If they agree on a subject, even though it be wrong, it is better than to disagree and be in the right, for this difference will abolish the divine foundation. Though one of the parties may be in the right and they disagree that will be the cause of a thousand wrongs, but if they agree and both parties be in the wrong, as it is in unity the truth will be revealed and the wrong made right.[24]

Disunity might sabotage efforts to implement a right decision and cause an effort to fail that otherwise might have succeeded. The paramount importance of unity over being right is underscored in the Bahá'í scriptures as follows: 'if two souls quarrel and contend . . . differing and disputing, *both are wrong*' (italics in the original).[25]

Unity and the need for organization

The consultation process is not just a practical mechanism for individuals to resolve personal problems or for informal groups to arrive at consensus; it is crucial to the functioning of the Bahá'í Administrative Order. Bahá'u'lláh forbade his religion to have a clergy, thereby abolishing a specialized leadership class to which believers turn for advice and guidance. The abolition of clergy is yet another implication of the oneness of humankind. Instead, he said that each local grouping of Bahá'ís should select nine or more members to administer local affairs through consultation. Under 'Abdu'l-Bahá and Shoghi Effendi, this system became regularized and routinized. A local community of Bahá'ís elects nine adults every April to serve on its *spiritual assembly* (its governing council). In many areas, the members of local spiritual assemblies vote annually to elect nine-member regional councils. Nationally, Bahá'ís are divided into electoral units, and each unit elects one or more delegates annually; the delegates gather annually to elect a nine-member national spiritual assembly. Every 5 years all of the national spiritual assemblies gather at the Bahá'í World Centre in Haifa, Israel, to elect the nine-member international Bahá'í governing council, the Universal House of Justice. All of these bodies function and make decisions through the consultation process.

Furthermore, many local Bahá'í communities appoint committees that involve the rank and file in collective decision making. The administrative component of the Nineteen Day Feast – the portion that follows worship and precedes the social portion – involves consultation of the local Bahá'í community with its local spiritual assembly about matters of common concern.

In addition, the Bahá'í Faith has specially appointed individuals whose primary purpose is to foster consultation and education in the Bahá'í community. The Universal House of Justice appoints

Counsellors (currently, 81 of them) at the international and con-
tinental levels whose main purpose is to meet with individual
Bahá'ís or with local or national spiritual assemblies to encourage
and educate them, give them suggestions, provide them with the
latest information and help them make decisions. The Counsellors
appoint *Auxiliary Board members* (currently, 990 worldwide) who
carry out similar duties in regions, and the Auxiliary Board members appoint *assistants* (who number in the thousands) whose area
might be several Bahá'í communities, one community or even a
specialized group in an area (such as youth, or Spanish speakers).
Committees, group projects and consultants create a culture of
consultation in the Bahá'í community.

Incompatibility of unity and partisanship

A distinctive aspect of the Bahá'í concept of unity is the rejection of
partisanship. Partisanship implies loyalty to an idea or ideology, a
political party or faction or a national, ethnic or racial identity that
overrides one's loyalty to humanity or to the totality of Bahá'u'lláh's
revelation. Partisanship is unity with strings attached, for it exalts
loyalty to one group over others. Partisanship is a roadblock to
the spiritual unity that is the ultimate goal of Bahá'í social and
spiritual processes.

Creating a community without partisanship is an immense challenge. One approach would be to convert only people of a single
ethnic or social background, but the Bahá'í emphasis on the oneness
of humanity demands an outreach to all strata of society. Defining
narrow bounds of orthodoxy would be another approach, but the
Bahá'í principle of independent investigation of truth encourages
Bahá'ís to arrive at their own understandings of truth and limits
efforts to suppress varying opinions. Consultation as a process that
produces group consensus on many matters helps to reduce partisanship but cannot prevent it.

The Bahá'í election process

Instead, the Bahá'í Faith has tackled partisanship at one of the
key points where it is expressed in systems of organization: the

election process. The Bahá'í authoritative texts explicitly forbid nominations, campaigning or even discussion of individuals before an election. A typical Bahá'í election begins with the gathering of the voters together (those unable to attend may vote by absentee ballot). Bahá'í prayers are read to create a spiritual atmosphere of unity. They are often followed by passages from the Bahá'í authoritative texts that stress the qualities or virtues one should consider when deciding privately whom one will vote for. A frequently read passage by Shoghi Effendi advises:

> It is incumbent upon the chosen delegates [the voters] to consider without the least trace of passion and prejudice, and irrespective of any material consideration, the names of only those who can best combine the necessary qualities of unquestioned loyalty, of selfless devotion, of a well-trained mind, of recognized ability and mature experience.[26]

After passages such as this one are read, absolute silence falls over the room. Each voter prays silently, meditates about the various choices that come to mind and votes. A list of all adult Bahá'ís eligible to vote and be voted for is provided to each person or is available for examination. The ballots are then collected and counted by appointed tellers. Since only a plurality, rather than a majority (50% plus one) is needed, one round of voting is adequate for electing a Bahá'í governing body, unless a tie needs to be broken.[27]

The Bahá'í authoritative texts give two reasons for avoiding the practice of nomination (and campaigning, which it implies). The first is that it is 'in fundamental disaccord with the spirit which should animate and direct all elections held by Bahá'ís' because it 'leads to the formation of parties' and produces 'corruption and partisanship'.[28] The second is that it kills 'in the believer the spirit of initiative and of self-development', prevents 'the development in every believer of the spirit of responsibility' and limits the possibility of 'maintaining fully his freedom in the elections'.[29] The Bahá'í Faith thus protects the individual's right to vote his or her conscience in an election and views the process of nominating as a fundamental infringement of that right.

One should add that elections are not a secular act or a convenient habit imported from outside society, but a spiritual and sacred act. Through his or her vote, the individual Bahá'í is participating in a process – one might even say a religious ritual – that reflects their spiritual maturity individually and communally and which is amenable to divine guidance. Voting is the act on which the entire edifice of Bahá'í organization is built. Shoghi Effendi refers to it as 'divine' and as 'fundamentally different from anything that any Prophet has previously established'.[30] Perhaps the best comparison in Christianity that one can offer to the Bahá'í election is the Eucharist, in which the body of Christ becomes present among the believers.[31]

It must be asked whether Bahá'í elections in practice actually follow the principles. Sociological research is necessary to answer that question in detail, but anecdotal evidence suggests that nominations are very rarely attempted,[32] and that Bahá'í culture has created a powerful aversion to the mentioning of names in connection with Bahá'í elections. Individuals attempting in obvious ways to influence an election would face the high probability that their efforts would come to the attention of Bahá'í institutions; the bigger the effort, the greater the likelihood of exposure. The consequence of exposure would be loss of ones right to vote and be voted for, thereby rendering counterproductive any effort to influence the voting.

Because Bahá'í elections involve a prayerful process that occurs without any mentioning of names or campaigning, there is no discussion of issues. In such an environment, no opportunities to express partisanship exist. Those elected, not having made any promises to the voters, are free from the need to represent a constituency or a particular platform and thus are not bound to support certain ideas and oppose others. They are considered responsible to God for their decisions, further weakening any sense of partisanship. But that does not mean they should be aloof from and uninterested in the voters. Rather, they should

> approach their task with extreme humility, and endeavour, by their open-mindedness, their high sense of justice and duty, their candour, their modesty, their entire devotion to the welfare and interests of the friends [the Bahá'ís], the Cause, and humanity, to win, not only the confidence and the genuine support and respect of those whom they serve, but also their esteem and real affection. They must, at all times, avoid the spirit of exclusiveness,

the atmosphere of secrecy, free themselves from a domineering attitude, and banish all forms of prejudice and passion from their deliberations. They should, within the limits of wise discretion, take the friends into their confidence, acquaint them with their plans, share with them their problems and anxieties, and seek their advice and counsel.[33]

The consultation process itself serves as another obstacle to partisanship, because of the important principle of non-advocacy of one's ideas and recommendations. According to this principle, once one mentions an idea in a decision making situation, the idea then belongs to the group; one can clarify it or elaborate on it, but cannot advocate for it. In fact, one is free to speak against it.

Because the Bahá'í electoral process has no room for campaigning or discussion of issues, the Bahá'í community is singularly lacking in its use of such labels as liberal, conservative, traditional or orthodox. It is not clear what such labels even would mean. The vast majority of Bahá'ís, never having heard such labels, have no identity as religiously liberal or conservative. Ethnic minorities are welcomed into the Bahá'í community and valued, are even favoured when there is a tie vote in a Bahá'í election between a minority and a non-minority, but are not represented by advocacy groups within the Bahá'í community or its administration.

Pressure tactics and lobbying

The ban on partisanship and advocacy also means that the norms of internal Bahá'í community discourse reject demonstrations, sit-ins, use of media pressure, public advancement of views or positions in opposition to institutional policies and other liberal democratic practices shaped by freedom of speech. The Bahá'í community strives to create institutions that are responsive to genuine needs and concerns without resort to pressure tactics, and to create an atmosphere of consultation in which frankness, tactfulness, trustworthiness, tolerance and fairness abound. In short, it seeks to create a community in which freedom of speech is a normative value, but extremes of speech are unnecessary. The only way that such an approach to discourse will work – and partisanship be avoided – is to create over the long term a community culture in which virtues are understood, valued and expressed, and in which spiritual unity remains the overriding goal.

Like any social system, the Bahá'í community experiences impulses towards dissatisfaction, dissent and occasionally opposition or even rebellion. At such moments, the boundaries on community discourse and membership are tested.

If an individual feels that an injustice has been committed in the Bahá'í community or that a member of a Bahá'í institution is corrupt, the Bahá'í authoritative texts state that the individual has a sacred duty to express his or her concern. One may consult with a Counsellor or Auxiliary Board member, who is able to take one's concerns to a Bahá'í institution. One may report one's concern to a local or national spiritual assembly. One may write to the Universal House of Justice about the matter. One always can appeal a decision to the next higher level of institution; decisions by local spiritual assemblies are appealed to the national spiritual assembly, and decisions by the latter are appealed to the Universal House of Justice. Since the Universal House of Justice is the highest institution in the system, one can appeal its decisions only to the Universal House of Justice itself.

Infallibility, covenant and dissent

The Bahá'í authoritative texts state clearly that the Universal House of Justice is guaranteed divine guidance. The members of the Universal House of Justice are ordinary human beings and are not infallible, but a majority is divinely guaranteed to decide that which is right.[34] Bahá'ís take the claim of guaranteed divine guidance seriously; a 1976 survey of 239 Ontario Bahá'ís attending the Nineteen Day Feast showed that 77 per cent believed the House of Justice was infallible, 16 per cent were not sure or did not answer, and 7 per cent did not believe the claim.[35] Such numbers reflect a significant level of trust in Bahá'í administrative institutions in general, and the fact that the Universal House of Justice's actions have, to date, confirmed most Bahá'ís' belief in its trustworthiness and reliability.

While religious institutions in other faiths have made claims to divine guidance, the Bahá'í claim is uniquely strong because it is backed by numerous authoritative texts. Bahá'u'lláh's claim to be

an infallible author of divine revelation – indeed, his claim to be
the return of Jesus Christ – are unambiguously stated in his own
writings. His appointment of his son 'Abdu'l-Bahá as his infallible successor and his authorizing 'Abdu'l-Bahá to interpret his
writings are also clearly stated and unambiguous. 'Abdu'l-Bahá's
establishment of the institution of the Guardianship, his appointment of Shoghi Effendi to that institution and his delineation of the
authority of the Guardian to infallible interpretation of the writings of Bahá'u'lláh and 'Abdu'l-Bahá is also a settled and clear matter. Finally, the writings of Bahá'u'lláh, 'Abdu'l-Bahá and Shoghi
Effendi all define the sphere of authority of the Universal House of
Justice: they give it guaranteed guidance in protection of the Bahá'í
Faith, in legislation on matters not covered by the authoritative
texts, in elucidation of matters that are obscure and in guiding,
organizing, protecting and developing the Bahá'í community. As a
result, it is very difficult for someone to say they accept Bahá'u'lláh
as a messenger of God but do not accept his line of successors.

    This lineage of leadership and authority is part of the Bahá'í
Covenant. The *Greater Covenant* refers to God's promise always
to provide humanity throughout history with guidance through
Manifestations (such as Abraham, Moses, Jesus, Muhammad,
Zoroaster, Krishna, Buddha, the Báb and Bahá'u'lláh) and to the
obligation of humanity to accept and obey the Manifestations. The
Lesser Covenant refers to the promise that in the Bahá'í Faith,
definitive guidance will continue through the institutions of the
Bahá'í Administrative Order and the obligation of the Bahá'í community to obey them. The Bahá'í authoritative texts describe the
Covenant as more than a contract or pact, but as a divinely inspired
and guided historical process.

    As a result, when a Bahá'í disagrees with a decision of the
Universal House of Justice – an experience that some active Bahá'ís
have – it represents more than a dilemma of conscience. Because
of the House's guarantee of divine guidance, it is also a dilemma
of faith. Of course, since no individual is guaranteed access to all
knowledge or to infallible analysis of it, it is reasonable for the individual to assume in most cases that the dilemma arises out of one's
own faulty reasoning, rather than from an error by the House of
Justice. But situations arise when a Bahá'í may become convinced
that the Universal House of Justice has made an error in a sphere
where the Bahá'í scriptures state it cannot. If a Bahá'í reaches this

conclusion, the most logical consequence would be to re-evaluate his or her membership in the Bahá'í community and possibly to withdraw from it, on the grounds that Bahá'u'lláh's claim to infallible divine revelation has been disproved. Withdrawal from membership in the Bahá'í community is a right all Bahá'ís retain and carries no spiritual penalties. This is in contrast to the situation in Islam, where withdrawal is usually considered an act of apostasy and many Muslims regard the proper penalty for apostasy to be death. It is also in contrast to many Christian groups, where membership is essentially an identity one inherits, regardless of what one actually believes.

Occasionally, Bahá'ís react to a disagreement with the Universal House of Justice by attempting to lobby against the decision. Such an effort may become partisan, a violation of Bahá'í principle requiring a response by the Bahá'í institutions. The most common response – after consultation with the individual has been attempted – is to sanction him or her in some way. Bahá'ís have various privileges of membership – the right to vote, to be voted for, to donate money to the Bahá'í Faith, to serve on Bahá'í institutions and their committees and to attend the Nineteen Day Feast – that can be suspended temporarily or indefinitely.[36] Such rights are restored once the cause for their suspension is resolved. In rare circumstances, the Universal House of Justice has determined that the person's behaviour indicates an unwillingness or inability to follow Bahá'í standards, and has removed the individual from membership in the Bahá'í community.

Covenant breaking

In very rare cases, dissidence may go beyond lobbying against a decision or institution. Sometimes a Bahá'í may decide to oppose the Bahá'í Administrative Order and advocate its replacement, perhaps because a higher source of guidance – usually a claim to personal divine revelation or inspiration – is invoked. Sometimes, such persons contact Bahá'ís in order to undermine their loyalty to Bahá'í institutions or to persuade them to reject the institutions. When that happens, the Universal House of Justice seeks to ascertain the facts and to convince the person to reconsider their actions, but if that fails, it may declare the person a Covenant breaker: a Bahá'í who has violated the terms of and is opposed to Bahá'u'lláh's Covenant.[37] From the perspective of Bahá'í theology, Covenant breaking is self-contradictory, for a person cannot simultaneously claim to be a follower of Bahá'u'lláh and reject the lineage of authority that explains and actualizes his teachings.

History has shown that persons who take such a position are usually motivated by a personal desire for power or by an idiosyncratic insistence that their understanding of Bahá'í scripture is right. Sometimes they say they wish dialogue with the Bahá'ís, but use it as an opportunity to try to pull Bahá'ís away from their institutions. As a result, Bahá'ís are instructed to avoid all contact with Covenant breakers and leave any discussions with them to appointed representatives of the Universal House of Justice.****

The strategy of requiring Bahá'ís to sever contact with Covenant breakers has been effective in maintaining the unity of the Bahá'í community. Covenant breakers usually offer a primarily negative message – an attack on Bahá'í institutions – rather than a set of positive teachings. Consequently, their recruitment of followers must focus on the Bahá'í community; they draw few members from outside the Bahá'í community, who are uninterested in attacks on institutions they have no knowledge of. If contact with the Bahá'í community is cut, the group is deprived of its principal source of new members.

As a result, the Bahá'í Faith is far more unified than other religions. Bahá'ís take the theological position that the Covenant prevents sect formation entirely, because Covenant breakers have left the Bahá'í Faith. Outsiders normally would utilize the criterion of *identity*: if someone says they are a Bahá'í, they are, regardless of their theology. But even this sociological approach to the issue

---

****The term sometimes used in Bahá'í scriptures is to shun covenant breakers. The scriptures also make it clear that the purpose of shunning is to protect the Bahá'ís from the covenant breaker's plans to set up an alternative form of the Bahá'í Faith and not to punish or deprive the person of opportunities to earn a livelihood. Violence against covenant breakers is forbidden. Business relationships with them are not forbidden (letter written on behalf of the Universal House of Justice, 29 October 1974, in *Lights of Guidance*, p. 186). There is no restriction on Bahá'ís associating with non-Bahá'ís who attack the Bahá'í Faith in print, for they are not attempting to create an alternative Bahá'í community.

of Bahá'í sect formation yields impressive results; the 'Bahá'í Faith' has five or six million members, while the Orthodox Bahá'í Faith has perhaps 100 members, and the various other groups together probably total another 100 at most. Such small communities are unable to maintain more than rudimentary institutions or even to print their own books; they must buy the writings of Bahá'u'lláh and 'Abdu'l-Bahá from the 'mainstream' Bahá'í Faith.

History has also shown that splinter groups usually last 30–50 years before lapsing into inactivity and gradually disappearing. For example, Ibrahim Kheiralla (1849–1929), the founder of the American Bahá'í community, broke from the Bahá'í Faith in 1900 when his request for a permanent position of authority over the American Bahá'í community was rejected by 'Abdu'l-Bahá. The alternative Bahá'í group that he founded, the 'Behais', had largely dissipated by 1910, when Kheiralla himself became uninterested in it. After a brief renaissance under new leadership in the 1930s, it declined again, and disappeared entirely by about 1950.

Ahmad Sohrab's New History Society, founded about 1930 as an alternative medium for expressing Bahá'í teachings, frequently published attacks on the Bahá'í community, but later it became a non-profit organization to promote intercultural exchange and understanding. It is no longer a religious organization and has no interest in the Bahá'í Faith. In 1993, the group donated Ahmad Sohrab's personal papers to the National Spiritual Assembly of the Bahá'ís of the United States.

The Orthodox Bahá'í Faith, founded about 1960 by Charles Mason Remey, has spawned three or four separate Bahá'í sects, together totalling a few hundred members at their peak, most of which have become fascinated by esotericism and apocalyptic interpretations of biblical prophecy. One group, the Bahá'ís Under the Provision of the Covenant, has set several dates for nuclear Armageddon and has currently split into two sects that are suing each other in the Montana court system.

Splinter groups can be influenced by intellectual trends in the mainstream community as well. For example, the *Behai Quarterly* was published by the 'Behais' in Kenosha, Wisconsin, in the late 1930s. The periodical published lengthy extracts from the writings of Bahá'u'lláh, reprinted from official Bahá'í publications without copyright permission. Its discussion of the teachings of the Bahá'í Faith focused on the same list of social principles that the mainstream Bahá'ís emphasized, usually phrased identically to the lists common in mainstream Bahá'í publications of the day. Ironically, the list of social principles used by the Behais – which was quite different from the teachings emphasized in the American Bahá'í community 30 years earlier, when their group was founded – was largely derived from the talks given by 'Abdu'l-Bahá when he visited the United States and Canada in 1912, even though the Behais rejected 'Abdu'l-Bahá's authority and accused him of corrupting Bahá'u'lláh's teachings.

The unity of the Bahá'í world is highlighted by a comparison to other religions. All major world religions are divided into sects or schools, numbering in the hundreds or thousands. Some sects are thousands of years old. Christianity has more than 33,000 sects.[38] Mormonism – a movement of similar size to the Bahá'í Faith, established within a decade of the latter's founding – has one large denomination with up to 14 million members, a reorganized branch that is a century and a half old and has 180,000 members, and several dozen smaller sects, some of considerable age, with a few hundred to a few tens of thousands of adherents.

To many it will seem ironic that, to maintain its unity, the Bahá'í Faith has a mechanism to expel or shun members. But no community or society can exist without establishing boundaries defining unacceptable individual behaviour – otherwise chaos or injustice would ensue – and boundaries cannot be maintained without specifying consequences for their transgression. Most religious groups have found it necessary to discipline clergy for violations of ethical norms; in the past most denominations in the United States disciplined members as well.

The Bahá'í Faith and secular partisan politics

The Bahá'í approach to unity has major implications for its approach towards the governance of secular society. The modern democratic nation state is founded on the assumption that powers must be divided: different powers are given to different branches, which exist to keep each other in check; often, within branches groups compete for dominance, thereby keeping each other in check. Although the founding fathers of the United States of America warned against the 'mischiefs of faction' a multiparty electoral system is now considered an essential component of a modern democracy.[39]

The Bahá'í rejection of partisanship is also a rejection of the notion that disunity must be used to control ambition and greed. Indeed, the Bahá'í system turns the equation around; it views partisanship as a common cause of ambition and greed and seeks to control them through consultation and creation of a virtue-centred community. The Bahá'í administrative system does not have separate legislative, executive and judicial branches; instead, all three functions rest in the local and national spiritual assemblies and the Universal House of Justice. A separate branch of advisors (the Counsellors, Auxiliary Board members and assistants) has consultative but no legislative, executive or judicial responsibilities.

The Bahá'í authoritative texts appear to support the value of secular government possessing branches; for example, Bahá'u'lláh praised the British governing system as possessing both a sovereign and a legislature, and Shoghi Effendi referred to the future world government as possessing an executive, a legislature and a 'tribunal'.[40] The Bahá'í authoritative texts apparently envisage the branches as potentially complementary rather than competitive.

Political parties, however, are not compatible with the Bahá'í approach to unity. Bahá'ís are forbidden to join political parties on the grounds that they exist to promote themselves at the expense of other political factions and that their platforms usually contradict one Bahá'í principle or another. Bahá'ís and Bahá'í organizations are also forbidden to become involved in partisan politics or to make campaign contributions. Historically, Bahá'ís who join a political party in spite of their religion's ban on such membership have had their Bahá'í community membership rights suspended.

The Bahá'í ban on partisan politics, on campaigning for office, and on contributing funds to political campaigns makes it virtually impossible for Bahá'ís to hold an elected position. There have been a few exceptions; Bahá'ís have served on local school boards in the United States where one need not declare a party affiliation or campaign. In one case a Bahá'í was elected mayor of Cottonwood Falls, Kansas – in spite of his refusal to join a party or campaign for office – because he was well-known and had an excellent reputation.[41] Since the selection of judges is often political, it is difficult for Bahá'ís to be chosen, but it has happened and a Bahá'í has even served on the US Court of Appeals for the Ninth Circuit.[42] While Bahá'ís are encouraged to serve their country as civil servants, the Universal House of Justice may require them to decline political appointments such as cabinet positions and ambassadorships because of their highly partisan nature.

Many individual Bahá'ís have put their efforts to serve humanity into nonpartisan avenues, and Bahá'í institutions have gained experience in dealing with governments in ways that avoid partisanship. Every resolution condemning the persecution of Iran's Bahá'ís that the US Congress has passed since 1982 has had bipartisan sponsorship and support. Subsequently, the United States National Spiritual Assembly has worked with other national organizations to achieve bipartisan support in Congress for ratification of UN human rights treaties designed to establish international standards against genocide and torture, and to abolish discrimination against minorities, women and children.

Civil disobedience, civil obedience and social change

The Bahá'í insistence on the principle of unity also determines the ways Bahá'ís can work for social change. Unity cannot exist in a society without the rule of law; hence the Bahá'í authoritative texts require Bahá'ís to respect and obey the governments and laws under which they live. Their obedience even extends to disbanding Bahá'í institutions voluntarily and suspending Bahá'í community activities if they are banned by the government. The exception is any government law requiring Bahá'ís to renounce or deny their religion, for such a law moves beyond the sphere of personal action and into the sphere of personal faith, over which the individual has no control.

Bahá'ís cannot participate in nonviolent civil disobedience as a mechanism for bringing about change in wider society, for it relies on violation of laws and the creation of a partisan atmosphere. Instead, Bahá'ís support social change through education, personal example, use of legitimate legal means (such as legal marches and educational efforts) and initiatives that may represent unusual ways of obeying laws.[43]

The techniques of nonviolent civil disobedience, as effective as they have been to bring about significant changes in social structure, are themselves possible only because changes in society over the last few hundred years have created conditions (a free press, democracy, public opinion) that make them effective. Nonviolent civil disobedience thus reflects a new level of maturation of human society. Bahá'ís favour creation of an even more mature society where innovative nonviolent civil *obedience* and efforts that create unity will replace civil disobedience and partisanship as mechanisms to bring about social change.

Conclusion

As Shoghi Effendi notes, the Bahá'í principle of the oneness of humanity 'is no mere outburst of ignorant emotionalism or an expression of vague and pious hope'.[44] Rather, it is an ethical imperative with an elaborate set of implications. It rejects splitting human beings into unequal divisions based on race, gender, education, class, citizenship or religious authority. It implies access to education for all. It implies that all must have a voice in the deliberations of society. It offers a mechanism – consultation – and the requisite values to bring about a consultative society.

Unity as a principle does not imply that humans are naturally united or that efforts to destroy unity will not exist or can be ignored. Instead, it implies the need for mechanisms to build and maintain unity. Elections that protect the right of the individual to vote his or her conscience and that prevent the creation of partisanship are a principal mechanism for creating unity; indeed, for Bahá'ís they are a sacred mechanism. Because unity in wider society is a Bahá'í goal, involvement in partisan politics is forbidden.

In order to protect humanity from egotism and the disunity it can create, Bahá'u'lláh created a Covenant whereby some of the authority given to him by God has been delegated to 'Abdu'l-Bahá, Shoghi Effendi and the Universal House of Justice. So clear and unambiguous is this chain of authority that efforts to thwart it have been few and, historically, have been spectacularly unsuccessful. 'Abdu'l-Bahá once noted that 'the pivot of the oneness of mankind is nothing else but the power of the Covenant'.[45] It is the power of the Covenant, Bahá'ís believe, that will guarantee their unity and thereby make eventually possible a unified civilization embracing all of humanity.

CHAPTER THREE

The divine and its relationship to creation

It has been noted that the Bahá'í Faith teaches three onenesses: the oneness of God, the oneness of religion and the oneness of humanity. The previous chapter covered the third oneness. This chapter considers the other two.

The unknowable essence, the primal will and creation

The word 'God' is convenient shorthand for something that is both knowable and unknowable, transcendent and immanent, describable and indescribable, personal and impersonal. It depends on the aspect of God one is discussing. Bahá'u'lláh describes the essence of God as ultimately unknowable, beyond human ken and reckoning:

> To every discerning and illuminated heart it is evident that God, the unknowable Essence, the Divine Being, is immensely exalted beyond every human attribute, such as corporeal existence, ascent and descent, egress and regress. Far be it from His glory that human tongue should adequately recount His praise, or that human heart comprehend His fathomless mystery. He is, and hath ever been, veiled in the ancient eternity of His Essence, and will remain in His Reality everlastingly hidden from the sight of men.[1]

He also describes the Divine Essence as 'the Inaccessible' and 'the Holy of Holies'.[2] But this does not mean that humans can know nothing about God. While God is beyond human understanding, it has attributes or qualities that can be described. Bahá'u'lláh speaks about *essential attributes,* such as seeing and knowing, which it by definition must be (God would not be God if God were not all-seeing or all-knowing). God also has *attributes of action,* such as will and command, things God can choose to do or not do.

The Essence also 'created' or emanated the Primal Will. It is eternal; there was never a time before which it did not exist. While it is co-eternal with the Essence, it is not its equal, because the Divine Essence is prior in terms of causation. The Bahá'í sacred texts call the Primal Will various things: the Command of God, the universal Mind, the First Remembrance and the Word of God. Some of the terms are drawn from Islamic mysticism and philosophy. In the Gospel of John, the Jewish philosophy of Philo of Alexandria, and the writings of some Greek philosophers, it is the *Logos* (the Word) and is described in the famous passage at the beginning of the John's evangel, 'In the beginning was the Word, and the Word was with God, and the Word was God'. To say the Word 'is' God reflects its epistemological status – in other words, it is an aspect of God that is relatively knowable; it is as close to knowing God as human beings can get. But the Bahá'í authoritative texts deny its ontological identity with God (that it is God in essence).

The Primal Will created the world. Bahá'u'lláh describes the world as coeternal with God as well; there never was a time when it did not exist. Because the world was originated by God, it is not identical with the unknowable Essence or with the Primal Will. Creation is a voluntary emanation from the Divine, just as light emanates from the sun.[3]

The Primal Will reflects the full range of divine attributes such as mercy, justice, love, patience, self-subsistence, might and knowledge. So does creation: 'From the exalted source [the Word], and out of the essence of His favour and bounty He hath entrusted every created thing with a sign of His knowledge, so that none of His creatures may be deprived of its share in expressing, each according to its capacity and rank, this knowledge. This sign is the mirror of His beauty in the world of creation.'[4] Bahá'u'lláh adds that 'Upon the reality of man, however, He hath focused the radiance of all of His names and attributes, and made it a mirror of His own Self. Alone of all created things man hath been singled out for so great a favor, so enduring a bounty'.[5] Thus humans are able to recognize and understand the divine attributes because the human essence, as part of physical creation, reflects all of them. Humans can love, so they can understand and experience God's love; humans can be merciful, so they can understand and experience God's mercy. The human soul is a mirror reflecting the attributes of the Primal Will, which in turn is a mirror reflecting the attributes of the Divine Essence.

Because all created things reflect divine attributes, human beings can learn about the Divine by studying nature. This has been referred to as the metaphorical nature of physical reality.[6] Physical reality provides a shadowy, or limited reflection, of divine reality. Nature mysticism (seeing the Divine manifested in the world around us) arises from this experience. So does the doctrine of pantheism (all things are part of God), though the Bahá'í scriptures reject pantheism as ultimately an inadequate understanding of reality and of the causal priority* of the Divine Essence.[7] The Bahá'í understanding of the physical world can be described as *panentheistic* (God reflected in nature), however.

In the range of things created by the Divine Essence, none of them is pure evil. The Bahá'í Faith thus denies the existence of a Satan. But nothing but God is pure good, either. Evil arises when human beings pursue narrow self-interest or improper ethical principles; when the 'good' they pursue is fully or partially selfish.[8]

The manifestation

In addition to most created things, which can reflect one attribute of God imperfectly, and human beings, which can reflect all the attributes imperfectly, Bahá'u'lláh postulates that periodically

---

* 'Causal priority' means that the Essence created the Primal Will, not vice versa; and the Primal Will created the world, not vice versa; thus even though all three have always existed, they are not the same thing, nor are they equal in status.

there is one being who can reflect all the attributes perfectly: the *Manifestation*:

> He hath ordained that in every age and dispensation a pure and stainless Soul be made manifest in the kingdoms of earth and heaven. Unto this subtle, this mysterious and ethereal Being He hath assigned a twofold nature; the physical, pertaining to the world of matter, and the spiritual, which is born of the substance of God Himself.[9]

The phrase 'born of the substance of God' echoes Trinitarian language. The Manifestation is a perfect reflection of the Primal Will, 'born' from it. In this sense, the Gospel of John was right: Jesus Christ was an expression of the Logos, the Word of God (though he was not the only expression of the Word). The Bahá'í authoritative texts also use the Sufi term 'Perfect Man' to describe the Manifestation.

The Manifestation provides human beings access to the Divine in human form, a perfect likeness of the Divine in all its attributes on earth. Bahá'u'lláh goes so far as to say that 'Were any of the all-embracing Manifestations of God to declare: "I am God", He, verily, speaketh the truth, and no doubt attacheth thereto. For it hath been repeatedly demonstrated that through their Revelation, their attributes and names, the Revelation of God, His names and His attributes, are made manifest in the world'.[10] No wonder that the lives of the various Manifestations are the subject of incredible stories and legends, that miracles are attributed to them and that people pray to them and venerate them.

The primary purpose of the Manifestations is education:

> In the kingdoms of earth and heaven there must needs be manifested a Being, an Essence Who shall act as a Manifestation and Vehicle for the transmission of the grace of the Divinity Itself, the Sovereign Lord of all. Through the Teachings of this Day Star of Truth every man will advance and develop until he attaineth the station at which he can manifest all the potential forces with which his inmost true self hath been endowed. It is for this very purpose that in every age and dispensation the Prophets of God and His chosen Ones have appeared amongst

men, and have evinced such power as is born of God and such might as only the Eternal can reveal.[11]

The Manifestations exist to teach us about our own selves. Since we live in society, and social relations are potentially both a means for and a detriment to attaining knowledge of our selves, the Manifestations educate humans on how to live together in society as well. Their primary purpose is to serve as educators and to some extent as exemplars.

The influence of the Manifestations does not end with their physical deaths; they continue to manifest their power in the world through the Holy Spirit. 'Abdu'l-Bahá describes the Holy Spirit as the 'Bounty of God' and the 'luminous rays which emanate from the Manifestations'. Answering the question of a Christian about the Trinity, he explained that 'the rays of the Sun of Reality' were focused on Jesus Christ, and from that focus the Bounty of God in turn was 'reflected upon the other mirrors which were the reality of the Apostles'. He explains that the 'descent of the Holy Spirit' on the Apostles refers to 'the glorious divine bounties' that are reflected in their realities.[12]

Progressive revelation

The Bahá'í authoritative texts assert that as long as there have been sentient beings on the Earth, there have been Manifestations. 'Abdu'l-Bahá says that 'there have been many holy Manifestations of God. One thousand years ago, two hundred thousand years ago, one million years ago, the bounty of God was flowing, the radiance of God was shining, the dominion of God was existing'.[13] Their ability to educate was determined by the needs and capacities of the society in which they lived; a society that used a language possessing only a few hundred words had a limited ability to understand and retain divine teachings and could absorb only so many ethical and theological innovations. 'Witness . . . how numerous and far-reaching have been the changes in language, speech, and writing since the days of Adam. How much greater must have been the changes before Him!' explains Bahá'u'lláh.[14] For this reason, one cannot read back into ancient history the cultural experience of the most recent Manifestations. Every Manifestation builds on the ethical and cultural norms of the society in which he or she[15] lives and provides new ethical and spiritual insights. In turn, these insights both demolish old social structures and understandings and necessitate the creation of new approaches to the world. Technological, cultural, social and ethical innovations result. The new society that is created is then ready for yet another Manifestation. This is termed *progressive revelation* in the Bahá'í authoritative texts. The Bahá'í authoritative texts do not provide a complete list of the known Manifestations. 'That the names of some of them are forgotten and the records of their lives lost is to be attributed to the disturbances and changes that have overtaken the world', Bahá'u'lláh notes.[16] In his writings, Bahá'u'lláh mentions Abraham, Zoroaster, Moses, Jesus, Muhammad, the Báb and himself as Manifestations. The terms 'Hinduism' and 'Buddhism' may not have existed at all in the Arabic and Persian of his day, or were still obscure neologisms; the words were coined in English in 1829 and 1801 respectively.[17] A word for Buddha existed in Persian, *but,* but it meant 'idol' because the Muslim invaders of India had smashed large numbers of Buddha statues. Hence Bahá'u'lláh was not in a position to discuss those traditions in any detail. But 'Abdu'l-Bahá, answering questions by American Bahá'ís, stated that the Buddha was a Manifestation, and Shoghi Effendi added Krishna to the official Bahá'í list. In another letter, Shoghi Effendi wrote about 'the religion of the Sabaeans', a group mentioned in the Qur'án and in Bahá'u'lláh's Kitáb-i-Íqán: 'very little is known about the origins of this religion, though we Bahá'ís are certain of one thing, that the founder of it has been a divinely-sent Messenger.'[18] The founder's name, however, has been lost.

This raises the number of Manifestations mentioned in the Bahá'í authoritative texts to ten: the Sabaean Manifestation, Abraham, Zoroaster, Moses, Krishna, Buddha, Jesus, Muhammad, the Báb and Bahá'u'lláh. To the list one can possibly add Sálih and Húd, two prophetic figures mentioned in the Qur'án and the Kitáb-i-Íqán, although their exact status is uncertain. Possibly one can add Noah and Adam as well, though it is not clear whether they should be regarded as historic figures, legendary figures or even as archetypal Manifestations. They lived too far back in the past, if they existed at all. The Bahá'í texts refer to 'Adam' in different symbolic ways, sometimes as the first

Manifestation of the current cycle of Manifestations, sometimes as the symbolic first human being.

Other sorts of prophetic figures

In Islam there was a distinction between a *rasúlulláh*, a divine messenger (here equivalent to a Manifestation), and a *nabí* or prophet. Abraham, Moses, Jesus and Muhammad were both messengers and prophets; Old Testament figures such as David (traditional author of the Psalms), Isaiah and Daniel were prophets but not messengers, because they stood in the shadow of a messenger (in this case, Moses) who revealed the basic laws and teachings of their religion. The Bahá'í authoritative texts also utilize the distinction between Manifestations – who are perfect vessels of the Divine Will – and lesser prophets, who are followers of the Manifestations and receive their power from them.[19]

The Bahá'í authoritative texts do not restrict the latter category just to prophets, however. God is capable of inspiring anyone with spiritual insights that they can share with their society. Bahá'u'lláh praised 'divine Plato' and philosophers who quest to understand the mysteries of God. 'Abdu'l-Bahá said that 'Confucius became the cause of civilization, advancement and prosperity for the people of China'; in other words, he carried out tasks similar to a prophet's, even though the Bahá'í authoritative texts do not define his status. John the Baptist came during the transition period between the dispensation of Moses and that of Jesus and is not clearly identified in the Bahá'í authoritative texts as either a lesser prophet or a Manifestation; he is described as the return of Elias and is often compared to the Báb. The apostles are subjects of praise in the Bahá'í sacred texts and their contributions to Christian scripture are acknowledged. The imams of Shi'ite Islam are understood to have been rightly guided. Both 'Abdu'l-Bahá and Shoghi Effendi are described as infallibly guided. Shoghi Effendi wrote that Joseph Smith could not be considered a prophet by Bahá'ís because 'we cannot possibly add names of people we (or anyone else) think might be Lesser Prophets to those found in the Qur'án, the Bible and our own Scriptures'. But he is reported to have orally described Smith as a 'seer'.[20] Clearly, in addition to the category 'prophet' there are divine philosophers, apostles, imams and other prophetic figures.

This is important when one turns to regions other than the
Middle East, where the Bahá'í authoritative texts offer few interpretations of religious history. The Hindu Vedas are understood
by Hindus to have been 'heard' by sages. Mahavira, founder of
Jainism, and Guru Nanak, founder of Sikhism, are not recognized
in the Bahá'í texts as Manifestations, but Bahá'ís can understand
them as prophetic figures who were inspired by the Holy Spirit.
Native American Bahá'ís are confident that their cultures received
divine guidance – the Bahá'í texts assure us that all people have –
and speculate whether Deganawidah, the White Buffalo Calf
Woman, Quetzalcoatl, Wiracocha and other spiritual teachers
were Manifestations or prophetic figures. Cultures all around the
world have figures that anthropologists call 'culture heroes', and
Bahá'ís in those cultures often are inclined to speak of them as
vessels of divine guidance for their people. Because of the Bahá'í
notion of progressive revelation of divine truth to humanity,
Bahá'ís usually emphasize the positive in other religious traditions, and they attract people from other religions to their Faith
by emphasizing how the previous religions were right, not by how
they were wrong.

The process of revelation

Religions usually regard their sacred texts as supernatural in origin. For the Bahá'í Faith, the sacred texts are confined to works
revealed by the Báb and Bahá'u'lláh. The process by which they
received or produced the texts is called revelation. Neither figure
received much material education, a point they emphasize. As
Bahá'u'lláh noted,

> Thou knowest full well that We perused not the books which
> men possess and We acquired not the learning current amongst
> them, and yet whenever We desire to quote the sayings of the
> learned and of the wise, presently there will appear before the
> face of thy Lord in the form of a tablet all that which hath
> appeared in the world and is revealed in the Holy Books and
> Scriptures. Thus do We set down in writing that which the eye
> perceiveth. Verily His knowledge encompasseth the earth and
> the heavens.[21]

The Báb described the rapidity and ease of his revelation in his most important book, the Persian Bayán:

> For if one from whose life only twenty-four years have passed [the Báb], and who is devoid of those sciences wherein all are learned, now reciteth verses after such fashion without thought or hesitation, writes a thousand verses of prayer in the course of five hours without pause of the pen, and produceth commentaries and learned treatises on such lofty themes as the true understanding of God and of the oneness of His Being, in a manner which doctors and philosophers confess surpasseth their power of understanding, then there is no doubt that all that hath been manifested is divinely inspired. . . . All these things are for a proof unto the people; otherwise the religion of God is too mighty and glorious for anyone to comprehend through aught but itself; rather by it all else is understood.[22]

There are eyewitness accounts of the Báb producing 50 pages of text in 2 hours, and over 100 pages in the course of an evening. Similar accounts exist about Bahá'u'lláh's mode of revelation:

> Mírzá Áqá Ján [Bahá'u'lláh's secretary] had a large ink-pot the size of a small bowl. He also had available about ten to twelve pens and large sheets of paper in stacks. In those days all letters which arrived for Bahá'u'lláh were received by Mírzá Áqá Ján. He would bring these into the presence of Bahá'u'lláh and, having obtained permission, would read them. Afterwards the Blessed Beauty [Bahá'u'lláh] would direct him to take up his pen and record the Tablet which was revealed in reply.

> Such was the speed with which he used to write the revealed Word that the ink of the first word was scarcely yet dry when the whole page was finished. It seemed as if some one had dipped a lock of hair in the ink and applied it over the whole page. None of the words was written clearly and they were illegible to all except Mírzá Áqá Ján. There were occasions when even he could not decipher the words and had to seek the help of Bahá'u'lláh. When revelation had ceased, then in accordance with Bahá'u'lláh's instruction Mírzá Áqá Ján would rewrite the Tablet in his best hand and dispatch it to its destination.[23]

Both the Báb and Bahá'u'lláh state that the receipt of revelation is a proof of their station as Manifestations. The resulting text is the creative word of God; 'every single letter proceeding from Our mouth', said Bahá'u'lláh, 'is endowed with such regenerative power as to enable it to bring into existence a new creation – a creation the magnitude of which is inscrutable to all save God'.[24] Their texts encompassed most of the prominent literary genres of the Islamic world: various types of poetry, mystical writings, theological texts, the epistolary genre (letters), treatises, scriptural commentaries and prayers. They were in Arabic, Persian or a unique mix of the two. In some cases they coined new Arabic words to express their ideas. At times they creatively bent or broke the complex rules of Arabic grammar, which became a source of polemic against them. Bahá'u'lláh's writings in pure Persian (using no words of Arabic origin) are original and unique.

Both the Báb and Bahá'u'lláh lived in an era when there was cheap paper, a well-established writing system, plenty of literate people around to serve as scribes and read their texts and cultural values that prized writing. These innovations occurred over many centuries. Neither Muhammad nor Jesus lived in such a world. The earliest fragments of the New Testament were written on papyrus decades after the crucifixion and consisted of a string of capital letters, often even without spacing between words, and with little or no punctuation. Moses, Zoroaster and Buddha may have had no access to writing at all. Consequently oral tradition was the principal vehicle for transmitting their revelations. Even Jesus offered some of his teachings in the form of short, pithy parables. The Buddha told stories and offered numbered lists of points (or his followers converted his teachings into numbered lists later). Zoroaster may have used hymns to convey his truths. These techniques would have improved the reliability of oral transmission, which rarely has the accuracy of writing.

One consequence of the improved technology is that Bahá'í scripture has a level of reliability, where transmission of the original teachings is concerned, that one does not see in the Bible and other earlier scriptures, except the Qur'án, the text of which appears to have been carefully preserved and relatively quickly written down. In a letter written on its behalf, the Universal House of Justice noted that

The Bahá'ís believe what is in the Bible to be true in substance. This does not mean that every word recorded in that Book is to be taken literally and treated as the authentic saying of a Prophet. A striking example is given in the account of the sacrifice which Abraham was called upon to make. The Guardian of the Faith [Shoghi Effendi] confirms that the record in the Qur'án and the Writings of Bahá'u'lláh, namely that it was Ishmael, and not Isaac as stated in the Old Testament, whom Abraham was to sacrifice, is to be upheld. In one of His Tablets 'Abdu'l-Bahá refers to this discrepancy, and explains that, from a spiritual point of view, it is irrelevant which son was involved. The essential part of the story is that Abraham was willing to obey God's command to sacrifice His son. Thus, although the account in the Torah is inaccurate in detail, it is true in substance.[25]

'Abdu'l-Bahá praised study of the Bible, and it is quoted by Bahá'u'lláh and 'Abdu'l-Bahá in their works. The Bahá'í approach to the Bible is very different from the approach of some Muslims, who argued that Christians and Jews had corrupted their scriptures to remove references to Muhammad, so their followers would not become Muslims. Bahá'u'lláh strongly rejected such a notion:

We have also heard a number of the foolish of the earth assert that the genuine text of the heavenly Gospel doth not exist amongst the Christians, that it hath ascended unto heaven. How grievously they have erred! How oblivious of the fact that such a statement imputeth the gravest injustice and tyranny to a gracious and loving Providence! How could God, when once the Day-star of the beauty of Jesus had disappeared from the sight of His people . . . cause His holy Book, His most great testimony amongst His creatures, to disappear also? What would be left to that people to cling to from the setting of the day-star of Jesus until the rise of the sun of the Muhammadan Dispensation? What law could be their stay and guide? How could such people be made the victims of the avenging wrath of God, the omnipotent Avenger? How could they be afflicted with the scourge of chastisement by the heavenly King? Above all, how could the flow of the grace of the All-Bountiful be stayed? How could the ocean of His tender mercies be stilled? We take refuge with God, from that which His creatures have fancied about Him![26]

While Bahá'ís devote most of their scriptural study to the authoritative Bahá'í texts, they also study the scriptures of the other religions, especially the Qur'án and Bible, because they are close in time to the Bahá'í scriptures and shaped their content. The scriptures of the world's religions are seen as sacred works that preserve and contain the creative word. Bahá'ís often include the scriptures of the world's major religions in their devotional programmes, where their symbolic and mystical power can inspire worship.

The Bahá'í view of other religions

Bahá'u'lláh and 'Abdu'l-Bahá both state that, while all religions share certain basic ethical and metaphysical principles, they differ because the revelation was shaped by the times and conditions in which it was received. The bewildering diversity of the world's religions – especially in ritual and practice – is attributed to the differing cultural contexts of the Manifestations and the varying interpretations by later generations, as well as to the problem of accurate transmission of the original teachings. In the past, there was no way to prevent the formation of sects, which broadened the diversity of a religious community but weakened its unity.

Bahá'í scholars have only begun to examine the teachings of the various religions in the light of the Bahá'í concepts of Divine Essence, Primal Will, Manifestation, revelation and progressive revelation. The concepts of Divine Essence and Primal Will have some parallels in such Hindu terms as Brahman and deity, in such Chinese concepts as Tao and T'ien and in such Buddhist notions as nirvana and the *dharmakaya* (dharma body) of the Buddha.[27] The idea of the Manifestation bears some resemblance to the Hindu notion of avatara and the Buddhist concept of bodhisattva. As more Bahá'ís of Hindu, Buddhist, Chinese and indigenous backgrounds examine the Bahá'í authoritative texts systematically, they will contribute new insights to understanding the Bahá'í concept of the Divine and its relationship to the world from their own religious and cultural milieus.

The principle of progressive revelation implies an underlying unity to all the religions; consequently, Bahá'ís approach the other faiths with appreciation. Bahá'u'lláh urges Bahá'ís to 'consort with all religions with amity and concord, that they may inhale from you the sweet fragrance of God'.[28] On the other hand, the Bahá'í concept of Manifestation implies that the latest Manifestation – Bahá'u'lláh – is in some sense the most important. Furthermore, the Bahá'í approach to the world's religions implies a Bahá'í theological interpretation of each one, as the Bahá'í teaching that Buddha is a Manifestation demonstrates. This theology is quite well developed in the case of Judaism, Christianity and Islam because Bahá'u'lláh, the Báb and 'Abdu'l-Bahá commented about those religions extensively. For example, the Bahá'í authoritative texts interpret events in Moses's life to explain why he does not always appear to be a sinless Manifestation; redefine the trinity; criticize Christian ritual and use of images; accept the crucifixion, which Muslims (interpreting a Qur'ánic verse) reject; accept Christ's distinctiveness and accept the title Son of God, but reject the idea that he was the only Manifestation of the Word; and state that Muhammad did indeed appoint his cousin and son-in-law 'Alí as his successor and the first Imám.

Bahá'u'lláh's teaching that the Divine continuously sends Manifestations to humanity implies that Bahá'u'lláh is not the last one. In his Kitáb-i-Aqdas, he made it clear that his dispensation would last 'a full thousand years' from the inauguration of his mission in 1853, and sometime after that period, another Manifestation would occur. Thus Bahá'ís have at least a 1,000 years to manifest ever more faithfully the teachings of Bahá'u'lláh in their lives, their faith community and the world. After that, they must patiently await the advent of the next Promised One.

CHAPTER FOUR

The path of individual transformation

The path of personal transformation outlined in the Bahá'í authoritative texts includes both an internal aspect (development of the self) and an external aspect (development of relationships with others). It has both a vertical aspect (relationship with the Divine) and horizontal aspects (relationships with other human beings). None of these aspects can be separated, for the development of the self occurs in relationship, and relationships are strengthened by the deepening of the self; furthermore, the development of the relationship with God is intimately connected to the development of one's relationships with people and things.

Bahá'u'lláh says that the purpose of the Manifestations is to make it possible for each person to 'advance and develop until he attaineth the station at which he can manifest all the potential forces with which his inmost true self hath been endowed'. As we saw in the last chapter, the potentials of the inmost true self include all the attributes of God. In another passage, speaking in the voice of God, Bahá'u'lláh exhorts the reader to 'turn thy sight unto thyself, that thou mayest find Me standing within thee, mighty, powerful and self-subsisting'.[1] True knowledge of one's self, in a sense, is knowledge of God. Thus the self – the immortal soul – is a powerful instrument for understanding the Divine, as mystics throughout the ages have discovered. The quest to discover and express one's true nature is even the central goal of 'godless' Buddhism.

Since the true self consists of all the attributes of God in potential form, learning how to manifest these attributes ever more perfectly is a central goal of life. Everyone can learn to be more loving, compassionate, kind and patient (to list just a few divine attributes); thus even atheists progress spiritually. While one cannot take material possessions or worldly accomplishments to the next life, one does take these spiritual accomplishments; they are one measure of how successful one's life was. Just as a developing foetus grows arms, legs and eyes in the womb – which are of limited use in such a cramped space – in this world we develop the spiritual instruments we need for the next life, which consists of worlds of infinite spiritual progress towards the Divine. Successful development of them leads to 'heaven' and may even make one's life in this world a sort of 'heaven'; a failure to develop them leads to distance from the Divine and 'hell'. While we continue to develop spiritually in the next world via divine grace and the prayers and dedicated acts of people in this world, our own choices and acts in this world lay a crucial foundation.

Prayer

Religion provides various instruments for developing our spiritual qualities. One is prayer and meditation. Shoghi Effendi noted that 'the core of religious faith is that mystic feeling which unites Man with God. This state of spiritual communion can be brought about and maintained by means of meditation and prayer'.[2] To assist the process, Bahá'u'lláh, the Báb and 'Abdu'l-Bahá have revealed hundreds of prayers. It was common for their followers to write to them and ask for special prayers, sometimes for use in one's personal devotions, sometimes to pray for another – a spouse, a child, a sick person, a recently deceased person – and these prayers have been published in prayer books. Many prayers focus on specific concerns, such as forgiveness, assistance, healing and grief. By praying divinely revealed words, one can be sure one is praying in a way that is spiritually beneficial (as opposed, for example, to praying for objects of one's desire). Furthermore, the revealed prayers are poetically uplifting and usually end with a list of qualities of God (the Forgiving, the Merciful, the Strong, the Beneficent, the Gracious) on which one can meditate.

Bahá'ís also pray to God in their own words. Bahá'u'lláh exhorts the believer to 'bring thyself to account each day ere thou art summoned to a reckoning; for death, unheralded, shall come upon thee and thou shalt be called to give account for thy deeds'.[3] Bringing oneself to account involves a frank conversation with God about ones desires and accomplishments, or lack thereof. It is a chance to meditate on one's strengths and weaknesses. It is also preparation for judgment at death.

In addition to the many prayers he revealed for various situations, Bahá'u'lláh also revealed obligatory prayers. Whereas Muslims have one obligatory prayer to say five times a day, often congregationally, Bahá'ís have three different obligatory prayers, they choose which one to say and they pray it privately and individually. The short obligatory prayer is to be repeated once a day 'at noon', which is defined as between noon and sunset:

> I bear witness, O my God, that Thou hast created me to know Thee and to worship Thee. I testify, at this moment, to my powerlessness and to Thy might, to my poverty and to Thy wealth.

> There is none other God but Thee, the Help in Peril, the Self-Subsisting.[4]

The medium obligatory prayer is to be said three times a day, in the morning (between sunrise and noon), at noon and in the evening (from sunset till 2 hours after sunset). This prayer is closest to Shi'ite practice, because Shi'ites could repeat their noon and afternoon prayers together, and their sunset and evening prayers together, thereby performing their five prayers at three time periods. The Bahá'í long obligatory prayer (which takes perhaps 6 minutes) can be said any time in a 24-hour period.

Both the medium and long obligatory prayers involve prostrations and other movements, which involve the body in the act of prayer. Bahá'ís are to perform ablutions (washing their face and hands) before reciting the obligatory prayers; ablutions must be performed even after taking a bath, underscoring the fact that ablutions are symbolic acts of purification. If water is unavailable, the verse 'In the name of God, the Most Pure, the Most Pure', can be recited five times instead. Women during their menses may replace the obligatory prayers with a specified verse.[5] When one performs the obligatory prayer, one is to turn towards the qiblih or 'point of adoration', which for Bahá'ís is Bahá'u'lláh's tomb outside Acre. The obligatory prayer is required of Bahá'ís from ages 15 to 70.

Bahá'í worship also includes a form of meditation: 'It hath been ordained that every believer in God, the Lord of Judgement, shall, each day, having washed his hands and then his face, seat himself and, turning unto God, repeat "Alláh-u-Abhá" [God is Most Glorious] ninety-five times'.[6] *Abhá* is a superlative form of the Arabic word *bahá*, 'glory, splendour', which Bahá'ís consider to be the Greatest Name of God. Bahá appears in the name of the Manifestation (Bahá'u'lláh) and in the term for a follower and for the religion. This practice is related to Islamic dhikr, 'remembrance', where Muslims repeat the 99 beautiful names of God (of which, Bahá'ís say, bahá is the hundredth and greatest name). It also resembles Hindu and Buddhist mantras and the recitation of short prayers and holy words in other religious traditions.

Unlike in Islam, none of these acts of worship are performed congregationally. They are part of one's private relationship with God, and no one can ask whether one is carrying them out. Bahá'u'lláh revealed only one congregational prayer, to be performed at a gravesite during a funeral. The prayer is said by one person on behalf of everyone; it is congregational in that sense (in Islam, a prayer leader recites the obligatory prayer and the audience performs the required prayer motions silently). In a sense, the congregational prayer for the dead involves a clerical function, in that one person says the prayer on behalf of everyone; but anyone, even a child, can recite the prayer.

Fasting

Both the Báb and Bahá'u'lláh enjoined a period of fasting. Interpreting an Islamic tradition that compared prayer and fasting to the sun and moon, Bahá'u'lláh explained that just as those two bodies were the greatest source of physical illumination, prayer and fasting are the brightest orbs in the heaven of religion. He called fasting 'the supreme remedy and the most great healing for the disease of self and passion' and noted that 'even though outwardly the Fast is difficult and toilsome, yet inwardly it is bounty and tranquillity'.[7]

The Bahá'í fast lasts for 19 days, from 2 March to 20 March. One fasts from sunrise to sunset, unlike the Muslim custom of fasting from first light to last light. In high latitudes, Bahá'ís may use clocks and fast from 6 a.m. to 6 p.m. The fast involves abstinence from eating, drinking and smoking tobacco. Bahá'u'lláh granted exceptions to those under age 15, over age 70, the ill, travellers, anyone performing heavy labour and women who are pregnant, menstruating or nursing.

The Bahá'í practice of fasting has many antecedents. The Ramadan fast is the Islamic precursor. Judaism has a Yom Kippur fast. In Catholicism it has become the Lenten practice of giving up something for 40 days, but in some Eastern Orthodox churches, Lent involves fasting. Only a century ago Protestants would periodically declare days of fasting for various reasons. Fasting is sometimes used in Hinduism, Buddhism and many indigenous religious traditions as well.

Studying the revelation

Bahá'u'lláh urges the believers to recite 'the verses of God every morn and eventide'.[8] Since revelation tells one how to live, believers need to read and meditate on it frequently. One also needs to study scripture as part of the process of investigating reality. Independent, personal investigation of the truth is an important principle, one that calls on Bahá'ís to read, observe, ponder and be inquisitive. The principle extends to choosing one's religion: the children of Bahá'ís should make their own commitment. It extends to the study of nature as well; science is an important expression of the investigation of reality. Since the truth expressed in nature and the truth expressed in revelation are both expressions of the Divine Will, they cannot be in contradiction, so religion and science ultimately are in harmony. The principle of harmony of science and religion is an important one in the Bahá'í authoritative texts.

Pilgrimage

One normally thinks of study of the revelation as a cognitive process of reading and contemplation. But another way to learn about the revelation and its message is to visit the places where it was revealed and where the Manifestation of God resided in his earthly life. For this reason, Bahá'ís are exhorted to perform pilgrimages if their circumstances permit. Pilgrimage to the House of the Báb in Shiraz is temporarily impossible because the building was intentionally destroyed by the government of Iran after the 1979 Islamic Revolution. Many other Bahá'í holy places in Iran have suffered the same fate. But it is possible to visit the sites associated with the life of Bahá'u'lláh and 'Abdu'l-Bahá in Haifa and Acre in northern Israel.

The Universal House of Justice, which has its seat in Haifa, conducts a series of 9-day pilgrimages throughout the year, except during the hottest summer months. The programme includes praying at the tombs of Bahá'u'lláh, the Báb and 'Abdu'l-Bahá; visiting the places in which Bahá'u'lláh and 'Abdu'l-Bahá lived, including Bahá'u'lláh's cell in the citadel in Acre; meeting with the members of the Universal House of Justice and touring the monumental buildings of the Bahá'í World Centre in Haifa.

Particularly noteworthy is the visit to the International Archives Building, a structure that is part archives, part museum and part reliquary. The visit begins with a viewing of the photographs and portraits of Bahá'u'lláh and the Báb, sacred images not normally viewed by Bahá'ís except under very special circumstances. The visit then turns to relics of various sorts: blood and hair of Bahá'u'lláh; clothes and personal items owned by Bahá'u'lláh, the Báb and 'Abdu'l-Bahá and original writings by them. The tour concludes with other items of historical significance, such as the sword used by Mullá Husayn at the siege of Fort Tabarsí.[9]

In the Middle Ages, Christian relics were believed to possess spiritual powers capable of blessing a place or owner, or bringing about miraculous cures for those who visit and pray to them. The purpose of Bahá'í relics is wholly different; they are physical reminders of sacred events, holy people and divine teachings. Thus they are primarily educational and inspirational.

Law and faith

The Bahá'í path of individual transformation includes morality and self-restraint. Bahá'u'lláh's laws include, among other things, complete abstinence from alcohol and habit-forming substances unless prescribed by a physician. Also forbidden is gambling, theft, murder, cruelty to animals, striking another person, gossip, backbiting and sexual relations outside of marriage. Bahá'ís are exhorted to wash regularly, perfume themselves and be the essence of cleanliness. They are encouraged to consult competent physicians and seek physical as well as spiritual healing. 'Think not that We have revealed unto you a mere code of laws', Bahá'u'lláh exclaims. 'Nay, rather, We have unsealed the choice Wine with the fingers of might and power'. He adds that 'the precepts laid down by God constitute the highest means for the maintenance of order in the world and the security of its peoples. . . . Know assuredly that My commandments are the lamps of My loving providence among My servants, and the keys of My mercy for My creatures. . . . From My laws the sweet-smelling savour of My garment can be smelled, and by their aid the standards of Victory will be planted upon the highest peaks'.[10]

While the Bahá'í Faith, like Judaism and Islam, is a religion of laws, it seeks to avoid the creation of an elaborate set of rules. Nor are all the laws binding on Bahá'ís at this time; Bahá'u'lláh started a process of gradually applying the laws, and the Universal House of Justice has continued the practice. Nor do the existence of laws minimize the role of faith. Bahá'u'lláh explained the following:

> The first duty prescribed by God for His servants is the recognition of Him Who is the Dayspring of His Revelation and the Fountain of His laws, Who representeth the Godhead in both the Kingdom of His Cause and the world of creation. Whoso achieveth this duty hath attained unto all good; and whoso is deprived thereof hath gone astray, though he be the author of every righteous deed. It behoveth every one who reacheth this most sublime station, this summit of transcendent glory, to observe every ordinance of Him Who is the Desire of the world. These twin duties are inseparable. Neither is acceptable without the other.[11]

Thus acceptance of the Manifestation of God for the age in which one lives – in this day, Bahá'u'lláh – is accorded high spiritual importance, but is inadequate without obedience to all the Manifestation's laws (a requirement no one can fulfil perfectly). In Christian terms, both faith and works are important. Only God can judge how well each individual has carried out these duties.

Since the Bahá'í Faith has laws, it can be said to have a definition of sin: actions that violate the laws of God. Bahá'u'lláh and 'Abdu'l-Bahá revealed many prayers to say for the forgiveness of sins, and human beings are referred to as 'sinners' in the Bahá'í authoritative texts. The emphasis, however, is not on the sinning, but on spiritual and moral tests: it is on the fork in the moral road and on both the right and wrong paths that follow from one's moral decision-making, not on the path of sin.

Marriage

Most of Bahá'u'lláh's laws have social implications, and thus they turn our attention from the individual's vertical relationship with God to the horizontal relationship with other human beings. Our social relations with others fall in a series of concentric circles encompassing ever larger groups of people: one's spouse, one's family, one's religious community and all of humanity. The latter two groups will be explored in Chapters Twelve and Five respectively.

The smallest and most intimate of the concentric social circles is the circle of marriage. Marriage is not required of Bahá'ís, though it is encouraged, and celibacy is discouraged. Bahá'u'lláh describes marriage as 'a fortress for well-being and salvation', sacralizing the institution and making it a vehicle for spiritual progress.[12] 'Abdu'l-Bahá elaborates that:

> . . . marriage must be a union of the body and of the spirit as well, for here both husband and wife are aglow with the same wine, both are enamoured of the same matchless Face, both live and move through the same spirit, both are illumined by the same glory. This connection between them is a spiritual one, hence it is a bond that will abide forever. Likewise do they enjoy strong and lasting ties in the physical world as well, for if the marriage is based both on the spirit and the body, that union is a true one, hence it will endure. If, however, the bond is physical and nothing more, it is sure to be only temporary, and must inexorably end in separation.[13]

Reference to being 'enamoured of the same matchless Face' refers to a common devotion to God and may be an allusion to the Bahá'í marriage vow, 'we will all, verily, abide by the Will of God'. By taking such a vow, the new couple is entering into a 'love triangle' of sorts that includes God and both of them. The resulting marriage, ideally, does not end with death, but continues forever in the next world.

Until very recently, throughout the world, the vast majority of marriages were arranged by the parents. Bahá'u'lláh forbids arranged marriages and says that first the couple must make their choice. 'Bahá'í marriage is the commitment of the two parties one to the other, and their mutual attachment of mind and heart', explains 'Abdu'l-Bahá. 'Each must, however, exercise the utmost care to become thoroughly acquainted with the character of the other, that the binding covenant between them may be a tie that will endure forever'.[14] Once they have chosen each other, however, they must seek permission to marry from their parents. Shoghi Effendi explains that Bahá'u'lláh established the law of consent 'to strengthen the social fabric, to knit closer the ties of the home, to place a certain gratitude and respect in the hearts of the children for those who have given them life and sent their souls out on the eternal journey towards their Creator'.[15] The Bahá'í approach, therefore, is half way between the traditional arranged marriage and the modern convention where parents have no say at all. It emphasizes family unity.

Many traditional marriages around the world also included the giving of a dowry. Bahá'u'lláh specified that the future husband should give a small dowry to the future wife. The amount, defined in grams of silver or gold, is symbolic only; a large dowry would make it impossible for the poor to wed or would be burdensome. The giving of the dowry apparently is representative of the husband's commitment to support his family. Currently the dowry law is binding on Middle Eastern Bahá'ís, but not on Bahá'ís elsewhere.

The emphasis on unity does not preclude divorce. Divorce is 'strongly condemned' and should be avoided whenever possible. But if a couple is unable to live together and they develop resentment and antipathy towards each other, they may commence a year of waiting, where they live separately and attempt to reconcile. If reconciliation proves impossible, a divorce is permissible.

The Bahá'í authoritative texts reject homosexuality as a proper expression of the sexual impulse, so gay marriage within the Bahá'í community is not permitted. The Universal House of Justice, however, has said that the Bahá'í Faith supports the right of all people to be free from discrimination, regardless of sexual orientation, and that the Faith does not impose its moral standards on others.[16]

Family life

While it is important for a couple to serve as helpmeets and spiritual partners to each other, the primary purpose of marriage is the procreation of children. Shoghi Effendi made it clear that the number of children is up to the couple, though they should plan to have at least one. The couple can also decide what form of birth control they use, although they should avoid techniques that cause abortion (such as an intrauterine device) because the Bahá'í authoritative texts say that the soul joins with the body at the moment of conception. The Universal House of Justice has also advised that couples should avoid permanent sterilization unless pregnancy would endanger the woman's life. Bahá'u'lláh has praised adoption as another way to build one's family.

It is in the arena of family life where the Bahá'í principle of equality of men and women must be practiced most profoundly, and where some of its limits are seen. 'Abdu'l-Bahá wrote that 'equality of men and women, except in some negligible instances, has been fully and categorically announced. Distinctions have been utterly removed'. There are no statements in the Bahá'í authoritative texts that men are superior over women or that women must obey men. Both men and women should have training so that they can pursue a vocation, hence women as well as men can be family bread winners. Bahá'u'lláh even stated that the curriculum for educating boys and girls should be essentially the same.[17]

But biology inevitably implies some distinctions between the roles of men and women. Shoghi Effendi's secretary, writing on his behalf, noted that 'the task of bringing up a Bahá'í child, as emphasized again and again in the Bahá'í Writings, is the chief responsibility of the mother, whose unique privilege is indeed to create in her home such conditions as would be most conducive to both his material and spiritual welfare and advancement. The training which the child first receives through his mother constitutes the strongest foundation for his future development'. 'Chief responsibility' does not mean sole responsibility; it is up to the husband and wife to decide what balance to set, based on their circumstances.

The Universal House of Justice has added that 'the members of the family all have duties and responsibilities toward one another and to the family as a whole' that 'vary from member to member . . . The parents have the inescapable duty to educate their children – but not vice versa; the children have the duty to obey their parents – the parents do not obey the children; the mother – not the father – bears the children, nurses them in babyhood, and is thus their first educator, hence daughters have a prior right to education over sons'. The House of Justice adds that 'a corollary of this responsibility of the mother is her right to be supported by her husband – a husband has no explicit right to be supported by his wife'. Particularly noteworthy in this passage is the reference to 'Abdu'l-Bahá's statement that if a family cannot educate both its sons and its daughters, the priority must be given to the daughters, because they will be the first educators of the next generation. In the last few decades, development experts have discovered the wisdom of this teaching in less developed parts of the globe.

The exemplar

'Abdu'l-Bahá is the exemplar for Bahá'ís in all the various aspects of personal transformation. He was devoted to Bahá'u'lláh, knew his revelation thoroughly, demonstrated it perfectly and lived a life of prayer and service. His title 'Abdu'l-Bahá, meaning 'servant of Bahá', signified his total devotion to the Bahá'í Faith and his devotion to service to all people. He married – one wife only, in spite of pressure to conform to the Middle Eastern practice of polygamy – and raised four daughters (his sons having died in infancy). Public education being non-existent in the prison city of Acre, the household included a classroom where all the children and grandchildren could receive lessons. He fed the poor in the town, cared for the sick and made sure there was a supply of food when nearby battles during World War One caused a regional famine. His love for everyone, his humour, his boundless encouragement and his wisdom in every circumstance have inspired generations of Bahá'ís. Asking oneself 'what would 'Abdu'l-Bahá do?' has been a question that has helped many Bahá'ís in their spiritual path.

CHAPTER FIVE

An ever-advancing civilization

The authoritative Bahá'í texts look at society both as an organism in its own right and from the point of view of the role of the individual in its advancement. Bahá'u'lláh exhorts people to be 'anxiously concerned with the needs of the age ye live in, and center your deliberations on its exigencies and requirements'. Elsewhere he adds that 'all men have been created to carry forward an ever-advancing civilization'.[1] Thus the improvement and advancement of civilization is both a purpose of individual life and a personal priority. Bahá'ís are encouraged as individuals and as communities to become engaged in efforts to improve society and to collaborate with like-minded individuals and organizations. Bahá'í principles such as equality of men and women, universal education, opposition to domestic violence, improving public health and alleviating poverty inspire their efforts. The main limitation that Bahá'ís observe is avoidance of partisan politics, for true social improvement cannot be brought about through disunifying means.

Work is worship

An important starting point in making social change is selection of a vocation. Bahá'u'lláh requires all to 'engage in some occupation'. There are several reasons for this. Bahá'u'lláh says that having 'attained the stage of fulfilment and reached his maturity, man standeth in need of wealth, and such wealth as he acquireth through crafts or professions is commendable and praiseworthy in the estimation of men of wisdom, and especially in the eyes of

servants who dedicate themselves to the education of the world
and to the edification of its peoples'. One stands 'in need of wealth'
because one must support a family and because to express one's
talents and capacities, one must have the means: a dwelling, a
work space, books, equipment, materials, etc. Wealth, expended
for these purposes, is a positive good. It is also needed to do works
of charity: 'the beginning of magnanimity is when man expendeth
his wealth on himself, on his family and on the poor among his
brethren in his Faith.'[2] Wealth can provide a means for carrying
forward an ever advancing civilization.

The purpose of wealth is not consumerism: 'food, drink, shelter
and a degree of material comfort are essential, but human beings
cannot and never will find fulfillment in these necessities.'[3] To assist
Bahá'ís to contemplate what part of their lifestyle is a necessity
and what part is a luxury, Bahá'u'lláh established the institution
of Huqúqu'lláh, 'the right of God'. In essence, it states that part of
an earner's wealth belongs to God and part belongs to the earner.
But unlike the biblical tithe, where Jews (and some Christians) give
10 per cent of their wealth to their religion, Huqúqu'lláh involves
giving 19 per cent of the increase of one's wealth to the Universal
House of Justice. The increase is measured in increments worth 19
mithqáls (69 grams, 2.22 troy ounces) of gold. Implementation of
the law is left to one's conscience; it is a spiritual obligation, not
something others can ask one about. One's residence and necessary furnishings and any essential business assets are exempt. It
is up to each individual or family to decide what is necessary and
what is a luxury, hence the law forces one to consider the nature of
one's lifestyle, the purpose of life and the purpose of wealth. One
needs furniture and clothing, but should it be fancy and expensive,
or basic? Does one need a small car, or an expensive one? One's
answer to these questions determines the amount of Huqúqu'lláh
one should pay.

In addition to being a source of wealth, an occupation is an
expression of one's spirituality; it is a form of worship. 'Abdu'l-
Bahá explains that 'in the Bahá'í Cause arts, sciences and all crafts
are counted as worship. The man who makes a piece of note-paper
to the best of his ability, conscientiously, concentrating all his forces
on perfecting it, is giving praise to God. Briefly, all effort and exer-
tion put forth by man from the fullness of his heart is worship, if
it is prompted by the highest motives and the will to do service to

humanity. This is worship: to serve mankind and to minister to the needs of the people. Service is prayer'.[4] Thus one's work potentially is sacralized; not only is it a vehicle for self-expression and a means for supporting one's family, but is a form of service to humanity and prayer to God.

There are several important implications of this principle. Since work 'has not only a utilitarian purpose, but has a value in itself, because it draws us nearer to God', 'inherited wealth cannot make anyone immune from daily work'. Furthermore,

> It is the duty of those who are in charge of the organization of society to give every individual the opportunity of acquiring the necessary talent in some kind of profession, and also the means of utilizing such a talent, both for its own sake and for the sake of earning the means of his livelihood. Every individual, no matter how handicapped and limited he may be, is under the obligation of engaging in some work or profession.[5]

If this proves impossible for some individuals because of illness or economic circumstances, it is incumbent on the wealthy or the government to provide them with a monthly allowance. Bahá'u'lláh forbade begging as a means to earn a living. Since homemaking 'is a highly honourable and responsible work of fundamental importance to society', it counts as 'work'. It is not yet clear what implications this principle has for retirement.[6]

The dawning place of the remembrance of God (Mashriqu'l-Adhkár)

The Bahá'í Faith unites its concepts of worship, work and service together into a single institution called the *Mashriqu'l-Adhkár*,[7] an Arabic phrase usually translated as 'the dawning place for the remembrance of God'. At the centre of the Mashriqu'l-Adhkár is the House of Worship, a special building dedicated to devotional activities, nine sided, with nine entrances, generally with a dome, generally set in beautiful, meditative gardens. The House of Worship is devoted to the Word of God; the writings of Bahá'u'lláh, the Báb and 'Abdu'l-Bahá, the Qur'án, Bible and the scriptures of other world religions are recited, sung or chanted in its sanctuary. Speeches and instrumental music are not to be heard in the space. Because of this restriction, a nearby auditorium is often provided where music, talks, audio-visual presentations and other activities can occur. On Holy Days it is common for the worshippers to start in the House of Worship's sanctuary with an uplifting programme of the Divine Word, complete with an acapella choir, then to move to the auditorium for an additional programme.

But the Mashriqu'l-Adhkár consists of more than a House of Worship. It is to be surrounded by 'a number of dependencies dedicated to social, humanitarian, educational, and scientific pursuits'. They will 'afford relief to the suffering, sustenance to the poor, shelter to the wayfarer, solace to the bereaved, and education to the ignorant' and could include such institutions as hospitals, schools, universities, orphanages, homes for the aged, libraries and guest hostels. Shoghi Effendi indicates that the Mashriqu'l-Adhkár exemplifies in tangible form the integration of Bahá'í worship and service. Eventually they are to be constructed in every town and village. Currently there are seven worldwide, and most have no dependencies yet.[8] In the meantime, Bahá'í communities rent or build Bahá'í Centres where worship, public gatherings, classes and social events can occur under the same roof.

Teaching, social action and public discourse

Bahá'ís seek to increase the size of their community because a new divine revelation does little good for humanity if the ranks of its lovers and servants are few. But they also seek to demonstrate the teachings through charitable and humanitarian efforts and to dialogue with others about ways their values can provide new insights and approaches to solving humanity's problems. These three approaches are termed, respectively, teaching the Faith, social action and public discourse.

The Bahá'í principle of independent investigation of truth shapes the ways Bahá'ís can teach their Faith because no one should ever be pressured, deceived or bribed into belief. One cannot be enrolled into the Bahá'í community simply because one's spouse is a Bahá'í;

one must genuinely believe in Bahá'u'lláh and accept his revelation. The Bahá'í authoritative texts stress the role of love, respect and hospitality in Bahá'ís' relations to others, and the Bahá'í concept of consultation establishes a culture of dialogue with others. As Bahá'u'lláh explained,

> If ye be aware of a certain truth, if ye possess a jewel, of which others are deprived, share it with them in a language of utmost kindliness and good-will. If it be accepted, if it fulfil its purpose, your object is attained. If any one should refuse it, leave him unto himself, and beseech God to guide him. Beware lest ye deal unkindly with him. A kindly tongue is the lodestone of the hearts of men. It is the bread of the spirit, it clotheth the words with meaning, it is the fountain of the light of wisdom and understanding.[9]

Teaching the Faith to others is a challenge that should strengthen one's faith and help transform one's character. As 'Abdu'l-Bahá noted, 'the intention of the teacher must be pure, his heart independent, his spirit attracted, his thought at peace, his resolution firm, his magnanimity exalted and in the love of God a shining torch. Should he become as such, his sanctified breath will even affect the rock; otherwise there will be no result whatsoever. As long as a soul is not perfected, how can he efface the defects of others. Unless he is detached from aught else save God, how can he teach severance to others!'[10] Teaching the Faith to others, thus, is part of the effort of personal transformation, as important as prayer, fasting and studying the Word.

The loving approach to teaching the Bahá'í Faith to others does not mandate an indirect effort. Bahá'ís can go door to door in places to teach others where it is socially acceptable. They can socialize in parks and other public spaces and befriend strangers. They can proclaim their beliefs on the media and invite the public to Bahá'í events. Such efforts make sense especially when the religion is small and unknown to the majority of the population.

Bahá'í communities have always been involved in expressing their teachings in the form of service. As already noted in Chapter Two, even in an environment of persecution, the Iranian Bahá'ís created private schools open to children of all faiths. Bahá'í

FIGURE 5.1 *A session at the Barli Development Institute for Rural Women in Indore, India (© Bahá'í International Community).*

communities in developing countries have established hundreds of social and economic development projects: schools, community gardens, tree-planting projects, women's literacy projects, public health projects and educational radio stations. In developed countries, social services are much better developed, hence Bahá'í communities (which are often small) tackle much more modest challenges; they provide tutoring services, clean parks, support soup kitchens and food banks and engage in multi-religious collaboration. Four *core activities* – spiritual education classes for children, junior youth and adults, and devotional programmes open to all – are priority outreach efforts of Bahá'í communities worldwide. The Universal House of Justice has recommended that Bahá'ís focus on specific villages or neighbourhoods in their efforts to proclaim the Faith and serve the public, so that their efforts have a greater impact. Efforts to serve and teach need to be balanced, complementary and coherent.[11]

Finally, Bahá'ís have always been in active dialogue with others about the ways their values relate to the problems of society. Bahá'u'lláh asked 'Abdu'l-Bahá to draft a book about social reform, *The Secret of Divine Civilization*, in 1875, in order to disseminate Bahá'í principles to Iranian reform-minded readers. During his travels in Europe, the United States and Canada in 1911–13, 'Abdu'l-Bahá articulated Bahá'í social principles to large audiences in an effort to change attitudes about racism, world peace, equality of the sexes and interfaith relations. The Bahá'í community had representation at the League of Nations and has a very active United Nations office, where its staff are involved in dozens of pressing international issues. Many National Spiritual Assemblies have similar offices in their national capitals. The Universal House of Justice and many National Spiritual Assemblies have published statements on such issues as world peace, the advancement of women, human rights, environmental degradation, global warming, poverty, governance and race unity. The purpose of such dialogue is twofold: to change cultural and social values that Bahá'ís see as impediments to the progress of society towards the Lesser Peace, and to discover the deeper meaning of their values, which are best explored in discussion with others and in efforts to implement them.

Global civilization

The civilization that the Bahá'í Faith seeks to advance is global in nature. History has seen a series of ever-larger stages in integration, 'starting with the family, the smallest unit in the scale of human organization', and successively replaced by 'the tribe, the city-state, and the nation'; the process will 'continue to operate until it culminates in the unification of the whole world, the final object and the crowning glory of human evolution on this planet'.[12] The technological advances of the last two centuries have shrunk the world into a neighbourhood and set in motion forces of globalization that match the vision of world unity Bahá'u'lláh offered a century and a half ago.

'Abdu'l-Bahá notes continuities between the family and global civilization. 'Simply enlarge the circle of the household and you have the nation', he notes:

Enlarge the circle of nations and you have all humanity. The conditions surrounding the family surround the nation. The happenings in the family are the happenings in the life of the nation. Would it add to the progress and advancement of a family if dissensions should arise among its members, fighting, pillaging each other, jealous and revengeful of injury, seeking selfish advantage? Nay, this would be the cause of the effacement of progress and advancement. So it is in the great family of nations, for nations are but an aggregate of families. Therefore as strife and dissension destroy a family and prevent its progress, so nations are destroyed and advancement hindered.[13]

For this reason, Bahá'u'lláh explained that the oneness of humanity implies the need to establish a global governing system. As an initial step, he calls for collective security. 'Be united, O concourse of the sovereigns of the world', he wrote, 'for thereby will the tempest of discord be stilled amongst you, and your peoples find rest. Should any one among you take up arms against another, rise ye all against him, for this is naught but manifest justice'.[14]

The lesser peace

He also called on all kings and rulers to limit their armaments and meet in an international summit to establish common treaties and institutions. He said that an international language and script should be selected to supplement local languages and allow easy world communication. The Bahá'í authoritative texts call for the eventual establishment of an international system of weights and measures, a world currency and an elected world legislature. They endorse global measures to ensure universal education and health care, to create equitable access to resources, and to diminish the extreme imbalances of wealth and poverty. This new stage in civilization is called the *Lesser Peace*.

Bahá'u'lláh's vision has gradually found expression in the international institutions that governments have found it necessary to create. Beginning with the International Telecommunications Union in 1869 and the Universal Postal Union in 1874, governments have created hundreds of international intergovernmental agencies to coordinate activities that transcend national boundaries. The

League of Nations and United Nations were subsequently founded, in 1919 and 1945 respectively, to provide an international deliberative body, though with limited powers in order to minimize intrusions on national sovereignty. The Bahá'í authoritative texts state that this progression of secular, political institutions will evolve as the problems of the world continue to multiply; globalization is forcing economic and financial integration on the nations, and environmental issues such as global warming demand international responses. The Universal House of Justice is enjoined in the authoritative texts to promote the Lesser Peace, and Bahá'í involvement in public discourse can help, but the governments and the public will have to do most of the work.[15] It may very well be that over the next century or two, regional institutions such as the European Union will provide a model for international integration, rather than a strengthened United Nations.

Establishment of the Lesser Peace will not produce solutions to all of humanity's problems; indeed, it may not even end all warfare. The United States fought a bloody Civil War 75 years after its unity was legally enshrined in its Constitution. But the Lesser Peace is an important step on a long and thorny path. In 1985 the Universal House of Justice wrote *The Promise of World Peace*, a statement to the peoples of the world that outlined a series of barriers to peace that must be overcome in order to create a just, peaceful world civilization:

> Racism . . . perpetrates too outrageous a violation of the dignity of human beings to be countenanced under any pretext. Racism retards the unfoldment of the boundless potentialities of its victims, corrupts its perpetrators, and blights human progress. . . .
>
> The inordinate disparity between rich and poor, a source of acute suffering, keeps the world in a state of instability, virtually on the brink of war. Few societies have dealt effectively with this situation. The solution calls for the combined application of spiritual, moral and practical approaches. . . .
>
> Unbridled nationalism, as distinguished from a sane and legitimate patriotism, must give way to a wider loyalty, to the love of humanity as a whole. Bahá'u'lláh's statement is: 'The earth is but one country, and mankind its citizens.' The concept

of world citizenship is a direct result of the contraction of the world into a single neighbourhood through scientific advances and of the indisputable interdependence of nations. Love of all the world's peoples does not exclude love of one's country. The advantage of the part in a world society is best served by promoting the advantage of the whole. . . .

Religious strife, throughout history, has been the cause of innumerable wars and conflicts, a major blight to progress, and is increasingly abhorrent to the people of all faiths and no faith. . . . The challenge facing the religious leaders of mankind is . . . to ask themselves whether they cannot, in humility before their Almighty Creator, submerge their theological differences in a great spirit of mutual forbearance that will enable them to work together for the advancement of human understanding and peace.

The emancipation of women, the achievement of full equality between the sexes, is one of the most important, though less acknowledged prerequisites of peace. The denial of such equality perpetrates an injustice against one half of the world's population and promotes in men harmful attitudes and habits that are carried from the family to the workplace, to political life, and ultimately to international relations. . . .

The cause of universal education, which has already enlisted in its service an army of dedicated people from every faith and nation, deserves the utmost support that the governments of the world can lend it. For ignorance is indisputably the principal reason for the decline and fall of peoples and the perpetuation of prejudice. . . .[16]

In short, world peace is not simply a matter of preventing warfare; it requires creation of a world culture based on a different set of values. Bahá'ís see the values advocated in the Bahá'í authoritative texts as the blueprint for a new civilization. The process of establishing them will be both religious (the Bahá'í community growing larger in numbers and capability) and cultural (gradual adoption of principles found in the Bahá'í writings, or parts of them, by societies). History suggests that the process will take centuries.

Reforming the economic system

One reason the process will be long is because the implementation of spiritual principles is a complex process. *The Promise of World Peace* notes that the current international system is set up 'callously to abandon starving millions to the operations of a market system that all too clearly is aggravating the plight of the majority of mankind, while enabling small sections to live in an unprecedented condition of affluence'.[17] But that does not mean the Bahá'í Faith advocates the abandonment of capitalism. 'The Cause is not an economic system, nor its Founders be considered as having been technical economists', Shoghi Effendi warned. 'The contribution of the Faith to this subject is essentially indirect, as it consists of the application of spiritual principles to our present-day economic system'.[18] One can find in the Bahá'í authoritative texts endorsement of private property, charging of interest on loans, profit sharing with workers, a graduated income tax, an inheritance tax, an explanation of the purpose of work and of wealth and advocacy of voluntary sharing of wealth.

In one tablet, 'Abdu'l-Bahá advocates the creation of a 'public treasury' in a village, into which one contributes based on one's income (the wealthy paying up to several times the percentage of the average worker). Unclaimed assets, voluntary contributions and taxes on livestock, mines and inheritance would round out the income. From the revenue would come payments for education, health care, taxes to other governments and support for orphans, the disabled and those unable to work. Hard-working people unable to earn enough to live would receive a subsidy from the public treasury.[19] The details of such a system will take trial and error to develop over a long period of time.

The most great peace

The Bahá'í authoritative texts talk of the Lesser Peace lasting centuries and involving the gradual spiritualization of humanity. During the Lesser Peace, humanity 'can be likened to a body that is unified but without life', the Universal House of Justice noted in a letter. 'The second process, the task of breathing life into this unified body – of creating true unity and spirituality culminating in the Most Great Peace – is that of the Bahá'ís, who are labouring consciously, with detailed instructions and continuing divine guidance, to erect the fabric of the Kingdom of God on earth, into which they call their fellow-men, thus conferring upon them eternal life'.[20]

The Most Great Peace is the Bahá'í vision of the biblical Kingdom of God on Earth, the paradisiacal future state promised by most of the world's religions. It is the goal towards which the Bahá'í community is striving. It is not known how much suffering humanity will have to endure before it is established. Most scriptures place the promised kingdom after an apocalypse, and Bahá'u'lláh warns humanity that an 'unforeseen calamity is following you'.[21] Thus Bahá'ís are not naive optimists about humanity's future. Rather, they look many centuries ahead, noting that a millennium ago, humanity lived under far more primitive and arbitrary conditions than today, and that cultural changes equally as revolutionary are possible over the next 1,000 years.

The Bible describes the Kingdom of God on Earth in highly metaphorical language; 'the wolf also shall dwell with the lamb, and the leopard shall lie down with the kid; and the calf and the young lion and the fatling together . . . And the cow and the bear shall feed; their young ones shall lie down together: and the lion shall eat straw like the ox. And the sucking child shall play on the hole of the asp, and the weaned child shall put his hand on the cockatrice' den. They shall not hurt nor destroy in all my holy mountain: for the earth shall be full of the knowledge of the LORD, as the waters cover the sea' (Isa. 11.6–9). Shoghi Effendi offers a far more concrete vision of the future; whether it describes society towards the end of the Lesser Peace or during the Most Great Peace is not certain:

> In such a world society, science and religion, the two most potent forces in human life, will be reconciled, will co-operate, and will harmoniously develop. . . . The economic resources of the world will be organized, its sources of raw materials will be tapped and fully utilized, its markets will be co-ordinated and developed, and the distribution of its products will be equitably regulated.

National rivalries, hatreds and intrigues will cease, and racial animosity and prejudice will be replaced by racial amity, understanding and co-operation. The causes of religious strife will be permanently removed, economic barriers and restrictions will be completely abolished, and the inordinate distinction between classes will be obliterated. Destitution on the one hand, and gross accumulation of ownership on the other, will disappear. The enormous energy dissipated and wasted on war, whether economic or political, will be consecrated to such ends as will extend the range of human inventions and technical development, to the increase of the productivity of mankind, to the extermination of disease, to the extension of scientific research, to the raising of the standard of physical health, to the sharpening and refinement of the human brain, to the exploitation of the unused and unsuspected resources of the planet, to the prolongation of human life, and to the furtherance of any other agency that can stimulate the intellectual, the moral, and spiritual life of the entire human race.[22]

Such is the long-term social goal of the Bahá'í Faith: creation of a world civilization where human potential can be fully expressed. The Bahá'í community has been striving towards that goal for over a century and a half, mostly by reaching out to peoples and cultures all over the globe, expanding its membership and building its own internal capacities. Because of its small size – perhaps 100,000 members in the year 1900, 400,000 in 1963, and 5 million today – the efforts of the Bahá'í community have mostly been focused inwardly, although there have already been notable successes in improving society as a whole. We now turn to the creation and development of the Bahá'í community over the last century and a half.

PART TWO

Development of the Bahá'í community

CHAPTER SIX

The Báb and the Bábí community, 1844–53

The Bahá'í Faith arose from the Bábí Faith, a religion that briefly flourished in Iran in the 1840s. It was established by 'Alí-Muhammad of Shiraz (1819–50), who in 1844 took on the honorific of *the Báb* (the Gate) and who declared himself to be the fulfilment of Islamic prophecies. The Twelver Shi'ite Islam that dominated Iran expected the return of the twelfth imam (a messianic figure), and the expectation was particularly strong in 1844.

Early life of 'Ali-Muhammad

The Báb was born 'Alí-Muhammad on the first day of Muharram, 1235, corresponding to 20 October 1819 on the Gregorian calendar. He was born in the southern Iranian city of Shiraz to a family of prosperous merchants. Both his father, Sayyid Muhammad Ridá, and his mother, Fátimih Bigum, were descendants of the Prophet, and their families had lived in Shiraz for generations. When 'Alí-Muhammad was 7 years old his father died, so responsibility for his upbringing fell to his maternal uncles, especially Hájí Mírzá Sayyid 'Alí.

The young boy was sent to a local teacher named Shaykh 'Ábid for 6 or 7 years for a private education (there being no public schools in Shiraz at the time). The teacher was Shaykhí, a controversial Shi'ite sect established by Shaykh Ahmad Ahsá'í (1756–1825). Members of 'Alí-Muhammad's family were also Shaykhís, which suggests that 'Alí-Muhammad was exposed to Shaykhí interpretations of Islam from a young age.[1] All accounts agree that 'Alí-Muhammad was a precocious, intelligent child, and was devoted to prayer at an early age.

While in his teens, 'Alí-Muhammad began to work in his uncle's business, and by the time he was 16 or 17 he was serving as a commercial agent for the family at their offices in Bushihr, an Iranian city on the Persian Gulf. Through this city flowed imports to Shiraz from India and the Arabian Peninsula. 'Ali-Muhammad seems to have been a successful merchant, and his later writings praise business as an important livelihood, but one which must be carried out with strict honesty and complete devotion to God. His own life apparently was extremely pious; he is known to have prayed much of the morning and afternoon on some days.

About 1840 or 1841 'Alí-Muhammad left the family business and travelled to Karbilá in Iraq, where the third Shi'ite imám, Husayn, is buried. There he attended a few classes given by Sayyid Kázim-i-Rashtí, the head of the Shaykhí movement. He remained in Karbilá 8 months and made an impression on many Shaykhís there.

'Alí-Muhammad may also have been exposed to Sufism (Islamic mysticism). Sufism was usually discouraged or opposed by the Shi'ite 'ulamá (learned), but Sufi writings have long circulated in Persian and Sufi orders were common there. He is known to have been in acquaintance with the leading Sufi in Shiraz. 'Alí-Muhammad, however, does not use much technical Sufi terminology in his later writings.

'Alí-Muhammad remained in Karbilá until His uncle, Sayyid 'Alí, journeyed there and implored Him to return to Shiraz. This he did in 1842. He married Khadíjih Khánum in August of that year and resumed His business. The couple had a son, Ahmad, who died before his first birthday. 'Alí-Muhammad's extended periods of prayer and His pious acts further developed His reputation as a mystic. Sometime before his declaration of his mission, 'Alí-Muhammad had a dream where he saw the severed head of the Imám Husayn and was privileged to drink seven drops of the Imám's precious blood. He privately made some sort of messianic claim to family members and it was accepted by His wife and His uncle, Sayyid 'Alí.

'Alí-Muhammad's writings before his declaration, however, do not demonstrate a prophetic consciousness. His earliest work was a short treatise, 'Journey towards God' that quoted the Qur'án and utilized Shaykhí ideas extensively.[2] In November or December 1843, some 6 months before declaring his mission, he started a commentary on a chapter (súrih) of the Qur'án, *Tafsír-i-súrih-i-baqarih* or 'Commentary on the Súrih of the Cow'. It utilized the usual tools of Qur'án commentary. The second half was composed some months after his declaration.

Declaration of the Báb

On 2 January 1844 Sayyid Káim-i-Rashtí (1793–1844), head of the Shaykhí sect, died in Karbalá without naming a successor. Since the Shaykhís believed that there was always a Perfect Shí'í on the earth, some of Rashtí's followers set out to find the new Perfect Shí'í. Furthermore, the Islamic year 1260 was about to begin – the thousandth year after the disappearance of the Twelfth Imám in 260 AH – and many Shaykhís expected that year to usher in the coming of the Muslim messiah, sometimes called the Imám Mahdí.* Among the prominent Shaykhís who initiated a search for the Mahdí was Mullá Husayn-i-Bushrú'í, and in May 1844 his travels took him to Shiraz.

Mullá Husayn encountered 'Alí-Muhammad on the afternoon of 22 May, accompanied him to his house, and had dinner with him. After dinner the subject of Mullá Husayn's search came up and 'Alí-Muhammad proposed that he himself fulfilled all the requirements for being the Promised One. After several hours of discussion, Mullá Husayn was convinced, and became his first official follower, thereby inaugurating what came to be called the Bábí Faith. 'Alí-Muhammad revealed the first chapter of a commentary on the Qur'ánic Súrih of Joseph (a work he titled the Qayyúmu'l-Asmá) that evening. It was to become one of his most important works.

---

*Islamic terminology on this point is complex and I am trying to simplify it for the reader. Both Sunnís and Shi'ites use the term Mahdí to refer to the Promised One who comes at the end of the age, though their understanding of the figure is somewhat different. Shi'ites also use the term *Qá'im*, 'He who arises', for the same figure. They identify the Promised One with the return of the twelfth imám, the twelfth in a series of infallible Shi'ite leaders, who supposedly disappeared from the earth in 260 AH (874 CE). For the sake of the reader I will use the terms Promised One and Mahdí and avoid the terms Qá'im and twelfth imam.

Over the next few months an additional 17 individuals accepted him as the Promised One. He gave them, and Mullá Husayn, the title 'Letters of the Living'. All of them had been Shaykhís. One, Fátimih Baraqání, later called Táhirih, was a brilliant scholar and poet, the foremost Bábí woman. Another, Quddús, emerged as a major leader.

'Alí-Muhammad assumed a title, the Báb (meaning 'the Gate' in Arabic). It suggested that he was claiming not to be the Promised One, but merely the gate to him.** A few scholars have argued that the Báb changed his mind about his claim; that first he merely claimed Báb-hood, but that after a few months his success led him to elevate his claim to Mahdí-hood. Had the Báb immediately made public his claim to be the Promised One, however, he would have been fiercely opposed by the Shi'ite clergy. The Báb himself says he gradually unveiled His claim, so as not to shock the public. His early claims were carefully phrased so that the later claims did not contradict them.

There is considerable evidence that the Báb understood himself to be the Promised One from the first night of His mission. Mullá Husayn seems to have understood the Báb to be the Promised One immediately. Only 5 months after the Báb's declaration, one of the Letters of the Living, Mullá 'Alí Bastámí, was arrested in Iraq for preaching that the Báb was the Mahdí. Clergy submitted as evidence at Bastámí's trial the Qayyúmu'l-Asmá itself, arguing that its Qur'ánic tone and style of revelation made it clear that the Báb was claiming prophethood. The judges – a panel that included both Sunní and Shi'ite jurisprudents – found Mullá 'Alí Bastámí guilty of spreading the Báb's heresy. Bastámí was sent to Istanbul and condemned to a life of hard labour, which caused his death shortly thereafter.

The Qayyumu'l-Asmá, which is one and a half times the length of the Qur'án, was completed over a 40-day period. In addition to stating the Báb's claim in indirect language, it foreshadowed his own martyrdom, admonished the shah, warned the Shi'ite clerical hierarchy, alluded to the coming of yet another prophetic figure after the Báb and called on the people of the West to issue forth

---

**The twelfth imam, before disappearing from the earth in 874, supposedly went into hiding and communicated to his followers through an individual called a Báb or 'gate'.

from their cities to aid his cause.[3] It was widely distributed in the first year of the Bábí movement and functioned as something of a Bible for the Bábís.

By writing *tafsír* or Qur'án commentary, the Báb was using a highly respected and venerable literary form; not one expected of a prophet. The Báb, however, used tafsír as His way to declare His station as well as to define His theology and to state His basic differences with traditional Shi'ite understandings of Islam. Thus he used an established literary genre in a radically new way. A unique aspect of the Báb's tafsír was that often he did not exegete the meaning of the text sentence by sentence or word by word, but offered symbolic interpretations of the text letter by letter ('the letter Alif in the first word of the súrih referreth to the favours (álá') of Thy Lord . . . Then the letter Nún referreth to the radiant light (núr) of Thy Lord . . .').[4] In this manner the Báb wrote entire, lengthy books on short chapters of the Qur'án.

Such an approach to commentary was not altogether new in Islam, but the extent the Báb did it was unique. He utilized esoteric and occult Islamic ideas, constructed elaborate arguments with astrological and alchemical metaphors, offered cabbalistic interpretations of words by substituting one word for another if the numerical values of the letters added up to the same sum, and played with Arabic grammar to construct neologisms of uncertain meaning. The resulting text could neither be proved nor refuted via logic; the insights were at least poetic and claimed divine inspiration. The works produced in this manner were described by the great Persian scholar Edward G. Browne as 'voluminous, hard to comprehend, uncouth in style, unsystematic in arrangement, filled with iterations and solecisms, and not infrequently quite incoherent and unintelligible to any ordinary reader'.[5] No doubt part of Browne's reaction was culturally shaped. To the seminary students who became many of the Báb's prominent followers, educated to appreciate nuance and allusion, the result was both philosophically brilliant and mystically profound, inspiring them to acts of great audacity in spreading the message and remarkable courage in defending themselves when attacked.

Early dissemination of the religion

As soon as the ranks of the Letters of the Living were complete, the Báb gave them missions to spread the new Faith. Mullá 'Alí Bastámí was sent to the holy Shi'ite shrine cities in southern Iraq, where he preached especially to the Shaykhís. Hundreds, both Persians and Arabs, and including a few prominent learned clerics, became followers until, as already mentioned, Bastámí was arrested, at which point Táhirih emerged as the leader of the Iraqi Bábís.[6] Another Letter of the Living returned to India, never to be heard from again.

Mullá Husayn, the Báb's first follower, was given the task of disseminating the new religion in Iran. Initially he went to Isfahan, a large city in central Iran, to build a Bábí community there. By August he was in Tehran; by September, in Mashhad, the largest city in Iran's northeast, his native area. While in Tehran he met Husayn-'Alí of Núr (1817–92), who later took on the title Bahá'u'lláh and founded the Bahá'í Faith. He was a wealthy nobleman, born in northern Iran, whose father was a palace official and noted calligrapher. Husayn-'Alí was raised in a cosmopolitan household where he rubbed shoulders with the country's leading officials and literati. In 1844 he was 27 and had an infant son, 'Abbás, born on the same night the Báb had first declared himself. Husayn-'Alí and his wife Navváb were known as the 'father of the poor' and the 'mother of consolation' for their efforts to feed the hungry and care for the sick. He immediately accepted the Báb and bent his energy and resources to the spread of the Faith. As a result, his home province of Mazandaran, north of Tehran along the Caspian seacoast, gradually became a major centre of Bábí activity.

Pilgrimage

On 10 September 1844 the Báb departed for Mecca, to join the annual pilgrimage. In Mecca he declared His claim publicly at the Kaaba and to the Sharif of Mecca, its custodian. But the Báb did not find acceptance. During this period he wrote extensively. Among His more important works were Khasá'il-i-sab'ih, which added a sentence to the Muslim call to prayer; Kitáb-i-Rúh ('Book of the Spirit'); Sahífih baynu'l-haramayn ('Treatise between the Two

Sanctuaries'); and Kitáb-i-Fihrist ('The Book of the Catalogue'), an invaluable list of the Báb's early works.

The Báb had planned to go to the Shi'ite shrine cities of Iraq after his pilgrimage, but the arrest of Mullá 'Alí Bastámí there made that impossible. Returning to Bushihr on 15 May 1845, the Báb proceeded to Shiraz, but was placed under house arrest because of the theological controversy his growing body of followers had created in that city. Notwithstanding his confinement, the Báb wrote very prolifically during this period. One work, the Tafsír-i-Súrih-i-Kawthar ('Commentary on the Chapter on Abundance'), was a 200-page commentary on a Qur'ánic chapter that is only a few lines in length.

Philosophical writings in Shiraz and Isfahan

About January 1846, according to the Báb himself, his writings shifted from a focus on interpretation of Islamic terms to a second, more philosophical stage, where he wrote about the unknowability of God, the nature of the Divine Will and its manifestation through messengers of God, and the creation of the world.

Because of a cholera outbreak, in September 1846 the Báb moved to Isfahan, where the governor, Manuchihr Khán, protected him and where the Báb could nurture a growing Bábí community. The need to maintain some secrecy about the Báb's whereabouts decreased His literary output, especially in reply to letters from followers. One major work revealed at the time was the Tafsír-i-Súrih-i-va'l-'asr ('Commentary on the Chapter on Time and Age'), a work interpreting the three verses (about 20 words) of a particular chapter of the Qur'án. It was composed spontaneously in response to a request by Mír Sayyid Muhammad, the chief cleric of the city. Much of the work, which is one third the length of the entire Qur'án, was revealed in a few hours, to the astonishment to those present. On another occasion, in 2 hours the Báb revealed a 50-page disquisition on the specific mission of Muhammad.

A growing community of followers

With the Báb under house arrest and often unreachable, the task of organizing Bábí sympathizers and converts fell on Mullá Husayn Bushrú'í, the first believer, and his associates. Mullá Husayn was particularly successful in Khurásán, his home province in north-eastern Iran, where converts soon numbered in the thousands. Another Letter of the Living, Mullá Yúsuf Ardabílí, created Bábí communities in Azerbaijan, Qazvin, Kerman and Yazd. As in Iraq, the Bábí message initially attracted Shaykhís, especially 'ulamá (clerics) and seminary students, although Sufis also joined. The new religion then spread through their social networks, reaching merchants, traders, artisans, urban intelligentsia and lower to mid-dle-rank state officials. Inhabitants of the cities and towns dominated. Relatively few rural land owners, peasants or tribal chiefs were reached, though some were, and they were often members of other persecuted Muslim minority sects.[7] It may be that increased competition from European merchants and European goods, and the consequent decline in the income of many merchants and artisans, were factors in the receptivity of these groups to a new religion. It is estimated that the Bábí population of Iran eventually reached 100,000 and constituted perhaps 4 per cent of the urban population and 3 per cent of the village population. It was virtually non-existent among Iran's three million nomads. It did not reach the Christian minority, although one Zoroastrian and a group of Jews are known to have accepted the Báb.[8]

The fortress of Mákú

The death of Manuchihr Khán in March 1847 ended the Báb's protected life in Isfahan. He was arrested and transported to Tabriz, and finally to the mountain fortress of Mákú, near the border of Turkey and Russia, where few of his followers could reach him. He reached Mákú in the late summer of 1847. At first the conditions of confinement in the fortress were severe, but gradually the Báb's captors gave him greater freedom of movement and the right to receive guests.

In Mákú the Báb had the time and opportunity to write extensively. His writings entered a third 'legislative' stage, where he penned works that openly announced His station as a Manifestation of God, abrogated Islamic law and offered a set of Bábí laws. He ordered his works proclaimed widely. Many of the terms and concepts mentioned in the earlier stages were defined and elaborated upon in the third stage, thus clarifying the meaning of many statements he had earlier made. The resulting works were some of his most important and influential.

The Persian Bayan was undoubtedly the most important work of the Báb and contains a lucid and systematic summary of his teachings. It was composed in Mákú in late 1847 or early 1848. The work consists of nine chapters titled *váhids* or 'unities', which in turn are usually subdivided into 19 *bábs* or 'gates'. The one exception is the last unity, which has only ten bábs. The Báb explained that completion of the Bayán would be the task of 'He whom God shall make manifest' a messiah figure to succeed the Báb, about whom he began to write extensively.

According to Moojan Momen, a scholar of the Báb, the Bayán sought to accomplish four things. First, it unequivocally stated the Báb's claim to be the return of the Imám Mahdí, the Shi'ite Promised One. Second, it abrogated Islamic law and replaced it with Bábí laws. Third, it incorporated the major features of the Báb's exegesis of the eschatological terms of the Qur'án, indicating the manner in which they had been fulfilled by his own appearance. Fourth, it emphasized the advent of 'He whom God shall make manifest'; indeed, one could argue that is the central theme of the entire work.[9]

The Bayán offered laws of behaviour for the Bábís that were based on the maxim that one should treat all things as God would treat them, that is, with gentleness and kindness. Bábís were never to spank their children, were to answer all cries by babies, make sure their doorways were tall enough so that even tall people could pass through them easily, carry no weapons in public, treat beasts of burden with kindness, change clothes often, wash often, help all travellers and keep all rivers and lakes clean.

The Báb's laws abolished polygamy except in the case of infertility, abolished the Shi'ite institution of temporary marriage and allowed men and women who were not related to see each other in public, contrary to Muslim customs of the day and prefiguring the Bahá'í emancipation of women a few decades later. He ordained a new solar calendar of 19 months of 19 days each, gave all the months names based on attributes of God, and changed the time of fasting to the month of Loftiness (which falls in March). He established a new institution similar to tithing, called Huqúqu'lláh.

In stark contrast to these laws and principles of behaviour were a series of harsh commandments to expel all nonbelievers from the central provinces of Iran, confiscate their property, annul marriages made between them and believers, destroy all books written by them and initiate jihad to spread the religion. But the harsh commands were made contingent on acceptance by 'He whom God shall make manifest' and thus appear to have constituted symbolic legislation designed to focus the Bábí community on acceptance of that figure.[10] In various writings, the Báb said to expect him 9 or 19 years after the initiation of the Báb's own ministry. He even hinted that his name would be Bahá.

Composed at the same time as the Persian Bayán was the Arabic Bayán, which consists of 11 *váhids* or 'unities', each with 19 *bábs* or 'gates'. It offers a concise summary of the Báb's teachings and laws. Each Bayán refer to the other and sometimes corresponding chapters and gates cover the same topics.[11]

The Báb also composed two works by the title of Dalá'il-i-sab'ih ('Seven Proofs'). The longer one was in Persian, the shorter one in Arabic; both were composed in Mákú in late 1847 or early 1848. Nicholas called the Persian Seven Proofs 'the most important of the polemical works that issued' from the Báb's pen.[12] The work was written to either a non-Bábí or to a follower whose faith had been shaken. The Arabic text summarized the seven proofs found in the Persian text. In the Seven Proofs, the Báb argued that the revelation of divine verses was sufficient proof of his truth; political sovereignty and holy war were not necessary. The work also expounded on the doctrine of progressive revelation through a series of divine messengers (Adam, Noah, Abraham, Moses, Jesus, Muhammad, the Báb and He whom God shall make manifest).

The day of resurrection

The imprisonment of the Báb in a remote fortress was a severe test for the Bábí community. Some expected the Mahdí to announce the beginning of a holy war (jihad) that would establish justice on the earth. Other, contradictory, Islamic traditions spoke of the martyrdom of the Mahdí and his companions, rather like the death of the Shi'ite Imám Husayn at Karbilá in 680 CE. The Báb hinted at his own martyrdom on several occasions and had rejected the idea that the Mahdí needed political power or military force to achieve his aims. Others argued that they should go to Mákú and forcibly free the Báb from his confinement, an act that presumably would trigger the holy war. A few Bábís armed themselves in anticipation of a holy war or an event like Karbilá.

In March 1848 Mullá Husayn went to Mákú from Khurásán and met with the Báb to discuss the situation and whether the time had come for the Bábís to arm themselves. The Báb apparently sent Mullá Husayn back to Khurásán to proclaim the beginning of the Qiyáma or 'Day of Resurrection', meaning the inauguration of a new religious dispensation, not the beginning of a holy war.

Mullá Husayn returned to Mashhad, the capital of Khurásán, where he was met by Quddús, the other leading member of the Letters of the Living. The proclamation of the Day of Resurrection caused unrest in the city and Mullá Husayn was held in police custody as a result. Quddús set out westward with a group of Bábís, apparently flying a black standard in fulfilment of an Islamic prophecy that when the Qá'im comes, an army would set out westward from Khurásán flying such a flag. Their goal may have been to free the Báb, or to experience a re-enactment of the Karbilá event.

After traveling several hundred kilometres westward, in late June 1848 Quddús and his band encountered first Táhirih, then Husayn-'Alí (Bahá'u'lláh), who were traveling eastward separately to join the Bábís in Khurásán. The three groups gathered in a hamlet named Badasht. Husayn-'Alí rented three gardens, one for each party. Those present, 81 in number, remained to deliberate for 22 days. Each morning Husayn-'Alí revealed a tablet to be read to the assembled group; if the works had survived, they might have been the earliest Bahá'í sacred texts. Bahá'u'lláh did not claim authorship, however, and issued them anonymously. The tablets gave many of those present new names, which were subsequently confirmed by the Báb. It was here that Fátimih Baraqání acquired the honorific *Táhirih*, the 'Pure One' and Mullá Muhammad-'Alí Bárfurúshí the honorific *Quddús*, 'Most Holy One', as they became known to history. Husayn-'Alí gave himself the honorific *Bahá*, 'Glory', and subsequently became known as Bahá'u'lláh.

It was the first time a large group of prominent Bábís had ever met together, and there were many issues to debate. They may have known about provisions of the Persian Bayán and its implications. Táhirih, present but veiled, represented the party that saw the Bábí movement as a new religion and that Islamic law had to be abrogated. Quddús represented those who opposed the abrogation of

Islamic law. Bahá'u'lláh mediated between the two. Discussion waxed hot, with Táhirih referring to Quddús as a 'pupil whom the Báb has sent me to edify and instruct' and Quddús referring to Táhirih as 'the author of heresy'.[13] Finally one morning Táhirih entered Bahá'u'lláh's tent where many had gathered. She was unveiled and boldly proclaimed the independence of the new Faith and the abrogation of Islamic law. The sight of the face of the 'Pure One' was so shocking that one man slit his own throat and ran screaming from the tent. Others, their faith shattered, immediately abandoned the religion and left the camp. Yet others contemplated the Islamic tradition that on the Day of Judgment, Fátimih, wife of the Imám 'Alí and an embodiment of spotless chastity, would cross the Sirát Bridge unveiled (Táhirih was regarded by the Bábís as the incarnation of Fátimih).[14] It was the proclamation of the emancipation of women that marked the beginning of the break with Islamic law. Subsequently, Táhirih's followers discarded their prayer rugs – which made it impossible for them to pray according to Islamic law – and broke the prayer seals on which their foreheads rested when they prostrated themselves.

Bahá'u'lláh's efforts to mediate between the two groups were largely successful and the Bábís at Badasht accepted that the Báb had inaugurated a new religion with its own laws. When the Badasht conference ended, Quddús and an unveiled Táhirih rode together in a howdah (a two-seat enclosure saddled to the back of a horse), an act so shocking that a mob of villagers, spying them, attacked the Bábís, killed several, and scattered the party. Word of the Bábí rejection of Islamic law began to spread across the country. The Bábí party continued westward towards Mazandaran in groups and often encountered hostilities. Further complicating the situation, the Shah died in October, creating a temporary power vacuum and raising messianic expectations. The new shah, however, appointed a new Prime Minister who determined to crush the Bábí movement.

Mullá Husayn, who had left Mashhad with an additional contingent of 202 Bábís, was too late to attend the Badasht gathering. When his group reached the forests and marshes of Mazandaran near the Caspian seacoast, they got lost. The brigands who offered to guide them tried to kill them, and they were attacked by local townspeople. Unable to continue safely, they encamped at the shrine of a local saint, Shaykh Tabarsí. The tomb was located inside a yard surrounded by a low wall. The Bábís proceeded to fortify the shrine. Bahá'u'lláh visited and encouraged them to arrange the release of Quddús, under house arrest in a nearby town. Quddús joined the force at the fort, at which point a count revealed 313 men inside. But the Bábís were ill equipped to fight; they had swords, daggers, seven muskets, and perhaps five horses. The Bábís also lacked military training. Bahá'u'lláh provided them supplies and sought to join the group, but he was arrested and jailed.

The occupational backgrounds of some 220 are known; more than 60 per cent were seminary students or clerics, while about 25 per cent were craftsmen, skilled and unskilled urban workers or peasants. Others were local villagers attracted to the messianic expectations of the Bábís.[15] When a 4,000-man local militia attacked them on 22 December 1848, however, the Bábís routed the soldiers, killed 70 or more (including the commander), and captured a large amount of ammunition, provisions and horses. The government responded by sending a more powerful fighting force and the siege of Fort Shaykh Tabarsí began.

The siege lasted until 9 May 1849 and ultimately involved 12,000 troops. The Bábís, surrounded and unable to obtain supplies, often went on the offensive and attacked the army camp at night, killing hundreds and capturing desperately needed provisions. In one case they even briefly captured the tent of the prince in charge of the siege. Army attacks on the earthworks of the fort, even when tunnelling succeeded in destroying two of its four towers, even after cannons pounded it day and night, failed. But eventually Mullá Husayn fell in the fighting. The last 200 starved and wounded survivors, promised an honourable surrender and safe passage home – sworn by the shah's commander upon the Qur'án – surrendered.[16] They were massacred, usually through methods of slow torture. But their legendary bravery has inspired Bahá'ís ever since.

Shaykh Tabarsí was the first of three Bábí conflicts with the state. In Nayríz, a town in central Iran, one neighbourhood largely converted to the Bábí Faith as a result of the urgings of a prominent clergyman who had become a Bábí named Vahíd. When an effort was made to arrest Vahíd in early June 1850, he and four to six hundred of the town's Bábí men took refuge in an old fort nearby, which they repaired.[17] It was besieged by as many as 5,000 soldiers. As in the case of Shaykh Tabarsí, the men in the fort often sallied forth and dispersed the larger and better trained army regiments. Eventually the fort was induced through deceit to surrender. Vahíd and his companions were captured and killed in late June or early July, 1850, within days of the martyrdom of the Báb. The Bábí quarter was plundered and burned and many of the Bábí men of the town, who had not participated in the defence of the fort, were executed. The Bábí women and children of Nayríz were brutalized and many died.[18]

A similar upheaval occurred in 1850 in Zanján, a city in north-western Iran. A large number of Zanjánís followed their beloved prayer leader, Hujjat, into the Bábí Faith in 1846. Hujjat was an Akhbárí Shi'ite, a minority interpretation at odds with the Usúlí position of the city's other clergy, who were jealous of Hujjat's eloquence and angered by his frank criticisms of their beliefs. Thus the conflict followed pre-existing theological divisions. Tensions between the two groups exploded into violence in May 1850. 3,000–4,000 men, women and children – about half the urban population – barricaded themselves into the eastern half of the walled town and in an old fort. They held out against as many as 20,000 soldiers for 5 months. Women cut off their hair and wound it around wooden cannons to hold them together; one woman, dressed as a man, joined the fighting, while other women helped at the barricades and nursed the wounded. Hujjat wrote an appeal to the shah, assuring him of their loyalty and their desire for peaceful coexistence. The troops gradually pushed the Bábí barricades back and killed their defenders. When Hujjat was killed, Bábí morale collapsed. The government issued a promise for peaceful surrender in return for amnesty. But once again a massacre of the men – only 100 of the original 1,800 had survived the fighting – resulted.[19]

Shaykh Tabarsí, Nayríz and Zanján were the largest and most notorious of the Bábí upheavals, but smaller acts of persecution against the Bábís occurred throughout the towns and cities of Iran. Sometimes armed mobs attacked Bábí homes; other times Bábís were arrested, paraded through the town square, and executed in gruesome fashion before the public. Estimates of the number of dead range from 4,000 to 20,000 men, women and children.

The fortress of Chihríq

The persecutions and upheavals weighed heavily on the Báb. He received the news of each upheaval at another fortress, Chihríq, farther from the Russian border, where he had been moved because the Russian government feared Bábism would spread into their Caucasian provinces and because the guards and villagers in Máků had become friendly to him. Confinement was again severe for a time. His stay in Chihríq ran from early May 1848 through July 1850, except for 3 months when he was taken to Tabriz.

While in Chihríq the writings of the Báb took another turn. The works he produced were more esoteric or mystical and less thematically organized. Two major books were produced, in addition to many minor works. The Kitáb-i-panj sha'n ('Book of Five Grades') was composed in March and April of 1850. The work consists of 85 sections arranged in 17 groups, each under the heading of a different name of God. Within each group are five 'grades', that is, five different sorts of sections: verses, prayers, homilies, commentaries and Persian language pieces. Each group was sent to a different person and was composed on a different day. Some of the sections represent further expositions of basic themes in the Báb's teachings; others consist of lengthy iterations of the names of God, and variations on their roots.

The Kitáb-i-asmá ('The Book of Names') is a 3,000-page book about the names of God. It also emphasizes that the Bábís must not let anything prevent them from recognizing He whom God shall make manifest. It was completed during the Báb's last days at Chihríq, before His execution.

Trial and execution

In July 1848, after the Badasht gathering but before the three upheavals had occurred, the Báb was taken to Tabriz and put on trial before the Crown Prince and a group of local Shi'ite clergy. His enemies later claimed that he had recanted His beliefs under the pressure of interrogation. The various accounts of the trial, however, all agree that the Báb boldly asserted his claim to be the Promised One expected by the Shi'ites. While the clergy sought the death penalty, the government, fearing public sympathy, preferred to have the Báb declared insane and keep him locked up. After the trial he was bastinadoed (a very painful beating of the soles of the feet) and sent back to the Chihríq fortress.

In 1850, however, the situation changed drastically. The majority of the movement's leaders were dead, the remnants scattered and dispirited. Public sympathy had waned. The new Shah and his Prime Minister had succeeded in crushing the Bábí insurrections at Shaykh Tabarsí, Nayríz and Zanján. It was now possible to execute the Báb.

The Báb's martyrdom, on 9 July 1850, in a public square in Tabriz before thousands of onlookers, was perhaps the most dramatic event connected with His life. All accounts – including those of neutral European observers and enemies of the Báb – agree that the first volley of bullets from a firing squad of Christian soldiers did not harm the Báb, but cut the ropes suspending him from the wall and freed him.[20] Bábí accounts state that the Báb had previously been conversing with a disciple when the guards came to take him to his execution and that the Báb said he had to finish the conversation. After the first volley freed the Báb, in the pall of gun smoke he returned to the holding area to complete his conversation. The guards found him there, allowed him to complete his instructions, and led him back to the square. A second firing squad of Muslim soldiers succeeded in killing him, though their bullets spared his face. His body was dumped in the dry moat outside the city walls, where Bábís rescued it at night and hid it for 59 years until it could be interred safely and with great dignity.

Aftermath

The death of the Báb, at age 30, left the Bábí community demoralized. Persecution and martyrdoms continued another 3 years. Many of the Báb's writings were destroyed. The Báb himself says the corpus exceeded 500,000 verses in length; the Qur'án, in contrast, has 6,300 verses. Shoghi Effendi mentions nine complete commentaries on the Qur'án, revealed during the Báb's imprisonment at Mákú, which have been lost without a trace.[21] Establishing the true text of some works can be difficult because of the existence of multiple copies with variant readings.

In addition to major works of theology, exegesis and mysticism, the Báb composed numerous letters to His wife and followers; epistles to the Shah of Iran, the Prime Minister and various clerics; prayers for various purposes; talismans, often in the form of a pentacle; and khutbihs (sermons, most of which were never meant to be delivered). Many have been lost; others have survived in compilations. The Bahá'í World Centre possesses 2,000 unique works, comprising at least five million words.

Before His death, the Báb designated Yahyá Núrí (1831–1912), younger half-brother of Bahá'u'lláh, as the figurehead of the community, and gave him the honorific Azal ('Eternity'). He never specified Yahyá's authority or responsibilities and did not name him successor or vicegerent. At the time Yahyá was still a teenager, had never demonstrated leadership in the Bábí movement and was still living in the house of Bahá'u'lláh. This suggests that the Báb appointed Yahyá a figurehead so as to divert attention away from Bahá'u'lláh, while allowing Bábís to visit Bahá'u'lláh and consult with Him freely, and allowing Bahá'u'lláh to write to Bábís easily and freely. The survival of the Bábí movement now fell largely on Bahá'u'lláh's shoulders.

CHAPTER SEVEN

The ministry of Bahá'u'lláh, 1853–92

The years immediately following the martyrdom of the Báb in 1850 were a time of confusion and anguish for the scattered and demoralized Bábí communities. No less than 25 persons declared themselves to be the Promised One of the Báb and sought to revive the community's spirit. Persecution continued unabated, including a second upheaval in Nayríz that resulted in the deaths of hundreds of Bábís. The Prime Minister, suspicious of Bahá'u'lláh's involvement in the Bábí Faith, banished him to the Shi'ite shrine cities of Iraq for a year (1851–2). He returned as the situation in Tehran went from bad to worse.

The plot and the black pit

In August 1852 a group of Bábís plotted to assassinate Iran's king in order to take revenge for the Báb's death and the continued persecution of the Bábís. The plot was a spectacular failure. One assassin was cut down on the spot and the other two were tortured to death. A severe government-sponsored pogrom against the Bábís of Tehran followed. Eighty-one were arrested. Many met a cruel death, being shot from cannons or chopped to pieces, sometimes after being force to walk to the scene of their execution with lighted candles thrust into slits cut in their flesh, or on horseshoes nailed to their feet. Both their bravery and the shocking brutality of their deaths were commented on by European witnesses and received coverage in western newspapers. Among those martyred was Táhirih, who was strangled.

Bahá'u'lláh was one of the Bábís arrested. All of his property was confiscated and for 4 months he was imprisoned in the

Síyáh-Chál or 'Black Pit', a former water reservoir for a public bath that had been converted into an underground prison. Forty Bábís were shackled with murderers and other criminals in two long rows along the walls. They were allowed outside daily for an hour to eat and exercise; no human waste was removed from the dungeon. Most of the Bábís were taken away, one per day, and executed. Much of the time Bahá'u'lláh had a heavy chain shackled to his neck that left scars for the rest of his life. 'The air we breathed was laden with the foulest impurities, while the floor on which we sat was covered with filth and infested with vermin', Bahá'u'lláh later recounted. 'No ray of light was allowed to penetrate that pestilential dungeon or warm its icy coldness'. Yet in spite of the conditions, the prisoners often chanted prayers, reportedly with such vigour that they could be heard in the nearby palace.

While in the Síyáh-Chál, Bahá'u'lláh received a revelation:

> During the days I lay in the prison of Tihrán [Tehran], though the galling weight of the chains and the stench-filled air allowed Me but little sleep, still in those infrequent moments of slumber I felt as if something flowed from the crown of My head over My breast, even as a mighty torrent that precipitateth itself upon the earth from the summit of a lofty mountain. Every limb of My body would, as a result, be set afire. At such moments My tongue recited what no man could bear to hear.[1]

At another time he 'beheld a Maiden . . . suspended in the air':

> Pointing with her finger unto My head, she addressed all who are in heaven and all who are on earth, saying: 'By God! This is the Best-Beloved of the worlds, and yet ye comprehend not. This is the Beauty of God amongst you, and the power of His sovereignty within you, could ye but understand . . . This is He Whose Presence is the ardent desire of the denizens of the Realm of eternity, and of them that dwell within the Tabernacle of glory, and yet from His Beauty do ye turn aside'.[2]

Bahá'u'lláh's revelations in the Síyáh-Chál marked the beginning of his ministry. It was the 'year 9', one of the dates the Báb gave for the advent of the Promised One. But Bahá'u'lláh did not announce his status as 'He whom God shall make manifest' for another decade; it remained a messianic secret, hinted at in his early writings. A short mystic poem titled Rashh-i-Amá ('Sprinklings from the Cloud', the 'cloud' referring to the Divine Essence) resulted from the imprisonment and is one of the oldest surviving works in Bahá'u'lláh's literary corpus.

Exile

In December 1853, convinced of Bahá'u'lláh's innocence in the plot to assassinate the Shah, the Iranian government released him from prison. But because he was a prominent Bábí, Bahá'u'lláh was banished from Iran. The Russian minister in Tehran offered him refuge in the Russian Empire, but he declined and departed for Baghdad, a city in Ottoman Iraq frequented by many Iranians intent on performing pilgrimage to the Shi'ite shrines nearby. He was accompanied by his family. His half-brother Yahyá, who had fled to the mountains and forests of northern Iran after the attempted assassination, decided to move to Baghdad as well and followed Bahá'u'lláh's party in disguise.

Iraq had a Bábí community, but it was dispirited and disunified. Bahá'u'lláh immediately set out to encourage and organize it, but his efforts were opposed by Yahyá, who spread rumours about Bahá'u'lláh's motivations and character. After a year of frustration and discouragement, in April 1854 Bahá'u'lláh abruptly departed Baghdad alone for the mountains of Kurdistan, leaving Yahyá to restore the community.

Bahá'u'lláh's 2-year retreat has been compared to Jesus's time in the wilderness; it gave Bahá'u'lláh the solitude to pray and prepare for his mission. He settled into a cave and soon attracted the attention of local Sufis, who invited him to take up residence in a seminary building in the nearby city of Sulaymaniyyah. As a result of his dialogue with prominent Sufis, he revealed another mystic poem, the Qasídih-i-Varqá'íyyih ('Ode to the Dove'). When the reputation of this new spiritual leader in Kurdistan reached the ears of his family in Baghdad, they suspected the leader's identity and sent a messenger, begging Bahá'u'lláh to return. He consented to do so, exactly 2 years after his departure.

Return to Baghdad;
Revelation of major works

Yahyá had had his chance to organize the Bábís; he had done little and his reputation suffered as a result. Bahá'u'lláh was thus free to meet with a growing stream of Iranian Bábí visitors, to encourage and to write. Over the next 7 years (1856–63) he composed five works of seminal importance to his ministry.

The Hidden Words (1858) consisted of two collections of ethical and mystical aphorisms, one in Arabic, one in Persian. Unlike most of Bahá'u'lláh's works, it was not revealed for a specific recipient. A sample of one aphorism from the Arabic and the Persian texts, respectively, give one a feel for the style and content:

O SON OF MAN!

Thou art My dominion and My dominion perisheth not; wherefore fearest thou thy perishing? Thou art My light and My light shall never be extinguished; why dost thou dread extinction? Thou art My glory and My glory fadeth not; thou art My robe and My robe shall never be outworn. Abide then in thy love for Me, that thou mayest find Me in the realm of glory.

O YE RICH ONES ON EARTH!

The poor in your midst are My trust; guard ye My trust, and be not intent only on your own ease.[3]

The *Haft Vádí* or Seven Valleys, in contrast, was a text about the mystic journey of the soul. It was revealed for Shaykh Muhíyu'd-dín, the Qádí (leader) of the Khániqayn Sufi Order, in a form that followed the basic structure of the classic Sufi text by Farídu'd-dín Attár titled *The Conference of the Birds*. The seven valleys represented seven stages in 'the wayfarer's journey from the abode of dust to the heavenly homeland'; the seven were the Valleys of Search, Love, Knowledge, Unity, Contentment, Wonderment and True Poverty and Absolute Nothingness. Shoghi Effendi calls it Bahá'u'lláh's 'greatest mystical composition'.[4]

Closely related to the Seven Valleys was the *Chahár Vádí* or Four Valleys, a mystical treatise that describes four 'valleys' or approaches to God (self, reason, love and heart) and four types of truth seekers.[5] The work was revealed for Shaykh Abdu'r-Rahmán-i Karkútí, another Sufi leader. Both works were in dialogue with Sufi concepts. The *Javáhiru'l-Asrár* or Gems of Divine Mysteries was revealed for an inquirer, Sayyid Yúsuf-i Sidíhí Isfahání, in 1860–1. Unlike the two treatises just discussed, it was in Arabic rather than Persian. The work addressed the question of how the Promised One of Islam could appear in the guise of an ordinary human being (the Báb) rather than apocalyptically. It interpreted important Qur'ánic concepts such as the Day of Judgment and the Resurrection. Some of its mystical insights overlap with concepts presented in the Seven Valleys; other aspects of the work appear in the *Kitáb-i-Íqán* or Book of Certitude.

The Book of Certitude was prompted by a series of questions by an uncle of the Báb, who had not completely accepted his nephew as a Manifestation and now sought guidance about the matter from Bahá'u'lláh. In January 1861 he visited Bahá'u'lláh in Baghdad, presented four questions in writing and witnessed some of the revelation of the reply. Within the span of 2 days and 2 nights, the 250-page response, the Book of Certitude, was completed and presented to him.[6]

A work of Qur'ánic and biblical exegesis, the book outlines the Bahá'í notion of the progressive revelation of God's will through a series of Manifestations, explains the symbolic meaning of the apocalyptic language of the New Testament and Qur'án, interprets numerous sayings attributed to Muhammad and the Shi'ite imams, upholds the purity of the Virgin Mary, defends the mission of the Báb, explains that the sovereignty of the Qá'im is purely spiritual rather than material or political, praises the heroism of the Bábís and enumerates the qualities of the true seeker after truth. Shoghi Effendi acclaims its style as 'original, chaste and vigorous' and describes its position in Bahá'í literature as 'unequalled by any work' except Bahá'u'lláh's *Kitáb-i-Aqdas* or Most Holy Book.[7] The Báb's uncle was convinced by its arguments and accepted the Báb as a divine Manifestation.

A notable feature of the work is what Christopher Buck has called its 'messianic secret' and what Nader Saiedi called 'veiled declaration'. In the book's closing, Bahá'u'lláh says it was *munzal*, 'revealed, sent down', and in other places he hints at his station as the Promised One of the Báb, but he never comes out and says it.[8] Nevertheless, a growing number of Bábís suspected Bahá'u'lláh's station as a divine Manifestation. Bábí pilgrims came to Baghdad to meet Bahá'u'lláh and Yahyá, were very impressed by the former, and generally were disappointed by the latter. Bahá'u'lláh's writings began to circulate in Iran, boosting his reputation among the Bábís and encouraging them. Bábís began to settle in Baghdad, giving that city a small but active Bábí community.

Declaration of his mission in the garden of Ridván

The Iranian government was not unaware of the revival of the Bábí community and complained to the Ottomans that Bahá'u'lláh resided too close to the Iranian border and to the Shi'ite pilgrimage centres. As a result, in the spring of 1863 Bahá'u'lláh was summoned to Istanbul. In late April he rented a garden on the eastern bank of the Tigris which he called *Ridván* or 'Paradise'. He retreated there for 12 days with several dozen followers. On the first day, April 20, Bahá'u'lláh declared to his companions and close associates that he was the divine messenger the Báb had prophesied.* It is not known how they reacted because none of those present recorded a memoir of the event. One family suspects their grandfather was present, but whenever they asked him he started to shake and was speechless, suggesting that the experience was too much to record.[9]

Bahá'u'lláh recorded in a tablet that he revealed three basic principles of his religion on that day: that the use of the sword (i.e. violence) was prohibited; that no new divine revelation could be expected for at least a 1,000 years; and that 'at that very moment', God was shedding 'the splendours of all His names upon the whole creation'.[10] The removal of the sword implies that religion must now be spread through peaceful means and that nonbelievers must have full rights with believers; otherwise, they would experience

---

*Today, Bahá'ís celebrate the first day of Ridván on 21 April because Bahá'u'lláh said it should be celebrated thirty-one days after the spring equinox, and the Bahá'í calendar currently fixes the spring equinox on 21 March. But in 1863, the equinox occurred on 20 March.

coercion. Reinforcing this insight is Bahá'u'lláh's statement that 'it is better to be killed than kill'.[11] The second principle implies the existence of a Covenant between God and humanity through Bahá'u'lláh. The third underlines the greatness of Bahá'u'lláh's revelation, compared to the revelations of the past, because it was the fulfilment of all the messianic promises. The third principle also underlines the fact that all things reflect names of God, and therefore there is nothing that is inherently unclean.

The 12 days Bahá'u'lláh spent in the Garden of Ridván has come to be called the Ridván Festival, the most important holy period in the Bahá'í calendar. The first, ninth and twelfth days (corresponding to the day of his declaration of his mission, the day his family joined him in the garden and the day he left the garden) are celebrated as holy days on which Bahá'ís should suspend all work. The Ridván event symbolically marked the break with the Bábí Faith and the beginning of a new religion, the Bahá'í Faith, based on the teachings of a new Manifestation: Bahá'u'lláh.

Istanbul and Edirne

On his departure from the Ridván garden, Bahá'u'lláh and his retinue began their long, three and a half-month overland journey to Istanbul. They remained there 4 months before being banished further to Edirne in European Turkey. During their stay in the Ottoman capital, many diplomatic officials called on Bahá'u'lláh, for they had heard of his movement, and many were impressed. Bábís visited and Bahá'u'lláh sent some of them back to Iran to proclaim the new Faith.

Bahá'u'lláh spent the next 5 years in exile in Istanbul and Edirne. Utilizing diplomatic contacts made in the Ottoman capital, he sent epistles to the reigning monarchs of Iran, Turkey and France announcing his claim to be God's latest messenger. Bahá'u'lláh's decision to write to the kings and rulers was based on historic precedent: Muhammad supposedly sent messages to the reigning monarchs of the world in his day and Jesus is said, in Muslim legend, to have sent an epistle to the Queen of Palmyra.

Bahá'u'lláh also sent numerous tablets to Iran's Bábís and dispatched teachers to explain his messianic claim. The result was the conversion of more than 90 per cent of the Bábís to the Bahá'í

Faith. Bahá'u'lláh's half-brother Yahyá, the figurehead leader of a now almost non-existent community, broke with him, attempted to have Bahá'u'lláh murdered and poisoned him, almost fatally. Consequently, Bahá'u'lláh ordered all the Bahá'ís to make a choice between himself and Yahyá; they could not remain in contact with both. Only a handful followed Yahyá.

Bahá'u'lláh also wrote a 412-page book, the *Kitáb-i-Badí'* or Wondrous Book, in 3 days, in response to seven questions from the judge of the Persian community in Istanbul about how he could claim to succeed the Báb and replace Yahyá as head of the community. The judge noted that the Báb had intentionally left it to 'He whom God shall make manifest' to complete the Persian Bayán. Bahá'u'lláh replied that the Book of Certitude was the expected completion of that work. He detailed the rebelliousness and perfidy of Yahyá and refuted claims that the Báb had given vicegerency to Yahyá.

The issue of who would be Bahá'u'lláh's successor also came up in Edirne. In response, Bahá'u'lláh penned the *Súriy-i-Ghusn* or Tablet of the Branch where he praised his eldest son 'Abbás (later titled 'Abdu'l-Bahá) as the 'Most Great Branch' and 'the Most Great Favor unto you, the most perfect bounty upon you' adding that 'through Him every mouldering bone is quickened'.[12] It clearly implied that 'Abdu'l-Bahá would succeed Bahá'u'lláh, but stopped short of an outright declaration.

The Ottoman authorities were alarmed by the open conflict between Bahá'u'lláh and Yahyá in Edirne. Unable or unwilling to determine the root cause of the strife between the two half-brothers, the government exiled Bahá'u'lláh and most of his followers to the city of Acre, in what is today northern Israel, in the summer of 1868. It was a heavily walled city to which many political exiles were sent; an impoverished place with no functioning aqueduct or public water system. The exile placed Bahá'u'lláh in the Holy Land, the land of many biblical prophecies. Yahyá and most of his handful of followers were sent to Famagusta, Cyprus.

Acre: The prison city

In Acre, Bahá'u'lláh, his family and a group of his followers, totalling about 70, were confined in the main citadel in a cluster of cells under severe conditions for more than 2 years. All but two fell ill from the poor-quality food and the lack of clean water. Three died. Bahá'í pilgrims, some walking on foot from Iran, were unable to meet Bahá'u'lláh, and had to content themselves with the sight of his hand waving a handkerchief out the window of his cell. One of Bahá'u'lláh's sons, Mihdí (1848–70), suffered a fatal injury and begged that his life be a sacrifice so that the pilgrims could see Bahá'u'lláh again. Several months after Mihdí's death, Bahá'u'lláh's party was allowed to leave the prison for rented spaces inside the city walls. The flow of Iranian Bahá'í pilgrims resumed, they brought letters to Bahá'u'lláh, and they carried his love, encouragement and written guidance to fellow Bahá'ís back home.

In spite of the severe confinement, Bahá'u'lláh continued to write to rulers, dispatching epistles to the monarchs of England, Austria and Russia. When he heard that Napoleon III had derisively commented about his first tablet, he dispatched a second epistle in 1869 – a year before the Prussians defeated Napoleon III and drove him into exile – predicting that 'for what thou hast done, thy kingdom shall be thrown into confusion, and thine empire shall pass from thy hands'. His epistle to Pope Pius IX, sent in 1868 or 1869 – a year or so before the newly formed Italian government stripped the Pontiff of secular power – contained an explicit declaration of Bahá'u'lláh's station: 'The Day of the advent of the Glorious Lord is at hand! . . . This is the Father foretold by Isaiah, and the Comforter concerning whom the Spirit [Jesus] had covenanted with you. Open your eyes, O concourse of bishops, that ye may behold your Lord seated upon the Throne of might and glory'.[13] The epistles to the kings and rulers, circulating in handwritten form in Iran, impressed many believers and caused a few seekers to accept Bahá'u'lláh.

The most important addition to Bahá'u'lláh's corpus in the early Acre period was the *Kitáb-i-Aqdas* or Most Holy Book, the book of laws of Bahá'u'lláh. As soon as Bábís and Muslims became Bahá'ís, they wanted to know what laws to follow: what obligatory prayer to say, how and when to fast, whether they could marry more than one wife, etc. Islam's sharí'ah law code provided a detailed body of guidance on these and many other matters, so they expected the new religion to provide the same. Bahá'u'lláh did not provide his laws until 1873, and he kept the Aqdas private a few additional years before giving permission for it to be circulated. The Book of Laws did indeed provide the principles for prayer, fasting, scriptural study, alms giving, Huqúqu'lláh and pilgrimage, and included laws regarding marriage, divorce and inheritance.** But the Aqdas provided more. It defined the basic features of the Bahá'í community: it established the institution of the House of Justice to govern the community and the House of Worship to serve as the centre of devotional life and charitable activities; inaugurated the Nineteen Day Feast to serve as its principal regular gathering for worship; listed the Holy Days on which Bahá'ís were to suspend work; and abolished the institution of clergy and all clerical responsibilities and prerogatives, such as the performance of rites and sacraments. Bahá'u'lláh also said that 'when the ocean of My presence hath ebbed and the Book of My Revelation is ended, turn your faces toward Him Whom God hath purposed, Who hath branched from this Ancient Root', in other words, turn to 'Abdu'l-Bahá as his successor upon Bahá'u'lláh's passing.[14]

The Aqdas also specified some principles for world order, such as the selection of a universal auxiliary language and script and the abolition of warfare. It specified punishments for murder, arson and adultery. It completed the advice and admonitions to kings and rulers, with sections devoted to the King of Prussia and to the 'Rulers of America and the Presidents of the Republics therein'. It prophesied that the banks of the Rhine would be 'covered with gore, inasmuch as the swords of retribution were drawn against you; and you shall have another turn. And We hear the lamentations of Berlin, though she be today in conspicuous glory'. He predicted a revolution in Iran and a future Bahá'í ruler for that country.[15]

The revelation of the Aqdas in about 1873 roughly coincided with further improvement of Bahá'u'lláh's conditions. The city's new governor was highly respectful of him. When he asked Bahá'u'lláh what he could do for him, Bahá'u'lláh asked that the aqueduct be repaired so the city had a supply of clean running water. The landlord from whom Bahá'u'lláh rented part of a house was so impressed with his tenant that when he heard 'Abdu'l-Bahá's bride had arrived in town but there were no marriage plans because there

---

**These laws have been described in Chapter Four.

was no place for the couple to reside, the landlord added a room to the rented area for the couple.

Mazra'ih and Bahjí

By 1877, it was possible for 'Abdu'l-Bahá to rent a former hunting lodge at Mazra'ih, 10 km from Acre. Bahá'u'lláh, for the first time in 9 years, was able to leave the city for a more comfortable residence in the countryside. Two years later (1879) a spacious mansion, Bahjí, just a few kilometres outside Acre, became available and 'Abdu'l-Bahá rented it for Bahá'u'lláh, which gave him ample space for his family, retinue and visiting Bahá'í pilgrims.

The last 19 years of Bahá'u'lláh's ministry (1873–92) saw a steady stream of important works emanate from his pen. Many of them, such as the *Lawh-i-Ishráqát* (Tablet of Splendours), *Lawh-i-Bishárát* (Tablet of Glad Tidings), *Lawh-i-Tajallíyyat* (Tablet of Effulgences) and *Lawh-i-Tarázát* (Tablet of Ornaments) elaborated on the spiritual and ethical principles of world order, stressing the importance of having a vocation, of the arts and sciences, obedience to government, the selection of an international auxiliary language, the establishment of the Most Great Peace, the banning of holy war and the necessity to educate children. These works provided elaboration on principles already stated in the Aqdas. Others, such as *Lawh-i-Hikmat* (Tablet of Wisdom) discussed Greek philosophers and philosophy. Several tablets praised 'Abdu'l-Bahá and hinted at his high station even further.

Two tablets were revealed in response to questions posed by Manikjí Limjí Hataria, a Parsee from Bombay who had moved to Tehran to ameliorate the persecution and suffering of Iran's Zoroastrians and who had once travelled to Baghdad to meet Bahá'u'lláh. The tablets discussed Zoroastrian topics and the purpose of religion. They helped to spark the interest of Zoroastrians in the Bahá'í Faith. Tablets sent to several Zoroastrian Bahá'ís were composed in 'pure Persian', with no use of words of Arabic origin; a feat rather like trying to write elegant English without the use of any words of Latin or French origin.

In his last year of life, Bahá'u'lláh produce three works of great significance. The Tablet of Carmel, revealed while Bahá'u'lláh visited Mount Carmel in Haifa a score kilometres south of Acre, alluded to the spiritual importance of that mountain, which was to become the site of the world centre of the Faith. While there, Bahá'u'lláh pointed out the spot where a tomb for the remains of the Báb was to be built.

He revealed his last lengthy work, *Lawh-i-Ibn-i-Dhib* or Epistle to the Son of the Wolf, several months before his passing. The Wolf had been a prominent Shi'ite mullá in Shiraz notorious for his cruel persecution of the Bahá'ís of that city; his son, the Son of the Wolf, was equally merciless. Bahá'u'lláh warned him of the consequences of his deeds, revealed a prayer for him to say to beg for forgiveness and provided a lengthy summary of Bahá'u'lláh's salient claims and teachings, mostly by quoting the most important passages from his corpus. Thus Epistle to the Son of the Wolf is a compilation of Bahá'u'lláh's writings by Bahá'u'lláh himself. A notable feature of the work is 're-revelation' where the passages included in the compilation are slightly different in phrasing from those in the original sources.

Finally, at some point in the last year or two of his life, Bahá'u'lláh revealed the *Kitáb-i-Ahd* or the Book of the Covenant, his last will and testament. In it he made it very clear that the Most Great Branch, or 'Abdu'l-Bahá, was to be his successor and that the passages in earlier works that had alluded to 'Abdu'l-Bahá did indeed refer to him. As a result, when Bahá'u'lláh passed away on 28 May 1892 and the will was read publically, there was initially no confusion or uncertainty on whom to follow.

Development of the Iranian Bahá'í community, 1853–92

Throughout Bahá'u'lláh's 39-year ministry (1853–92), the community of his followers steadily grew in size, understanding and capacity. If the Bábí community had indeed grown to as much as 100,000 members at its peak in about 1850, a much smaller community – perhaps half or less – survived to learn about Bahá'u'lláh's claim in the 1860s to be He whom God shall make manifest. Gradually, the vast majority of the Bábís accepted his claim and became Bahá'ís.

Two other, smaller, groups formed as well. Azalís followed Bahá'u'lláh's half-brother Yahyá. It is not known how large they became; perhaps the membership reached 5,000. Ten or twelve became prominent members of Iran's Constitutional Revolution of 1906 and thus became known to history. The community never was very organized and subsequently shrank. It is not known whether it exists at all in the early twenty-first century.[16]

The other surviving group decided to follow neither Yahyá nor Bahá'u'lláh and came to be called Bayánís, for they followed the writings of the Báb and particularly the mother book of his corpus, the Bayán. The Bayánís had a few local communities in Iran in the nineteenth century. It is not known how long the group persisted.

A few Bábís, confused by the rival claims, drifted away. Probably over 90 per cent of the Bábí community became Bahá'ís by the 1870s. Gradually, they learned the teachings of the new religion through teachers Bahá'u'lláh sent, pilgrimage to Acre to meet Bahá'u'lláh and the circulation of Bahá'u'lláh's writings. Pilgrims carried many letters to Bahá'u'lláh and brought his replies back to Iran. In addition, Shaykh Salmán, an illiterate Bahá'í, walked between Acre and Iran every year for decades in order to carry letters back and forth. As a result, the Bahá'í community gradually came to adopt the Bahá'í obligatory prayers, Bahá'í fasting customs, Bahá'í holy days and the payment of Huqúqu'lláh to Bahá'u'lláh. Local communities began to meet together to pray, study the Bahá'í sacred writings and teach the Faith to their friends and relatives. Because it was impossible to print Bahá'u'lláh's books in Iran, in 1881–2 Bahá'u'lláh sent one of his sons to Bombay to arrange for the printing of the Kitáb-i-Íqán.[17]

Initially, local leadership was informal and was sometimes provided by former mullahs (Shi'ite clergy) who had become Bahá'ís. The arrival of manuscript copies of the Kitáb-i-Aqdas in Iran had a powerful impact. In 1878, a Bahá'í in Tehran spontaneously organized a 'consultative assembly' of prominent local Bahá'ís based on the command in the Aqdas to establish Houses of Justice. The nine members consulted together, established a local Bahá'í fund, discussed the selection of a local place of worship and made plans to disseminate the Bahá'í Faith in Tehran and the rest of the country. The body lasted about 4 years until Bahá'u'lláh asked the group to disband on the grounds that its establishment was premature.[18]

A few years later – starting in 1886 – Bahá'u'lláh appointed *Hands of the Cause of God*, eminent individuals possessing spiritual rank in the Bahá'í community to whom he could entrust sensitive and important tasks. Over a few years he appointed four of them; two had been on the consultative assembly. One had been an Islamic clergyman who converted to the Bahá'í Faith as an adult; the other three were sons of Bábís. They travelled extensively around Iran, meeting Bahá'í communities, deepening their knowledge of the Bahá'í teachings, encouraging efforts to teach the Faith to others, dealing with dissent and disagreements and carrying out international trips on behalf of Bahá'u'lláh and (later) 'Abdu'l-Bahá. They often were arrested and imprisoned.[19]

In the 1860s, the Bahá'í population was largely confined to the Shi'ite populations of Iran and Iraq. But by the mid-1880s the Bahá'ís began to reach out to Iranian Jews and Zoroastrians. Both were Persian-speaking groups who had imbibed Persian culture and understood some aspects of Shi'ism, such as its stress on martyrdom. By the late nineteenth century, the younger and more educated members of both groups sought a more modern approach to the world and became attracted to the Bahá'í Faith's modernistic ideas and its claim to fulfil scriptural prophecies (the Jewish Messiah; the Zoroastrian Shah Bahrám). The result was the eventual conversion of perhaps 10 per cent of Iran's Jews to the Bahá'í Faith, though in some cities such as Gulpaygán the conversion may have been over 75 per cent. Particularly attracted were the Jadíd-i-Islam, Jews who had earlier been forcibly converted to Islam. A third to a half of Iran's Zoroastrians became Bahá'ís.[20] Particularly noteworthy was Haj Mehdi Arjmand (1860–1940), a Jew who became a Bahá'í about 1878, learned Arabic, mastered the Qur'án, studied the Bible in great depth and debated with American Protestant missionaries in Hamadan in the mid-1890s about the claim that Bahá'u'lláh fulfilled biblical prophecies. The conversion of Jews and Zoroastrians to the Bahá'í Faith continued until about the 1930s. It ended as the Jewish and Zoroastrian Bahá'ís assumed a greater Bahá'í identity, intermarrying more with Bahá'ís of Muslim background than with Jews or Zoroastrians and following Bahá'í funeral practices.

Spread of the Bahá'í Faith in the Middle East and central, south and southeast Asia

In addition to the strengthening and diversification of the Iranian and Iraqi Bahá'í communities, the ministry of Bahá'u'lláh saw the religion spread as far west as Egypt, as far south as Sudan, as far north as Russian Central Asia, and as far east as Indonesia and China. The exile of Bahá'u'lláh caused the Faith to reach Anatolia, European Turkey, Syria, Palestine and Egypt, for Bahá'ís followed Bahá'u'lláh and settled where he resided or in cities nearby, such as Baghdad, Mosul, Istanbul, Edirne, Cairo, Alexandria, Port Said and Beirut. Persecution of Iranian Bahá'ís in Egypt resulted in the exile of seven of them to Khartoum, Sudan, from 1868 to 1877. Other Iranian Bahá'ís remained in Egypt, however, and taught the Faith to Sunni Muslims and local Christians; the first Christian became a Bahá'í in 1868. In 1888 two Lebanese Christians became Bahá'ís in Egypt and, a month after Bahá'u'lláh's passing in 1892, they travelled to Europe and the United States, where one settled.

Bahá'ís fleeing persecution in Iran moved northward to Russian Central Asia and the Caucasus region, where the Russian government tolerated them. When a group of Muslims martyred a Bahá'í in Ashgabat in 1889, the Russian government prosecuted the murderers, sentenced two to death and ordered four others exiled to Siberia. Both the Bahá'ís and the Muslims were shocked by the verdict. The Bahá'ís requested that clemency be shown to the murderers, and in consequence the government reduced their sentences to exile. Considerable respect for the Bahá'í community resulted. Because the government protected the Bahá'ís' safety, the Bahá'í population of Ashgabat soon rose to several thousand and it became the largest Bahá'í community in the world.[21]

No Bábí community formed in India during the lifetime of the Báb, even though one of the Letters of the Living was Indian and three Indian Bábís fought at Shaykh Tabarsí. In the 1850s the Afnán family – the relatives of the Báb, who were merchants – established an office in Bombay and began to teach the Faith in that city. Bahá'í teachers travelled to India to teach the Faith to Muslims and Parsees as early as the 1860s. A thousand Parsees became Bahá'ís over the next 50 or 60 years.[22]

Particularly important was the work of Jamál Effendi, an Iranian who became a Bábí in Tehran in the early 1860s. As a result of a request from the handful of Bahá'ís in Bombay for a teacher, Bahá'u'lláh sent him to India about 1875. He arrived in Bombay and travelled around the subcontinent for some three years, proclaiming the Faith to local government leaders and debating mullás. He met the founder of the Arya Samaj, Maharishi Dayanand Saraswati, and told him about the Bahá'í Faith. He visited Dhaka in modern

Bangladesh. He travelled to Colombo, Sri Lanka, where Buddhist leaders opposed his teaching efforts. Numerous people became Bahá'ís, including a young man named Sayyid Mustafá Rúmí.[23]

In May 1878, accompanied by Rúmí, he travelled to Burma, establishing Bahá'í communities in Rangoon and Mandalay over the next 6 years. The new Bahá'ís were of both Shi'ite and Sunni backgrounds. Possibly Theravada Buddhists became Bahá'ís as well; it is not known when the Burmese Bahá'í community began to teach the Faith to them. In 1884–5 Jamál Effendi and Sayyid Mustafá Rúmí visited Malaya, Singapore, Bangkok, Java and Sulawesi. While numerous people declared their belief in Bahá'u'lláh, the area was too remote for follow-up and no permanent Bahá'í communities resulted. Rúmí eventually returned to Burma, where he married into an Indo-Burmese family, became fluent in Burmese and English, and remained there the rest of his long life (he died in 1945 at age 99).[24] Jamál Effendi travelled extensively around India for several more years, then in 1889 made a trip northward from Srinagar and possibly Kabul across the western edge of Tibet to Xinjiang province of China and then to Central Asia. He was the first Bahá'í teacher known to visit Tibet. He was not the first Bahá'í in China, because the Afnán family had earlier opened a trading office in Shanghai.

Bahá'u'lláh's final years

Bahá'u'lláh coordinated all these efforts from his residence at Bahjí through correspondence, instructions to pilgrims and appointed representatives. In 1890 he met Edward G. Browne, Professor of Arabic at Cambridge University. Browne left a moving pen portrait of Bahá'u'lláh, who at that time was 72:

> The face of him on whom I gazed I can never forget, though I cannot describe it. Those piercing eyes seemed to read one's very soul; power and authority sat on that ample brow; while the deep lines on the forehead and face implied an age which the jet-black hair and beard flowing down in indistinguishable luxuriance almost to the waist seemed to belie. No need to ask in whose presence I stood, as I bowed myself before one who is the object of a devotion and love which kings might envy and emperors sigh for in vain!

FIGURE 7.1 *Mansion of Bahjí where Bahá'u'lláh passed away (© Bahá'í International Community).*

A mild dignified voice bade me to be seated, and then continued: – 'Praise be to God that thou hast attained! . . . Thou hast come to see a prisoner and an exile. . . . We desire but the good of the world and the happiness of the nations; yet they deem us a stirrer up of strife and sedition worthy of bondage and banishment. . . . That all nations should become one in faith and all men as brothers; that the bonds of affection and unity between the sons of men should be strengthened; that diversity of religion should cease, and differences of race be annulled – what harm is there in this? . . . Yet so it shall be; these fruitless strifes, these ruinous wars shall pass away, and the "Most Great Peace" shall come. . . . Do not you in Europe need this also? Is not this that which Christ foretold? . . . Yet do we see your kings and rulers lavishing their treasures more freely on means for the destruction of the human race than on that which would conduce to the happiness of mankind. . . . These strifes and this bloodshed and discord must cease, and all men be as one kindred and one family. . . . Let not a man glory in this, that he loves his country; let him rather glory in this, that he loves his kind. . . .'[25]

In May of 1892 Bahá'u'lláh was 74 years old and in declining health. He passed away in the early hours of the morning on 29 May. Huge crowds came to his funeral from Acre and the surrounding villages; crowds who, 24 years earlier, had feared him as a heretic and had jeered or threatened him and his followers in the city's narrow streets. For days afterward, the mansion of Bahjí was thronged by mourners paying their respects.[26] A suitable tomb being unavailable, Bahá'u'lláh was buried under the floor of the northernmost room of the house of one of His sons in law. The building became his mausoleum, a place to which Bahá'ís make their pilgrimage, and the direction in which they face daily when saying their obligatory prayers. His Will and Testament was read aloud to his family and close associates. It clearly appointed his eldest son, 'Abbás, as his successor. The family of Bahá'u'lláh and all the Bahá'ís turned to him. No doubt they wondered how the Faith would grow without its Prophet and what changes 'Abbás would institute to ensure its future.

CHAPTER EIGHT

The ministry of 'Abdu'l-Bahá, 1892–1921

When Bahá'u'lláh passed away in 1892 his eldest son, 'Abbás, was 48 and was highly respected in the Bahá'í community and by the residents of Acre. He had served as his father's chief lieutenant, as liaison with government officials, as greeter of Bahá'í pilgrims and other visitors and as a correspondent with prominent Arab reformers. Edward G. Browne was immensely impressed when he met him in 1890:

> Seldom have I seen one whose appearance impressed me more. A tall strongly-built man holding himself straight as an arrow, with white turban and raiment, long black locks reaching almost to the shoulder, broad powerful forehead indicating a strong intellect combined with an unswerving will, eyes keen as a hawk's, and strongly-marked but pleasing features – such was my first impression of 'Abbás Effendi, 'the master' (Áká) as he par excellence is called by the Bábís [Bahá'ís]. Subsequent conversation with him served only to heighten the respect with which his appearance had from the first inspired me. One more eloquent of speech, more ready of argument, more apt of illustration, more intimately acquainted with the sacred books of the Jews, the Christians, and the Muhammadans, could, I should think, scarcely be found even amongst the eloquent, ready, and subtle race to which he belongs. These qualities, combined with a bearing at once majestic and genial, made me cease to wonder at the influence and esteem which he enjoyed even beyond the circle of his father's followers. About the greatness of this man and his power no one who has seen him could entertain a doubt.[1]

FIGURE 8.1 *Portrait of 'Abdu'l-Bahá (© Bahá'í International Community).*

In 1875, Bahá'u'lláh encouraged his son to write a book, *The Secret of Divine Civilization*, in order to spread Bahá'í social reform principles. It advocated the ratification of a Constitution for Iran, election of a parliament by the people, universal education, codification of the nation's laws and various other modernizing efforts, justified partly through the use of quotations from the Qur'án and sayings attributed to Muhammad. The work was published anonymously in Persian in order to avoid the stigma that it was a 'Bábí' text. The book was followed in 1886 by *A Traveller's Narrative*, a history of the Bábí Faith, also published anonymously. In 1893, shortly after becoming the head of the Bahá'í Faith, 'Abbás wrote *A Treatise on Politics*, a short work on the relationship between the government and the governed and the role of religion in governance.

Clearly, the new head of the Bahá'í Faith was very experienced and capable. To underline his subservience to his father's legacy, 'Abbás soon took the title of *'Abdu'l-Bahá*, meaning servant of Bahá.

Opposition to 'Abdu'l-Bahá

'Abdu'l-Bahá had an immediate problem with some members of Bahá'u'lláh's family. Bahá'u'lláh had had three wives; as a wealthy aristocrat this was common. His first marriage, to Navváb, was arranged by his family when he was 18, in 1835. With her he had seven children, four of whom died in childhood and one in adolescence, leaving 'Abdu'l-Bahá and his sister, Bahíyyih Khánúm. Bahíyyih Khánum had chosen not to marry so that she could devote her energy to serving Bahá'u'lláh and 'Abdu'l-Bahá.

The second marriage, to Mahd-i-'Ulyá, a widowed cousin of Bahá'u'lláh, occurred in 1849, during the life of the Báb, and produced six children, of whom three boys and one girl reached adulthood. Finally, while in Baghdad Bahá'u'lláh took a third wife, Gawhar Khánúm, with whom he had one daughter.[2] 'Abdu'l-Bahá's eldest half-brother, Muhammad-'Alí (1853–1937), had been called by Bahá'u'lláh the 'Greater Branch' (a title lesser than 'Abdu'l-Bahá's, the 'Most Great' Branch) and in his will and testament Bahá'u'lláh declared Muhammad-'Alí second in rank in the Faith after 'Abdu'l-Bahá. Nine years younger than 'Abdu'l-Bahá, he had always been in 'Abdu'l-Bahá's shadow and came to resent him. Muhammad-'Alí saw that if he could eliminate or neutralize 'Abdu'l-Bahá in some way, he could claim the right to lead the Bahá'í community.

Even before Bahá'u'lláh's funeral, Muhammad-'Alí grabbed two cases of Bahá'u'lláh's papers, probably hoping to obtain the will and testament. Later, he claimed that 'Abdu'l-Bahá withheld pension payments from his brothers and accused 'Abdu'l-Bahá of antigovernment plots. When 'Abdu'l-Bahá broke ground on Mount Carmel for the tomb of the Báb, Muhammad-'Alí claimed he was really building a fort with an arsenal for storing weapons. In order to spread his influence in Iran and undermine 'Abdu'l-Bahá's prestige, he forged or modified tablets attributed to Bahá'u'lláh. He argued that 'Abdu'l-Bahá claimed to be a Manifestation of God or even claimed divinity and consequently had disqualified himself from leadership of the Bahá'í community, thereby leaving Muhammad-'Alí in charge. 'Abdu'l-Bahá's response to the attacks was consistently humble. At first he sought to remain silent, but eventually he felt compelled to write in length about the nature of the plots against him.

As with the earlier conflict created by Yahyá against Bahá'u'lláh in 1868, the community eventually had to make a choice whom they would associate with. Ultimately, very few chose Muhammad-'Alí, who lived to see the utter failure of his efforts. The Iranian Bahá'í community nearly universally ignored his claims and remained loyal to 'Abdu'l-Bahá. The only exceptions were two or three ambitious Bahá'ís who hoped that Muhammad-'Alí would provide them opportunities for leadership. The Ottoman Turkish government, however, reinstated 'Abdu'l-Bahá's confinement in Acre in 1898 and set guards over his house to watch all comings and goings, a situation that lasted 10 years.

For a time, the attacks on 'Abdu'l-Bahá's leadership and personality caused severe confusion for many Bahá'ís and terrible anguish for 'Abdu'l-Bahá. While any conflict in a religion that proclaims unity as its principal teaching is to be detested, the mere act of emphasizing unity is not sufficient to prevent ambition or overcome jealousy.* History shows that many religions face very similar challenges to leadership on the death of the Founder. Judas's betrayal of Jesus, the controversy between Paul and James, the civil war between 'Alí and Uthman in Islam, and the plots against Buddha by his cousin Devadatta are examples of similar conflicts in other religions.

---

*The problems of maintaining unity in the face of ambition and other human weakness was discussed in Chapter Two.

Expansion of the faith to the occident

In spite of the opposition, 'Abdu'l-Bahá moved forward in his efforts to expand and develop the Bahá'í community. Within months of assuming the role of Head of the Faith, two Lebanese Bahá'ís reached Europe and the United States. Ibrahim George Kheiralla (1849–1929), an Orthodox Melkite Christian, had been a member of the first graduating class of Syrian Protestant College in 1870 and later settled in Cairo. In 1889 he heard of the Bahá'í Faith from Iranian Bahá'ís who had settled in the city and joined the Faith. He headed to St Petersburg and Berlin in June 1892, weeks after Bahá'u'lláh's passing, in order to find his fortune. He arrived in New York in December 1892 and began classes on the Bahá'í Faith in June 1894 in Chicago. By 1899 he had attracted some 1,500 to the Bahá'í Faith.

His 12 lessons proved to have two primary audiences. One was middle class to upper class mainline Protestants, some of whom were active in their churches and some of whom had been attracted to Spiritualism, Theosophy, esoteric Masonic groups and Vedantism. The other group was first-generation Lutheran immigrants of Scandinavian and German backgrounds, usually of working class status, a few of whom had been interested in Swedenborgianism. The Anglo-Saxons tended to convert as individuals and women joined more often than men; the immigrants tended to convert as families. The Chicago and Cincinnati Bahá'í communities contained both groups; Kenosha, Wisconsin, was almost exclusively Scandinavian and German; the New York, Washington, Boston and the San Francisco area communities were almost exclusively Anglo-Saxon and middle to upper middle class.[3]

Kheiralla could not read Persian and probably had access to few of Bahá'u'lláh's Arabic works, so his understanding of the Bahá'í Faith was incomplete. He taught that Bahá'u'lláh was the return of the Father and 'Abdu'l-Bahá was the return of Christ, a station 'Abdu'l-Bahá was neither given by Bahá'u'lláh nor claimed. Kheiralla's lessons taught the Bahá'í the idea of progressive revelation and interpreted biblical prophecies to refer to the Bahá'í Faith. Kheiralla taught the American Bahá'ís to say two 'Bahá'í' prayers, but Kheiralla seems to have authored both of them. He did not talk about obligatory prayer or fasting and may not have known

about them, although he did teach them to say the Greatest Name
95 times daily. But he asked all new American Bahá'ís to write
a letter to 'Abdu'l-Bahá declaring their Faith, and 'Abdu'l-Bahá
wrote back to them in Arabic.

In 1898–9 Kheiralla brought a group of Americans on pilgrimage. The experience confirmed their faith in 'Abdu'l-Bahá; as one
put it, 'The Greatest Branch ['Abdu'l-Bahá] is all and more than
anyone could ask. He is the perfect ideal of Christ'. But they also
discovered, to their shock, that much of what Kheiralla had taught,
including reincarnation, was either rejected by the Bahá'í authoritative texts or was irrelevant to them: 'The main facts are all true
. . . that God manifested in the flesh on earth – established his
kingdom – departed and left the regency to his Son Abbas Effendi
['Abdu'l-Bahá] The Christ. The rest is all *knowledge* . . . it will be
all straight before any of us attempt to teach it'.[4]

When the pilgrims returned to the United States in early 1899,
controversy immediately erupted because Kheiralla insisted that
everything he taught was correct, while the pilgrims insisted it was
not. Kheiralla had written a book summarizing his teachings and
he had hoped to publish it and make money, of which he had very
little. 'Abdu'l-Bahá sent a series of Persian Bahá'í teachers to nego-
tiate with Kheiralla, but ultimately the efforts failed and Kheiralla
established a rival group, so he was declared a Covenant breaker
around 1900.

The 1,500 American Bahá'ís were mostly confused. Kheiralla's
group started out with a few hundred members, but soon shrank
to a few dozen, even with the encouragement of Muhammad-'Alí
and 'Abdu'l-Bahá's other half-brothers. Thanks to the efforts of the
visiting Persian teachers, the group that remained loyal to 'Abdu'l-
Bahá ultimately retained perhaps half of the nineteenth-century
converts. The rest drifted away.

'Abdu'l-Bahá was a major factor in retaining the bulk of the
American Bahá'ís. Over the next decade, over 100 undertook a
long ocean journey to meet him, and invariably they returned
home impressed by his person and fired with the desire to spread
the Faith. 'Abdu'l-Bahá carried out a massive correspondence with
individuals worldwide. His letters have been described as 'mas-
terpieces of Persian epistolary genre. They are marked by direct-
ness, intimacy, warmth, love, humour, forbearance, and a myriad
of other qualities that reveal the exemplary perfection of His

personality. 'Abdu'l-Bahá addresses everyone as an equal in the service of Bahá'u'lláh'.[5] Some American Bahá'ís received 20 or 30 tablets from him, often with prayers for them to say for their personal spiritual struggles.

Even though the community was shrunken and initially discouraged, by 1906 American Bahá'ís had taken the Bahá'í Faith to France, England, Germany, Canada and Hawaii. They began to publish pilgrim's notes of their meetings with 'Abdu'l-Bahá, summaries of the Bahá'í teachings, collections of 'Abdu'l-Bahá's tablets, booklets of Bahá'í prayers and translations of the writings of Bahá'u'lláh. A publishing society was one of their first permanent agencies.[6]

Development of the Iranian Bahá'í community

At the same time, 'Abdu'l-Bahá devoted considerable attention to development of the Iranian Bahá'í community. In 1897 he called on the four Hands of the Cause of God, resident in Tehran, to establish a consultative body in Iran's capital. Initially they served on it and appointed additional members. In 1899 they appointed a group of prominent male believers (women and men being unable to meet together at the time) to elect the members other than themselves by secret ballot. The body included one Bahá'í of Zoroastrian background and another one of Jewish background, and thus was representative of all the ethnic groups found within the community. The body was eventually called the *Central Spiritual Assembly,* because it served both as the local coordinating council of the Tehran Bahá'ís and the national consultative body for the Bahá'ís of Iran.[7]

One of the Central Assembly's first tasks was to establish a school for boys, the Tarbíyat School, in Tehran. Apparently a Bahá'í organized a traditional school in his house about 1897 and it eventually expanded to involve several teachers in a building of its own. By 1903 it had achieved government recognition. The Tarbíyat School developed into one of Iran's finest private schools. It added a school for girls in 1911.[8]

In order to train people capable of answering difficult questions about the Bahá'í Faith, in 1903 Sadru's-Sudúr, a former Shi'ite cleric who had become a Bahá'í, established a small school that gave classes on the Bahá'í scriptures, Qur'án and Islam. His effort was encouraged by 'Abdu'l-Bahá in a series of tablets. It represented the first formal effort to establish Bahá'í scholarship, which otherwise was already developing, thanks to the capable pens of several former Shi'ite clerics. When Sadru's-Sudúr died 3 years later, 'Abdu'l-Bahá directed Mírzá Na'ím to continue the school. Sadru's-Sudúr's students became important teachers and administrators of the Bahá'í Faith in the early twentieth century. 'Abdu'l-Bahá also asked him to write the first textbook for teaching the Bahá'í Faith to children. In 1908, 'Abdu'l-Bahá sent a tablet to Fá'izih Khánum and encouraged her to start a school to train Bahá'í women to be teachers, since women could not attend Sadru's-Sudúr's classes. This launched the effort to educate Bahá'í women in Iran. By 1924, 102 women had completed the courses.[9]

As the Central Spiritual Assembly gained in experience, it appointed committees to assist poor Bahá'ís, resolve disputes, deepen Bahá'ís' understanding of the teachings of their Faith, explain the Faith to inquirers and educate Bahá'í women. When several Bahá'ís graduated from the Tehran medical school, it encouraged them to establish a clinic. Because Iran lacked a stable banking system or any reliable government services, in 1917 it organized what was in effect a private bank, the *Shirkat-i-Nawnahálán* or 'Children's Company'. Bahá'í children deposited money in it for safe keeping and adults could purchase shares in it. The assets were loaned out to Bahá'ís to grow their businesses, and the depositors and shareholders were paid interest or dividends. It continued to grow until it was confiscated after the Islamic Revolution of 1979. Because the Iranian Bahá'í community had an engine for economic growth and saving and because the Bahá'í teachings encouraged education, the community's poverty and illiteracy began to decrease and it eventually achieved a prosperity notably higher than its fellow citizens, an accomplishment that both defied and exacerbated the persecution the community continued to experience.[10]

The Central Spiritual Assembly aided many local Iranian communities to establish local coordinating councils. No doubt many also received tablets from 'Abdu'l-Bahá asking them to organize. Mashhad had a coordinating council by 1905; Tabriz and Qazvin by 1910; Abadeh by 1911. Both the Jewish and Zoroastrian Bahá'ís elected coordinating bodies.[11]

The effort to form consultative bodies extended beyond Persia. Ashgabat, Tiflis and Baku, all in the Russian dominions just north of Iran, had coordinating councils by 1902; Samarkand formed one by 1910.[12] The first American Bahá'í pilgrims returned home in 1899 with a copy of the Kitáb-i-Aqdas, and a Lebanese Bahá'í friend of Kheiralla's translated it into English, providing knowledge about Houses of Justice. Starting in the last months of 1899 and extending through mid-1901, the Bahá'ís in Chicago, New York City, northern New Jersey and Kenosha elected coordinating bodies. By 1910, consultative bodies had been elected in Washington, Boston, Spokane, the San Francisco Bay area and Los Angeles as well. Most, but not all, had nine members and were elected annually. Some included women; some were male-only, though women could vote.[13] There was no standardized title for them, though 'Abdu'l-Bahá usually used the term 'Spiritual Assembly' in his tablets to them. In 1910, 1911 and 1912, he stated that women could serve on local Spiritual Assemblies in North America, though the Islamic culture of Iran made their membership on Assemblies impossible in that country for another four decades. As a result, the Iranian Bahá'ís focused on women's education.

The Occidental Bahá'ís also became involved in the practical needs of their communities; efforts Bahá'ís now call social action and public discourse. The Kenosha Bahá'ís, inspired by the Kitáb-i-Aqdas, opened a weekend industrial school in 1907 to teach sewing and other useful skills to youth. 'Abdu'l-Bahá praised the effort, which appears to have been the first economic development effort by Occidental Bahá'ís. Chicago, Kenosha, the San Francisco Bay area and Washington, DC had all established Bahá'í children's classes by 1912. Chicago had a young people's group as well. A Paris Bahá'í opened a school for poor children to which the other Paris Bahá'ís contributed materially. May Maxwell started one of the first Montessori classrooms in Canada to educate her daughter, Mary. American Bahá'ís helped arrange Maria Montessori's first visit to the United States and published about the Montessori technique. British Bahá'ís helped start the Save the Children organization. American and British Bahá'ís were involved in the peace movement, before World War One.[14]

Knitting together the Bahá'í world

The increased diversity of the Bahá'í world and the varying talents in its different parts prompted 'Abdu'l-Bahá to encourage the international movement of Bahá'í teachers. Bahá'í teachers were already circulating around Iran and Central Asia on a regular basis and were often supported financially by the local communities. As already noted, 'Abdu'l-Bahá asked several prominent Iranian teachers, including the great scholar Mírzá Abu'l-Fadl, to visit the United States and Europe between 1900 and 1904 to deepen the new Occidental believers in the basics of the Faith. Several young Persians settled in the United States and Europe at 'Abdu'l-Bahá's direction. 'Abdu'l-Bahá also sent a Persian Bahá'í to Crimea in 1902 to teach Leo Tolstoy the Faith, because the Russian novelist and philosopher had heard of the Faith and was sympathetic.[15]

Starting in 1904, he directed Occidental Bahá'ís to visit India, Burma, Central Asia and Iran, sometimes as members of teams that included Persian teachers. The presence of westerners helped impress British civil servants and prominent Indians and Burmese that the Bahá'í Faith was not just a Muslim sect, but an international faith, and inspired the local believers to teach relatives and acquaintances. By 1910, the first Hindus and Sikhs had become Bahá'ís in India. In Iran, the visits of western Bahá'ís proved the international spread of the Faith, were immensely encouraging for the local believers and encouraged the Bahá'í women to envision a day when they would be emancipated. Correspondence between Iranian and American Bahá'í governing bodies, which started as early as 1902, was strengthened, and correspondence between women's groups began.

In 1908 Sidney Sprague, an American who had become a Bahá'í in Paris, settled in Tehran and soon became the headmaster of the Tarbíyat School for boys. His presence greatly increased contact between the Iranian and American Bahá'ís and helped stimulate the Washington, DC Bahá'ís to form the Persian American Educational Society in 1909. The Society dedicated itself to providing human resources, scholarships and materials to the Bahá'í schools. By 1911, four American Bahá'í women settled in Tehran. Two were physicians; the other two, nurses. Their presence made it possible for the Tarbíyat School to open a facility to educate girls and for the Sehat Hospital to treat women patients. Their presence also demonstrated to those wishing to persecute the Iranian Bahá'ís that the community now had active coreligionists in the west. The Americans learned Persian and received a stream of encouraging tablets from 'Abdu'l-Bahá, which helped them adjust to the culture shock and endure the resistance and occasional hostility of Bahá'í men, whose consciousness of the equality of the sexes was still developing. American Bahá'í women continued to make important contributions to the Iranian Bahá'í community until the 1970s. The first woman elected to the National Spiritual Assembly of the Bahá'ís of Iran, in 1954, was an American.[16]

Houses of worship

The increasing capacities of Bahá'í communities prompted them to purchase or build places for worship. In November 1902, with 'Abdu'l-Bahá's permission, the Ashgabat community – a score miles north of the Iranian border in Russian Central Asia – broke ground for a *Mashriqu'l-Adhkár* or 'Dawning Place for the Remembrance of God'. The grand structure, complete by about 1912, was nine-sided with a dome and had a monumental main entrance flanked by minaret-like towers. 'Abdu'l-Bahá told them that the Mashriqu'l-Adhkár should have ancillary institutions such as an orphanage, old people's home, library, hospital, guest hostel and school, and efforts to establish a few of them began.[17]

Inspired by the effort, in March 1903 the Chicago Bahá'ís wrote 'Abdu'l-Bahá and received permission to build a House of Worship. Other American communities followed, but 'Abdu'l-Bahá told them to support Chicago first, thereby converting the local effort into a national project. In 1909, delegates from Bahá'í communities all across the United States, plus Montreal, met in Chicago and elected the nine-member Executive Committee of the *Bahai Temple Unity*, an organization empowered to complete a House of Worship in Wilmette, a suburb of Chicago.[18]

'Abdu'l-Bahá was very pleased and continuously encouraged Bahá'í communities throughout the world to organize themselves, worship together regularly and develop agencies for meeting their needs. Many rented halls for regular meetings or, in the case of

Iran, used designated rooms in houses for regular worship. The all-Bahá'í village of Kungyangoon, in the Irrawaddy River delta of Burma, built a Bahá'í centre when the village's mosque was destroyed in a wind storm. The Bahá'ís of Mandalay, Burma, established a 'Young Men's Bahai Association' patterned after the YMCAs that Christian missionaries were establishing. Iranian communities created private schools open to children of any religion, using teachers trained at the Tarbíyat School; by 1918–19, some 20 Bahá'í schools across the country enrolled several thousand children, representing more than 10 per cent of all the children in primary and secondary education in the country.[19]

Strengthening Bahá'í devotional practices

The early years of the twentieth century saw considerable development in Bahá'í worship, particularly in the United States. The first pilgrims returned to the United States in 1900 with a translation of the Middle Obligatory Prayer and began to use it. By 1902, the Chicago Bahá'ís knew the dates of four of the nine Bahá'í Holy Days, and had heard of two others. Not only did they commemorate them, but they sent postcards to the other Bahá'í communities a month in advance so the others could commemorate them as well. American Bahá'ís began to observe the fast (2–20 March) by 1903, and in 1906, 489 American Bahá'ís signed a supplication to 'Abdu'l-Bahá that said they were fasting that year.[20]

American Bahá'í communities often held Sunday morning services in the 1900–12 period, for which several Bahá'ís composed hymns, using the standard forms of American Protestant hymnody and themes or passages drawn from the Bahá'í scriptures.[21] 'Abdu'l-Bahá had some of the hymns translated into Persian so they could be used in Iran as well. To give Bahá'í communities a common form of worship, 'Abdu'l-Bahá encouraged the establishment of the Nineteen Day Feast. The term 'Feast' refers not to eating as much as to the Feasts of Saints in the Christian calendar and other celebratory events. 'Abdu'l-Bahá described it as the 'Supper of the Lord' to the Kenosha Bahá'ís and linked it to the last meal of Christ. Bahá'u'lláh had established the practice of giving hospitality once every 19-day Bahá'í month in the Kitáb-i-Aqdas, but did not specify whether it was to be done by each household or by the community as a whole, or whether it was for the purpose of community worship or for reaching inquirers.

In 1905, 'Abdu'l-Bahá held a Feast for visiting pilgrims and urged them to establish the practice of a community-wide Feast primarily for Bahá'ís. This inspired one American Bahá'í to travel all across the North American continent, hosting sample Feasts. Iranian Bahá'ís already had been holding small devotional meetings in private homes and sponsored community-wide Feasts when local conditions permitted. Because of persecution, neighbourhood Feasts and Feasts for extended families remained common.[22]

Persecution

Opposition to the Bahá'í Faith was a serious problem in parts of Iran, particularly Isfahan and Yazd, and limited the development of Bahá'í communities. Some Shi'ite clergy held an implacable hatred against the new Faith because of its claim to a revelation superseding Muhammad's; others sensed political advantage to persecuting it. The government generally was opposed to riots, murders and disorder and thus often restrained efforts to persecute the Bahá'ís, particularly in Tehran where there were many Europeans to witness events. European diplomats pressured Iran to stop persecuting the Bahá'ís because their newspapers often carried stories about incidents, because the persecuted Bahá'ís appealed to local consulates for assistance, and because 'Abdu'l-Bahá asked western Bahá'ís to speak to their governments or to Iran's ambassadors about the attacks on their coreligionists. Improved communications sometimes limited persecution as well because Bahá'ís sent telegrams to Tehran reporting attacks against them.

In spite of these measures, however, the worst persecution since the 1850s broke out in 1903. Two hundred Bahá'ís in the city of Isfahan had to take refuge in the local Russian consulate while mobs pillaged their houses and shops until the Russian and British consulates pressured the local government to restore order. In the town of Yazd and its nearby villages, nearly 200 Bahá'ís were killed over a month. Many more were left homeless. Others subsequently moved away from both areas, settling in safer places such as Tehran, Khurásán or Ashgabat. Because Bahá'u'lláh had told the Bahá'ís not to resist persecution there was no resistance, as had occurred during the Bábí period, and this may have reduced the total number of deaths. Iranian Shi'ite culture highly honours martyrdom, hence the brave deaths of the peaceful Bahá'ís made a powerful impression on their neighbours and often stimulated conversions. 'Abdu'l-Bahá anonymously composed an account of the persecutions and had it translated into English and published, which helped to strengthen the Bahá'í identity of western believers as well.[23]

The Iranian constitutional revolution, 1905–13

The persecution of the Yazd and Isfahan Bahá'ís in 1903 was facilitated by a weakening of Iran's central government because of resistance to some of its modernizing reforms and the conviction of other citizens that the government was reforming too slowly. In 1905, the conflict precipitated the Constitutional Revolution. The Bahá'ís' support for the ideals of Constitutional reform was solid, even enthusiastic; both Bahá'u'lláh and 'Abdu'l-Bahá had advocated establishment of a Constitution and a representative parliament for Iran, and the civic freedoms such a government could provide could free the Bahá'í Faith from ongoing opposition. Some Bahá'ís wrote in favour of the Constitution and spoke in support of it to friends and prominent people.

But it soon became clear that any pro-Constitutional activities by Bahá'ís would allow the powerful Shi'ite clergy – who were opposed – to paint the Constitutionalist movement as Bahá'í-inspired and directed, which would severely weaken it. Hence 'Abdu'l-Bahá restrained the Bahá'ís from getting involved, in spite of criticism from pro-Constitutionalist forces and their western supporters, and urged the Bahá'ís to be sources of unity instead. In June 1911, when the second Parliament considered allowing representation of Iran's religious minorities in the Parliament, 'Abdu'l-Bahá urged the Bahá'ís to seek parliamentary seats for the Hands of the Cause. But severe partisanship in that body, a Russian invasion of Iran in December 1911, and internal dynamics of the Iranian Bahá'í community caused 'Abdu'l-Bahá to reverse his position in 1913 and tell the Bahá'ís not to seek seats in the Parliament.[24]

Freedom for 'Abdu'l-Bahá

Iran was not alone in facing a revolution. The Ottoman Empire experienced the Young Turks Revolution in 1908, which overthrew the Sultan. The Young Turks freed all political prisoners, including 'Abdu'l-Bahá; in 1908 his 55 years of exile and imprisonment came to an end. No longer were Ottoman guards watching his household. The members of his family who had opposed him witnessed the total failure of their efforts to restrict or re-imprison 'Abdu'l-Bahá.

Freedom gave 'Abdu'l-Bahá the opportunity to inter the remains of the Báb properly in the tomb he had been building for them on the slopes of Mount Carmel in Haifa. Bahá'u'lláh had pointed out the spot to him in 1890 and had overseen the efforts to hide the Báb's remains in various places in Iran for over 40 years. At some point 'Abdu'l-Bahá had the remains secretly brought to Acre, where they were hidden in his sister Bahíyyih Khánum's bedroom. The Burmese Bahá'ís commissioned a special marble sarcophagus for them. On 21 March 1909, he had the remains ceremonially brought to Haifa, placed in the sarcophagus and interred in the Shrine of the Báb with great care and dignity.

That task completed, 'Abdu'l-Bahá arranged his work so that he would be free to travel. In August 1910 he left Haifa for Egypt, where he remained a year. The Egyptian newspapers gave him extensive, favourable coverage; prominent Egyptians came to meet him and were very impressed; and the Bahá'í communities of Cairo, Alexandria and Port Said greatly benefitted from his talks and personal meetings.

Travels in the occident

In August 1911, 'Abdu'l-Bahá took a steamer to Marseilles, from which he went to Thonon-les-Bains in the French Alps, Switzerland, London and Paris. Returning to Egypt in December, he set out again in March 1912 for New York City. From there, for 8 months he travelled south to Philadelphia and Washington, north to New England and Montreal and west to Buffalo, Pittsburg, Cleveland, Cincinnati, Chicago, Kenosha, Minneapolis, Denver, the San

Francisco area, Los Angeles and Sacramento. He gave over 400 talks to a combined audience of perhaps 93,000 people and was the focus of over 350 newspaper articles. He spoke to the National Association for the Advancement of Colored People, at six settlement houses, in one African American church and one Japanese American church, three synagogues, and before a large Syrian American audience, in addition to liberal Protestant churches, Theosophical groups, six universities, women's associations, Esperanto societies and peace societies. Departing New York on 5 December 1912, he travelled to London, Edinburgh, Paris, Stuttgart, Vienna and Budapest, returning to Egypt in June 1913 and Haifa in December 1913, 7 months before the beginning of World War One.

The list of prominent people who met him is very long, and he made an indelible impression on many of them. 'For the first time I saw a form noble enough to be the receptacle for the Holy Spirit', Kahlil Gibran commented after his three personal visits with 'Abdu'l-Bahá. 'He is a very great man. He is complete. There are worlds in his soul. And oh what a remarkable face – what a beautiful face – so real and so sweet'. Gibran's unique portrait of Christ in *Jesus, Son of Man* (published 1928) was based on his encounters with 'Abdu'l-Bahá. Howard Colby Ives, a Unitarian minister at the time, noted that 'the impressive thing, and what I have never forgotten, was an indefinable aspect of majesty combined with exquisite courtesy . . . Such gentleness, such love emanated from Him as I have never seen'.[25]

'Abdu'l-Bahá's public talks provided the Bahá'ís with an entirely new approach to explaining their Faith. The combination of principles and the way he emphasized them was new, even though he had spoken about them to pilgrims and had written about them in various tablets. The most important principle he emphasized was the oneness of humanity. He demonstrated it by encouraging Louis Gregory, an African American lawyer, and Louisa Mathew, an English woman, to marry, and by adding a Japanese American Bahá'í to his entourage during his trip to California. He stressed independent investigation of truth and its corollaries of free choice in choosing one's religion and the abolition of clergy. From these two principles flowed most of the rest of the principles he spoke about: equality of men and women, the oneness of the religions of the world, the need for religion to be a cause of unity and harmony, that religion must be in accord with science and reason, that human beings must free themselves from religious and patriotic prejudices, the need to establish universal peace, the importance of universal education and spiritual solutions to economic questions. His advocacy of votes for women garnered headlines. His call for world peace before peace societies had an extra urgency; at least six times in North America he warned that Europe was a powder keg and a great, destructive war there was coming soon.[26]

His talks to the Bahá'ís had a different character. He usually offered them towards the end of his visit to a city when he knew the Bahá'ís somewhat and they had already heard his public presentations. He stressed the life and teachings of Bahá'u'lláh, the martyrdoms and sacrifice of the Persian Bahá'ís, the unity the Bahá'í Faith was bringing to diverse races and religions around the world and the glorious future for humanity that was in store if the Bahá'ís consecrated themselves to service to humanity and to teaching the Faith to others. He spoke about Bahá'u'lláh's Covenant, how it guaranteed the unity of the Bahá'í Faith and the necessity to obey him as Centre of the Covenant. He warned against association with the small Covenant-breaking groups that existed in Chicago and Kenosha, which had been stirred into activity by his visit. He often spoke about the Universal House of Justice that was to be established in the future and its role in safeguarding the unity of the Bahá'í Faith.

His impact on the Bahá'ís was profound. Hundreds of Bahá'ís made a lifelong dedication to the Faith, devoted their lives to teaching and ultimately brought thousands into the community. Many children of Bahá'ís, when later asked what year they accepted the Faith, said 1912; 'Abdu'l-Bahá had made a special effort to meet with the Bahá'í children. He often added young adult Bahá'ís to his entourage for part of his trip; later they became members of National Spiritual Assemblies, Hands of the Cause and Auxiliary Board members, and helped establish the Bahá'í Faith in dozens of countries around the world.

His demonstration of race unity transformed the attitudes of many Bahá'ís towards race, a transformation of which the marriage of the Gregorys was a constant witness and reminder. The acceptance of blacks as equals laid the foundation for the acceptance of the Bahá'í Faith by such important African Americans as Alain Locke, a founder of the Harlem Renaissance; Robert Abbot, founder of the *Chicago Defender*; Nina Gomer Dubois, first wife of W. E. B. DuBois; Robert Hayden, the great poet; and Dizzy Gillespie, the famous jazz trumpeter. Over the next few decades, the number of African American Bahá'ís swelled from a few dozen to over 10,000 and their role in the American Bahá'í community became prominent and important.

Many non-Bahá'ís were very impressed and became friends of the Bahá'í community. W. E. B. DuBois wrote several articles about 'Abdu'l-Bahá's visit for *The Crisis*, the monthly magazine of the NAACP, and named 'Abdu'l-Bahá 'Man of the Month' in the May 1912 issue. A prominent British Bible scholar, Thomas Cheyne, wrote a book, *The Reconciliation of Races and Religions*. When Agnes Alexander, a travelling Bahá'í teacher, arrived in Japan in the 1920s, the American ambassador pledged to help her teaching efforts because he had met 'Abdu'l-Bahá in New Hampshire in 1912.[27]

World War One and aftermath

The Bahá'í community needed all the maturity it had developed from his Occidental visit, because 7 months after 'Abdu'l-Bahá returned to Haifa, World War One erupted. Cables and letters between Ottoman-controlled Palestine and the Occident ceased; except for an occasional postcard, all communications with 'Abdu'l-Bahá was cut. With no communication between Iran and the United States possible, the Persian-American Educational Society collapsed. The effort to build a Bahá'í temple in Wilmette slowed. American Bahá'ís were torn by controversy over whether to support the war effort or champion world peace; some of the supporters of the latter were investigated by the precursor agency of the Federal Bureau of Investigation. Other Bahá'ís followed esoteric interpretations of the Bahá'í texts and opposed all efforts to organize the Bahá'í communities further. Cut off from 'Abdu'l-Bahá's loving advice and encouragement, the American Bahá'ís struggled.

'Abdu'l-Bahá was cut off from Iran as well, where conditions were chaotic and several Bahá'ís were martyred. Pilgrims were unable to come to Haifa; 'Abdu'l-Bahá had little correspondence; there were shortages of everything. He also faced severe dangers. The Ottomans, suspicious of him, threatened to crucify him and his family on Mount Carmel. Fearful that battles between the Ottomans and the advancing British army would cause suffering in Haifa and Acre, 'Abdu'l-Bahá directed the Zoroastrian Bahá'ís who had settled lands he had purchased in the Jordan valley to raise grain, which he brought to Haifa and stockpiled in various places, including the Shrine of the Báb. When General Allenby's forces approached northern Palestine in September 1918, food supplies ran short, many people hoarded supplies, and starvation loomed for the poor. 'Abdu'l-Bahá distributed the grain to needy families – he personally knew many of them – and prevented suffering. His humanitarian efforts may have been one reason the British knighted him 1920. Their occupation of Palestine freed 'Abdu'l-Bahá, his family and the Bahá'í holy places in Haifa and Acre from any threats once and for all.[28]

While efforts to assist the local population occupied much of his time during the war, 'Abdu'l-Bahá did give a series of short talks about 70 famous early believers that were later compiled into a book, Memorials of the Faithful. The animating theme behind the stories in their great love for Bahá'u'lláh. He also penned 14 tablets to the Bahá'ís of the United States and Canada in 1916 and 1917 collectively known as the Tablets of the Divine Plan. The tablets gave them the responsibility to take the Bahá'í Faith to nearly the entire world; they listed 120 territories and islands in the Americas, Africa, Australia, the islands of the Pacific and Europe. He divided North America into five regions – Canada and the north-eastern, central, southern and western parts of the United States – and drafted two tablets to each region where he spoke of that region's spiritual potential, listed places that had to be opened to the Faith, and provided prayers to say for guidance and assistance. The remaining four tablets were addressed to the entire continent. He recommended that teachers learn the local languages, outlined the spiritual prerequisites for success and stressed the spiritual capacities of the American Indians and Eskimos. He spoke particularly about reaching Greenland, establishing the Faith in Panama, and opening Bahia (now Salvador), Brazil, to the Faith (because of the similarity of its name to the word Bahá'í).[29] In a sense, he had been preparing the American Bahá'ís for this mandate of spiritual conquest for almost two decades, and had particularly prepared them through his talks about teaching the Faith in 1912.

Five of the tablets arrived, written in tiny print on postcards, in 1916. They were published and had a powerful impact on the Bahá'ís, who reinvigorated their commitment to teaching the Faith. But the rest had to await the end of the war and arrived in 1919. At the American national Bahá'í convention in April 1919, all 14 tablets were unveiled, a Bahá'í sent by 'Abdu'l-Bahá from Haifa spoke, and the convention was electrified by the vision they offered. One Bahá'í, Martha Root, left before the convention ended to wind up her affairs and head to South America to teach the Faith. She spent most of the next 20 years travelling, earning a scant living by writing travel articles for newspapers about the places that she visited, lecturing about the Bahá'í Faith in every venue she could, proclaiming it to local newspapermen and converting the resulting articles into pamphlets in the local languages, finding able translators to translate Bahá'í literature for free and introducing the Faith to royalty and peasantry alike.[30]

As soon as the Tablets of the Divine Plan were disseminated across the United States, Hyde and Clara Dunn of San Francisco read them and immediately decided to move to Australia. They arrived there in April 1920. Inspired by the unveiling of the tablets and by 'Abdu'l-Bahá's tablet to Martha Root praising her South American efforts, Leonora Holsapple settled in Bahia, Brazil, in 1921 and started the first Bahá'í community in South America. In that year, also, Agnes Alexander, a Hawaiian Bahá'í who had settled in Japan in 1914 to spread the Faith there, visited Korea to teach the Faith for the first time.[31]

The Tablets of the Divine Plan also inspired the American Bahá'ís to establish committees to coordinate the teaching work in each of North America's five regions. The Bahai Temple Unity, heretofore tasked primarily to build a House of Worship, now assumed the character of a national coordinating body. In 1916 'Abdu'l-Bahá gave the Bahai Temple Unity responsibility to review all Bahá'í literature before publication to ensure its basic accuracy. In 1919, the Bahai Temple Unity appointed a Teaching Committee to coordinate the efforts the Tablets of the Divine Plan mandated. The Tablets also seem to have inspired an effort to organize the American Bahá'ís more systematically; the Chicago Bahá'í coordinating body became more active and the Cleveland Bahá'ís formed a 'House of Spirituality', the first new local consultative body formed in America since 1910. Work on the House of Worship was reinvigorated and a design for the structure was selected in 1921. To further strengthen the American Bahá'í community, 'Abdu'l-Bahá sent Fazel Mazandarani, a prominent Persian Bahá'í teacher, on a North American tour in 1920–1. 'Abdu'l-Bahá himself hoped to travel again. The Bahá'ís of India begged him to come; at one point he speculated that he might go to India, China and Japan, cross the Pacific to the western United States, cross the American continent and the Atlantic to Europe, and return to Haifa from the west.[32] But at war's end he was 74 and even though his health was reasonably good, it was hard to know how long it would remain strong. Consequently, he dedicated himself to meeting pilgrims and writing. Several very significant works resulted. In December 1919 he wrote a lengthy tablet to the Central Organization for a Durable Peace, a private organization based at the Hague. In it, he noted that the League of Nations was incapable of establishing world peace and advocated the establishment of a worldwide body of representatives chosen by the national Parliaments and confirmed by the national executive, who in turn would elect a smaller body, the Supreme Tribunal, which would settle disputes between nations and coordinate international affairs. In 1920 and 1921 he revealed tablets to August Forel, a prominent Swiss scientist and psychiatrist who had become a Bahá'í, about the relationship of the mind and the soul, the powers of the soul, the Divine Essence and its relation to the created world and the Bahá'í social principles. In 1921 he wrote a tablet commending the work of the Save the Children Fund, an organization started by a friend of a British Bahá'í.[33]

Throughout 1921, 'Abdu'l-Bahá's health was fragile and he began to refer to his imminent passing. In mid-November 'Abdu'l-Bahá addressed a lengthy tablet to the American Bahá'í community about the importance of firmness in the Covenant. Two weeks later he fell ill. An American Bahá'í physician who happened to be on pilgrimage at the time was summoned, but 'Abdu'l-Bahá passed away at 1 a.m. that night, 28 November 1921. The doctor had been a bitter opponent of the Bahá'í Faith until he met 'Abdu'l-Bahá in New York in 1912 and had a change of heart. He had the privilege of closing 'Abdu'l-Bahá's eyes.

Thousands attended his funeral 2 days later, including the British High Commissioner of Palestine, the Governor of Jerusalem, the Head Mufti of Haifa, the Bishop of the Greek Catholic Church of

Haifa, one of the leading figures in Haifa's Jewish community and prominent Muslim and Christian poets and orators. Newspapers around the world carried lengthy obituaries.

'Abdu'l-Bahá's entire grief-stricken family was there except his eldest grandson, Shoghi Effendi Rabbani, who was studying at Oxford University at the time. 'Abdu'l-Bahá's sister, Bahíyyih Khánum, oversaw the funeral and made the decision to inter 'Abdu'l-Bahá in a chamber in the Shrine of the Báb. She consulted 'Abdu'l-Bahá's Will and Testament for burial instructions and noted that it was addressed to Shoghi Effendi, who was on his way from Britain. It was not read publically until 3 January 1922, after Shoghi Effendi had arrived. At that point, the 24-year-old Shoghi Effendi and the world learned that 'Abdu'l-Bahá had appointed his eldest grandson *Guardian of the Cause of God,* a position in the Faith not previously mentioned. It was a shock to Shoghi Effendi, on whom a life-long burden of immense weight and importance had been placed. The Bahá'í Faith had entered a new era with a new leader and a new set of priorities.

CHAPTER NINE

The ministry of Shoghi Effendi, 1921–63

Shoghi Effendi's life, in a sense, had been a preparation for the responsibilities thrust upon him. Born 1 March 1897, he was 'Abdu'l-Bahá's oldest grandchild; 'Abdu'l-Bahá had had four daughters who survived to adulthood and who bore him 13 grandchildren, 'Abdu'l-Bahá's sons having all died young. 'Abdu'l-Bahá told everyone, when his eldest grandson was still a small boy, that he should be addressed with the term *Effendi* added to his name; it was a Turkish title equivalent to 'sir' or 'mister' and is indicative of respect. A special relationship developed between the two of them; Shoghi Effendi adored his grandfather and 'Abdu'l-Bahá guided his spiritual development and education.

Shoghi Effendi began his studies in the one-room school 'Abdu'l-Bahá started in the household, where Persian, Arabic and sometimes English and French were taught.[1] Later Shoghi Effendi was sent to live in Haifa across the bay from Acre and attend the Jesuit Collège des Frères, where he learned French. As a teenager he went to Beirut to attend another Catholic school, then transferred to the preparatory High School of the Syrian Protestant College (today known as the American University of Beirut). He obtained his high school diploma in 1912, at age 15. He went to the Syrian Protestant College 1913–17, completing his Bachelor's degree in the latter year, one of ten Bachelor's degree graduates. The school had as many as 35 Bahá'í students from around the Middle East because 'Abdu'l-Bahá had encouraged them to go there, then come to Haifa on school vacations to pray in the shrines and learn from the believers there. Shoghi Effendi did an additional year of graduate work.[2] 'Abdu'l-Bahá had wanted him to get the best possible education available locally, and he had done so.

FIGURE 9.1 *Portrait of 'Abdu'l-Bahá and Shoghi Effendi together (© Bahá'í International Community).*

Shoghi Effendi returned to Haifa in the summer of 1918 to serve as his grandfather's chief secretary. For almost 2 years he translated tablets into English – which he had learned well in Beirut – and accompanied his grandfather on visits to governmental officials. In 1920 he headed to Oxford University to study further and perfect his English in order to serve 'Abdu'l-Bahá better. It was in England, on 29 November 1921, when he received the shocking news that 'Abdu'l-Bahá had passed away the night before.

The aftermath of 'Abdu'l-Bahá's passing

It took a month for Shoghi Effendi to return to Haifa. No one – Shoghi Effendi included – knew what 'Abdu'l-Bahá's Will and Testament contained until it was read aloud on 3 January 1922. Shoghi Effendi thought that perhaps it might empower him to establish the Universal House of Justice, the worldwide governing body of the Bahá'í Faith that Bahá'u'lláh had said would be created in the future. Instead, the Will established twin institutions to guide the Bahá'í Faith. Shoghi Effendi was appointed the *Guardian of the Cause of God* (*valí amru'lláh* in Arabic). He was not yet 25 years old. The Guardian was empowered to interpret the Bahá'í sacred texts and protect the Faith from division and disunity. He was to appoint a successor Guardian from among the male descendants of Bahá'u'lláh, the decision to be publically ratified by a committee of nine Hands of the Cause of God.

The second institution was the Universal House of Justice, about which Bahá'u'lláh had written extensively. The Guardian was to be the irremovable head for life of the Universal House of Justice. The House was to be elected by all the members of all the National Spiritual Assemblies, who constituted an electoral college. The National Spiritual Assemblies in turn were to be elected by delegates elected by the Bahá'ís locally around the world. The Universal House of Justice was empowered to legislate on matters not covered by the authoritative Bahá'í texts, but not interpret them (as that was the Guardian's responsibility). The House could elucidate on obscure matters. 'Abdu'l-Bahá made the authority of the twin institutions absolutely clear:

> The sacred and youthful branch, the Guardian of the Cause of God, as well as the Universal House of Justice to be universally elected and established, are both under the care and protection of the Abhá Beauty [Bahá'u'lláh], under the shelter and unerring guidance of the Exalted One [the Báb] (may my life be offered up for them both). Whatsoever they decide is of God. Whoso obeyeth him not, neither obeyeth them, hath not obeyed God; whoso rebelleth against him and against them hath rebelled against God; whoso opposeth him hath opposed God; whoso contendeth with them hath contended with God; whoso

disputeth with him hath disputed with God; whoso denieth him hath denied God; whoso disbelieveth in him hath disbelieved in God; whoso deviateth, separateth himself and turneth aside from him hath in truth deviated, separated himself and turned aside from God. May the wrath, the fierce indignation, the vengeance of God rest upon him![3]

The Will and Testament also specified the responsibilities of the Hands of the Cause, who were to be appointed by the Guardian. A large portion of the Will condemned the rebellion of Muhammad-'Alí and of his brothers, detailed their nefarious deeds, set them in the context of Yahyá's earlier rebellion, and made it clear they had cut themselves off from the Bahá'í community, so they had no authority over it and no right to its property. This was important because Bahá'u'lláh had designated Muhammad-'Alí's station as second to 'Abdu'l-Bahá's and Muhammad-'Alí had used this fact to claim the right of succession.

The shock of learning of his appointment intensified Shoghi Effendi's crushing grief for the loss of the grandfather he loved more than life itself. It nearly paralyzed him. His aunt Bahíyyih Khánum, 'Abdu'l-Bahá's sister, was a pillar of strength and encouragement and sent cables to the Bahá'í world informing them of Shoghi Effendi's new responsibilities. He followed it up with an inspiring and poignant letter to the Bahá'ís of the world dated 22 January 1922.[4]

'Abdu'l-Bahá's passing also stirred the Covenant breakers into action. Muhammad-'Alí filed in court for a share of 'Abdu'l-Bahá's property and demanded custody over the Shrine of Bahá'u'lláh, next to the crumbling mansion of Bahjí where he lived. When the British and Muslim authorities refused his claims, Muhammad-'Alí's younger brother forcibly took the keys for the Shrine from its caretaker. It took Shoghi Effendi 15 months of patient work with the Palestinian authorities to get them back. If that blow were not enough, in early 1922 the Iraqi authorities seized Bahá'u'lláh's house in Baghdad, which was a designated place of Bahá'í pilgrimage. Shoghi Effendi coordinated an international campaign to get it back, an effort that has not succeeded to this day.

Shoghi Effendi was also pressured by family members to behave like 'Abdu'l-Bahá: to wear oriental garb (he had switched to western clothing), go to mosque on Friday, and spend long hours entertaining

Muslim clerics. Some family members and veteran Bahá'ís felt he was not ready to assume the responsibilities that had fallen on him. He invited various prominent Bahá'ís from Burma, Egypt, England, France, Germany, Iran and the United States to come on pilgrimage and discuss the next steps to take. Many arrived by late February and discussions began then, though they continued with others later.[5] Some Bahá'ís felt that the election of the Universal House of Justice was the logical next step to take, partly because 'Abdu'l-Bahá had often spoken about the Universal House of Justice but had never mentioned the Guardianship, so they were already familiar with that body, partly because they thought the Universal House of Justice would be able to steady and strengthen the young Guardian, and partly because a few of them hoped to serve on it.[6]

Shoghi Effendi, however, saw a major problem with the idea: there were no National Spiritual Assemblies to elect it, and they would take time to establish. Therefore, after discussions, Shoghi Effendi sent the Bahá'ís back to their national communities with instructions to work towards establishment of National Spiritual Assemblies. He wrote the 'fellow workers in the Cause of Bahá'u'lláh' a lengthy letter on 5 March 1922 about the crucial importance of establishing local Spiritual Assemblies wherever nine or more Bahá'ís resided, and National Spiritual Assemblies for every nation with a Bahá'í community. The letter quoted extensively from 'Abdu'l-Bahá's tablets about 'the sacredness of their nature, the wide scope of their activity, and the grave responsibility that rests upon them'. It described the spiritual qualities their members should possess and the consultative atmosphere that should prevail in their deliberations.[7]

Then, utterly exhausted, in broken health, in profound grief and feeling inadequate to carry out his responsibilities, Shoghi Effendi left for the mountains of Switzerland, where the solitude of hiking in the Bernese Alps could partially heal his soul. He returned to Haifa in early December, refreshed and able to tackle his work once again. He returned to Switzerland often in later years to renew his spirit, though for a much shorter time.

Priorities of the guardianship

Shoghi Effendi appears to have grasped immediately the importance of 'Abdu'l-Bahá's Will and Testament, which he later called 'the Charter of Bahá'u'lláh's New World Order'.[8] It laid out a system for electing local and National Spiritual Assemblies; he immediately began to implement it. In turn, the Assemblies would make other accomplishments possible. One was the election of the Universal House of Justice, which not only needed National Spiritual Assemblies to serve as electors, but potential members who had gained administrative experience and acquired the spiritual prerequisites of membership. The Assemblies would also provide the organizational capacity to carry out 'Abdu'l-Bahá's Tablets of the Divine Plan – called by Shoghi Effendi 'that Holy Charter wherein 'Abdu'l-Bahá's mandate investing them [the North American Bahá'ís] with their world mission is inscribed' – to establish the Bahá'í Faith in every country and significant territory on Earth.[9] Much of Shoghi Effendi's time, over the next 36 years, was devoted to these two priorities.

A third important priority stemmed from Bahá'u'lláh's Tablet of Carmel, 'the Charter of the World Spiritual and Administrative Centers of the Faith' as Shoghi Effendi called it, which spoke of Mount Carmel and said 'ere long will God sail His Ark upon thee, and will manifest the people of Bahá who have been mentioned in the Book of Names'.[10] Shoghi Effendi explained that the tablet laid the foundation for the holy places to be built on the mountain, including the Shrine of the Báb and the Seat of the Universal House of Justice, whose members are the 'people of Bahá' referred to in the tablet. Bahá'u'lláh and 'Abdu'l-Bahá had explained, either orally or in writing, many details about the design of the Bahá'í holy places on the mountain. 'Abdu'l-Bahá had built a simple stone mausoleum for the remains of the Báb half way up the north-facing slope. Shoghi Effendi devoted much time to planning the gardens, terraces and buildings to be erected on Mount Carmel, as well as acquiring holy places in and near Acre, restoring them, and laying out gardens around many of them.

In addition to the 'three distinct processes' set in motion by 'the three Charters', there was an inevitable fourth priority for Shoghi Effendi: writing and translating.[11] In 1921, relatively few works of Bahá'u'lláh were available in English, and the English was often poor and confusing. Even fewer works were published in other western languages. Furthermore, the effort to explain and interpret the meaning of the texts, revealed in an Islamic cultural context and now vital to a growing body of followers of western Christian backgrounds, had scarcely begun.

Building the administrative order

Efforts to form local and National Spiritual Assemblies began immediately. Ethel Jenner Rosenberg was one of the English Bahá'ís in
Haifa during January, February and March 1922. Shoghi Effendi
instructed her to write to leading Bahá'ís in London, Manchester
and Bournemouth – the three localities with Bahá'ís – and ask
them to assemble a list of all the Bahá'ís in their locations. When
Rosenberg returned to Britain, she helped the London Bahá'ís, as
defined by the resulting membership list, to elect a ten-member
Spiritual Assembly on 17 June 1922. To these ten, one representative from Manchester and Bournemouth were added, the twelve
serving as the 'All-England Bahá'í Council'. By early April 1923,
Manchester and Bournemouth were able to elect local Spiritual
Assemblies as well. Two more letters from Shoghi Effendi to the
London Bahá'ís explained that the local Spiritual Assembly election should occur on 21 April of every year and that the Assembly
should have no more than nine members.[12]

Once the three communities had formed Spiritual Assemblies,
it was possible to elect a National Spiritual Assembly. The
British Bahá'ís decided that six members would be chosen by the
London Bahá'ís, two by the Manchester Bahá'ís and one by the
Bournemouth Bahá'ís, in approximate proportion to the sizes of
the communities. No convention was held; the communities voted
by mail. In October 1923 the National Spiritual Assembly of the
Bahá'ís of Great Britain held its first meeting. It was one of three
National Spiritual Assemblies recognized by Shoghi Effendi that
year. The other two were for Germany and Austria and for India
and Burma.[13]

It was easier for smaller, newer Bahá'í communities to elect
a National Spiritual Assembly than for the larger communities,
which had a longer history of inappropriate habits to overcome.
North America already had an annual Bahai Temple Unity convention, which elected an Executive Board. But legally, authority
was invested in the convention, not the Executive Board; the entire
convention appointed committees, for example. A nominating
committee nominated members to the Board, and the convention
voted on their slate of candidates. Alternate members were elected
to the Board and were present for deliberations with full voting

rights if the regular members were unable to attend. In contrast, the Will and Testament of 'Abdu'l-Bahá specified that authority was invested in the Spiritual Assembly, not in those who elected it. There could be no alternate members.[14]

Bahá'í voting customs were well-established in the East: there were no nominations, campaigning or mention of names, instead the voters prayed and voted for those whom their conscience and their rational consideration brought to mind. The earliest elections for the Chicago local governing body in 1901 and 1906 had followed the voting system of the East as well, but it had not been followed at the national level. It was not until 1925 that the North American Bahá'ís were able to implement all these changes. Shoghi Effendi recognized the Bahai Temple Unity Executive Board as an official National Spiritual Assembly in that year.[15]

The sudden emphasis on organization in America was a shock to some Bahá'ís and apparently a few drifted away from the Faith, which they regarded as 'the spirit of the age' and therefore unorganizable. But the overall effect was positive because now there was something to join and build. The number of American Bahá'ís, about 1,500 in late 1899, was about the same in 1906 (1,280), 1920 (1,234), 1922 (1,368) and 1926 (1,247); the higher number reported to the US census in 1916 (2,884) reflects inclusion of many friends of the Faith at a time when membership was poorly defined. But the 1936 census showed genuine growth to 2,584, and by 1947 the number of American Bahá'ís had reached 5,174. It thus appears that without organization, the American Bahá'í community had been a revolving door, with about the same number drifting away as joining.[16]

Persecution made it difficult for the Persian Bahá'í community, numbering from 100,000 to 200,000 members, to implement Shoghi Effendi's guidance about organization. A proper national Bahá'í election required local membership lists so that local Assemblies could be elected by recognized voters. Ideally a national convention was held where the delegates could assemble, consult and vote together. Before the beginning of the Guardianship, the Bahá'í Faith lacked an official membership standard; in the United States, American Bahá'í communities submitted membership data to the US census in 1906, 1916, 1926 and 1936 for a national count of religious communities, and in the first two cases local communities sometimes submitted two lists, one of people whom they could count on to attend events and one of a larger community of interested people.* Persecution in Iran had produced a community of believers willing to martyr themselves for their Faith, but some believers were unwilling to commit themselves to the Faith on paper. It also proved difficult to elect local spiritual assemblies outside of the larger towns and cities; throughout the 1930s the country was divided into about 20 administrative districts with an Assembly in each. It was not until 1934 that a national Bahá'í membership list could be compiled that was reasonably complete. That year the Central Spiritual Assembly was replaced by a National Spiritual Assembly for Iran. But the victory was soon accompanied by another setback for the Faith, because later that year the Iranian government began a process that led to the closing of all the Bahá'í schools.

Other communities worked towards establishing a National Spiritual Assembly as well. Egypt and Sudan formed a joint National Spiritual Assembly in 1924; Iraq's formed in 1931; Australia and New Zealand elected a joint body in 1934. North of Iran, the Bahá'ís in Caucasia (Azerbaijan, Armenia and Georgia) and Turkistan (now called Turkmenistan) formed National Spiritual Assemblies by 1925. Turkistan had several thousand Bahá'ís in over 30 local Bahá'í communities; the very large community in Ashgabat had a completed Bahá'í House of Worship that included Bahá'í schools and well-organized Bahá'í youth groups.

The turmoil following the establishment of the Soviet Union left the Bahá'ís living in its southern republics relatively free, but starting in 1928 the Soviet government began a crackdown. They arrested Spiritual Assembly members and other well-known Bahá'ís, closed the Bahá'í schools, forced the Bahá'í youth groups to become part of the Communist youth group system and confiscated the House of Worship, which they leased back to the Bahá'í community. Some Bahá'ís were exiled to Siberia; others were deported to Iran; others began to migrate back to Iran where conditions were better. One observer has suggested that Bahá'í beliefs contradicted 'the Communist thesis about the backwardness of religion: its adherents were broadminded, tolerant, and

---

*After 1936, the Supreme Court ruled that the US Census could no longer collect religious membership statistics.

international in outlook' and for this reason the Bahá'ís 'attracted the attention of the Soviet communists to a much greater degree than might be warranted by the numerical strength of its supporters'. Shoghi Effendi asked the American Bahá'ís to appeal to the Soviet authorities, but their efforts were ineffective. A change of government policy in 1934–6 brought a temporary lessening of government restrictions and the House of Worship was even given back to the Bahá'ís, but in 1938 leniency came to an end. Five hundred Bahá'í men were arrested; 600 Bahá'í women and children fled south to Iran. All Bahá'í communities were disbanded and their activities banned. Hundreds of Bahá'ís were exiled to Siberia, where many died; others, or their children, re-established contact with the Faith only after the fall of Communism in 1989. The House of Worship was converted into an art gallery, then during World War Two into a factory. A severe earthquake that razed Ashgabat in 1948 severely damaged it, and it was demolished in 1963.[17]

Bahá'í activities in Iraq and Egypt were also limited by persecution. The one or two hundred Bahá'ís in Germany and Austria were relatively free until the Nazis, whose ideology was antithetical to basic Bahá'í principles, banned the Bahá'í Faith in June 1937. They confiscated all Bahá'í property and records and imprisoned some Bahá'ís. Bahá'ís of Jewish background, such as Lidia Zamenhof, daughter of the founder of Esperanto, were sent to concentration camps.[18]

As a result, Shoghi Effendi had few tools to work with to achieve the worldwide diffusion of the Bahá'í Faith. The Iraqi, Egyptian and German Bahá'í communities were small and persecuted; the Iranian community was large, but persecuted; the Central Asian communities were being destroyed; the thousand Indian Bahá'ís had no resources to spare; the thousand or two Burmese Bahá'ís were extremely poor and isolated; the Australian community was still tiny, with a hundred or so members; the British community was small (a hundred or so) and soon would be caught up in the European conflict. That left the few thousand North American Bahá'ís, who had been the recipients of the Tablets of the Divine Plan.

Interpreting the Bahá'í revelation

Consequently, Shoghi Effendi showered the North Americans with epistles that clarified, interpreted and explained aspects of the

Bahá'í teachings. Selected letters from 1922 to 1932 have been published in a 200-page book, *Bahá'í Administration*. They focused on the spiritual and practical principles behind the organization of the Bahá'í community: guidance about the role and functioning of committees, the election of delegates to the national convention, their duties and the purpose of that annual meeting, the maintenance of proper membership (and voting) lists, the use of consultation, the spirit and method of Bahá'í elections, the importance of regular observance of the Nineteen Day Feast, the strengthening of Bahá'í publishing, and the voluntary, spiritual nature of giving to the Bahá'í fund. Shoghi Effendi stressed the necessity of teaching the Faith, both the crucial role of individuals in teaching and the need for committees to support and follow up on their efforts, and encouraged a series of 'World Unity' conferences to proclaim Bahá'í principles. He repeatedly emphasized the significance of the Bahá'í House of Worship in Wilmette, the basement level of which was being completed during the 1920s, and elaborated on the purpose of the institution of the Mashriqu'l-Adhkár. He standardized the system of transliteration of Bahá'í terms in Arabic and Persian. The letters also dealt with the big picture: the qualifications to be a believer, the duties of every Bahá'í, the gradual recognition of the Bahá'í Faith as an independent religion, the dedication of Bahá'ís to interracial amity, non-participation in political affairs, and the rising menace of social chaos in the world. In one particularly memorable passage, he noted that 'One thing and only one thing will unfailingly and alone secure the undoubted triumph of this sacred Cause, namely, the extent to which our own inner life and private character mirror forth in their manifold aspects the splendor of those eternal principles proclaimed by Bahá'u'lláh'.[19]

Starting in 1929, Shoghi Effendi began a series of lengthy epistles that constituted some of the most weighty and significant interpretations of the Bahá'í Faith penned by the Guardian. 'The World Order of Bahá'u'lláh' (February 1929) described the nature and animating purpose of the Bahá'í Administrative Order. 'The World Order of Bahá'u'lláh: Further Considerations' (March 1930) outlined the distinguishing features of the Bahá'í world order, the divine civilization it sought to build and its differences from the ecclesiastical and political institutions established by Christianity and Islam. 'The Goal of a New World Order' (November 1931) reviewed the guiding principles of world order, contrasted them

with the impotence of statesmanship, delineated the implications of the principle of the oneness of mankind and reminded
the Bahá'ís of 'Abdu'l-Bahá's warning that yet another world war
would break out. 'The Golden Age of the Cause of Bahá'u'lláh'
(March 1932) stressed the decline of religious and political institutions, the relationship of the Bahá'í Faith to the religions of the past
and the necessity of a new divine revelation and the divine polity
it brought.

'America and the Most Great Peace' (April 1933) highlighted
and praised the historic accomplishments of the American Bahá'ís
and sought to inspire them to retain their leadership and 'spiritual
primacy' in the Bahá'í world. 'The Dispensation of Bahá'u'lláh'
(February 1934) described in great detail, utilizing new translations of numerous passages from the Bahá'í authoritative texts, the
stations of the Báb, Bahá'u'lláh and 'Abdu'l-Bahá, the nature of
the Bahá'í Administrative Order, and the relationship of each to
the other. The epistle provided a theological clarity and precision
that Christianity, in its quest to understand the nature of Christ,
took centuries to achieve. 'The Unfoldment of World Civilization'
(March 1936) traced human evolution through to the chaos of the
present day, describing the universal fermentation and decline of
the age of transition, explaining the decline of the institutions of
Christianity and Islam and the breakdown of political and economic structures and promising the rise of the Bahá'í community
and the eventual achievement of world unity.

These seven epistles were published as a 200-page book, *The
World Order of Bahá'u'lláh,* in 1938. Two later letters were of
greater length and were published separately. *The Advent of Divine
Justice* (December 1938) described in 75 pages the American Bahá'í
community as the 'chief remaining citadel' of the Bahá'í Faith –
war or persecution having engulfed most of the rest – and stressed
the historical importance of the plans they were engaged in. The
letter elaborated on the three 'prerequisites' for their 'success' in
all their endeavours: 'a high sense of moral rectitude in their social
and administrative activities, absolute chastity in their individual
lives, and complete freedom from prejudice in their dealings with
peoples of a different race, class, creed, or color'.[20]

A rectitude of conduct, 'with its implications of justice, equity,
truthfulness, honesty, fair-mindedness, reliability, and trustworthiness' must be manifested in all the interactions of Bahá'ís with

fellow humans. A 'chaste and holy life' with 'its implications of modesty, purity, temperance, decency, and clean-mindedness',

> involves no less than the exercise of moderation in all that pertains to dress, language, amusements, and all artistic and literary avocations. It demands daily vigilance in the control of one's carnal desires and corrupt inclinations. It calls for the abandonment of a frivolous conduct, with its excessive attachment to trivial and often misdirected pleasures.[21]

Racial prejudice was 'the most vital and challenging issue confronting the Bahá'í community at the present stage of its evolution':

> A long and thorny road, beset with pitfalls, still remains untraveled, both by the white and the Negro exponents of the redeeming Faith of Bahá'u'lláh. On the distance they cover, and the manner in which they travel that road, must depend, to an extent which few among them can imagine, the operation of those intangible influences which are indispensable to the spiritual triumph of the American believers and the material success of their newly launched enterprise.[22]

The Advent of Divine Justice is particularly significant because it connects the mystical core of the Bahá'í Faith – one's relationship with God – to personal transformation, Bahá'í ethics, the development of one's character, the moral qualities and virtues one must develop and express in one's life and their manifestation in concrete, personal efforts to spread the Bahá'í Faith.

The Promised Day is Come (March 1941) sought to set the 'world afflicting ordeal' of World War Two in the context of sacred history. Much of the 130-page epistle consisted of new translations of Bahá'u'lláh's letters to the kings and rulers of the world, to the Pope and to numerous Muslim and Christian ecclesiastics. By ignoring or rejecting God's Manifestation, these leaders had set into motion powerful historical and spiritual forces. All the dynasties but one – that of Queen Victoria, who is said to have received Bahá'u'lláh's letter to her positively – were swept from power; the caliphate collapsed; many of their empires were defeated or broken up; the moral and spiritual authority of the Christian and Muslim institutions were compromised; religious orthodoxy crumbled; the pillars of religion were weakened; and the 'three false gods' of nationalism, racialism and communism and their 'war-engendering, world-convulsing doctrines' spread and to some extent replaced them. But the war 'is not only a retributory and destructive fire, but a disciplinary and creative process, whose aim is the salvation, through unification, of the entire planet'. A 'great Age' is to come, the 'fitting climax' of social evolution; a world civilization will be 'born, flourish, and perpetuate itself, a civilization with a fullness of life such as the world has never seen nor can as yet conceive'. Therefore, it is the duty of the Bahá'ís,

> however confused the scene, however dismal the present outlook, however circumscribed the resources we dispose of, to labor serenely, confidently, and unremittingly to lend our share of assistance, in whichever way circumstances may enable us, to the operation of the forces which, as marshaled and directed by Bahá'u'lláh, are leading humanity out of the valley of misery and shame to the loftiest summits of power and glory.[23]

Shoghi Effendi's last major work – his only real book, the previous ones being epistles – was *God Passes By*, his 1944 review of the first century of Bahá'í history, published on the centenary of the declaration of the Báb. Its masterful grasp of the details of Bábí and Bahá'í history, its judgments of the motivations of participants and the significance of events – judgments that reflect Shoghi Effendi's authority as Guardian and interpreter as much as his skills as historian – its overview of relevant secular forces and contexts, and its lyrical English reveal Shoghi Effendi's intellectual and literary capacities at their peak. Much of the work of future Bahá'í historians will consist of expanding on the trajectory of Bahá'í history he defined.

New authoritative translations

Shoghi Effendi devoted a considerable fraction of his ministry to translation. The purpose of his education had been to prepare him to translate Bahá'í authoritative texts into English because heretofore the translations had often been wooden, vague and confusing. As Guardian, Shoghi Effendi had the authority to interpret the meaning of the sacred texts, a crucial need when taking words and phrases developed in the context of an Islamic civilization and setting them into a western language developed in the context of Christian civilization. As a result, he did not delegate translation to others, though he did ask others to review and comment on his drafts. Shoghi Effendi's philosophy of translating revelation favoured beauty, poetry and musicality over literalism, because scripture has a power to uplift, transform and inspire the reader that is lost in a literal rendering. This is easiest seen when comparing Shoghi Effendi's translation of Qur'ánic verses that appear in the Bahá'í scriptures with standard translations. For example, the statement that God is closer to human beings than their 'jugular vein' (50:16; Sale, Yusuf Ali) or 'neck vein' (Dawood, Rodwell) is translated 'life vein' by Shoghi Effendi.[24] He also chose to use an elevated King Jamesian style because it was dignified, conveyed a sense of sacredness and was familiar to English speakers, thereby creating a sacred language for Bahá'í scripture. While tastes in Bible translations have subsequently changed, Shoghi Effendi's translation norms remain the standard for new authoritative translations of Bahá'í scriptures into English.

Shoghi Effendi's first major translation was of 'Abdu'l-Bahá's Will and Testament. His first translations of Bahá'u'lláh's works were the Kitáb-i-Íqán (1931) and Hidden Words (1932). In 1935 he assembled and translated a 200-page compilation, Gleanings from the Writings of Bahá'u'lláh, which was followed by a second more devotional volume of Bahá'u'lláh's writings, Prayers and Meditations (1938). His final translation of Bahá'u'lláh's writings was Epistle to the Son of the Wolf (1941). One also must mention his 700-page translation of The Dawn-breakers: Nabíl's Narrative of the Early Days of the Bahá'í Revelation (1932), an account of the lives of the Báb and Bahá'u'lláh through 1853 by one who was an eyewitness of many of the events. It took him 2 years to read all the background material, edit and translate the work, and add extensive footnotes from other sources.[25] The book was extensively illustrated by photographs by an Australian Bahá'í woman, whom he sent to Iran to obtain the images the book needed. His purpose was to set out an authentic record of the early history in magnificent English to inspire future generations of Bahá'ís in their service to the Faith.

Shoghi Effendi's attention to the literary needs of the Bahá'í community was not limited to writing and translation. In 1923, John Ebenezer Esslemont, a distinguished British Bahá'í and a close associate of Shoghi Effendi, published an introductory textbook, *Bahá'u'lláh and the New Era*. It was by far the most comprehensive and accurate introduction ever produced, partly because Esslemont spent years accumulating and organizing the information, and partly because 'Abdu'l-Bahá had read and approved several of the chapters. Shoghi Effendi, seeing the book's potential, made its translation a priority, thereby providing a standard introduction to the Faith to Bahá'ís of the east and the west, regardless of their cultural backgrounds. By 1969 it had been translated into about 100 languages.[26] It has gone through five editions to keep its contents current. Shoghi Effendi also approved the American National Spiritual Assembly's idea to produce regularly a book that would survey the latest news and cultural and literary developments in the Bahá'í community. *The Bahá'í World* was first published in 1925.

Developments in Haifa and Acre

Shoghi Effendi continued 'Abdu'l-Bahá's efforts to develop the Bahá'í World Centre. In 1929 he was able to obtain from the Covenant breakers the Mansion of Bahjí outside Acre, where Bahá'u'lláh passed his last years, restored it and opened it to pilgrims. When 'Abdu'l-Bahá's sister, Bahíyyih Khánum, passed away in 1932, he interred her about half way up the slope of Mount Carmel not far from the Shrine of the Báb and erected an elegant monument over her resting place. Her mother, her brother Mírzá Mihdí and 'Abdu'l-Bahá's wife Munírih were reinterred nearby to form the 'Monument Gardens', which Shoghi Effendi made the focus of a 'far flung arc' on which to set the major buildings of the future Bahá'í World Centre.[27] He expanded the Shrine of the Báb, completing the basic, square sandstone building 'Abdu'l-Bahá envisaged, and set up the rear three rooms as the first archives area. He also developed the gardens around the Shrine and began the process of beautification of the sacred spot.

Implementing the divine plan

The steady increase in administrative experience and knowledge of the Bahá'í teachings deepened and strengthened the capacities of the North American Bahá'ís and allowed Shoghi Effendi to give them new teaching goals. In 1936 he wrote the National Bahá'í Convention and stressed the importance of settling at least one Bahá'í in every state in the United States and every republic in Latin America (including the Caribbean) by the end of the first Bahá'í century (1944). In 1935, 11 of the 48 contiguous states did not have Bahá'ís and 26 did not have local spiritual assemblies. Only two Latin American countries had Bahá'ís. There was an immense amount of work to do.[28]

A year later, desiring to formalize the teaching effort, Shoghi Effendi gave the North American Bahá'ís the Seven Year Plan. It laid out even more ambitious goals: by 1944 there was to be at least one local Spiritual Assembly in every state in the United States and at least one in every Canadian province, the Bahá'í Faith was to be established in every republic in Latin America (meaning at least one Bahá'í in each), and the exterior of the Bahá'í House of Worship in Wilmette was to be completed.[29] To inspire the Bahá'ís, Shoghi Effendi penned frequent epistles of encouragement to them; much of *The Advent of Divine Justice* focused on the spiritual and historical significance of the Seven Year Plan.

New techniques were necessary to achieve the goals. Growth of the North American Bahá'í community in the 1920s and early 1930s had heavily relied on travelling Bahá'í teachers who visited cities for a time to give public lectures on spiritual and personal development topics, offer more informal talks about the Faith to those attracted, enrol new Bahá'ís and elect a local Spiritual Assembly. Other travelling teachers would then return from time to time to give talks to deepen the Bahá'ís' understanding of their new Faith and attract new believers. The technique tended to produce Bahá'í communities that were dependent on visiting teachers, however, and the number of such teachers was insufficient for the new goals. Consequently, the National Spiritual Assembly began to encourage the use of *firesides,* where Bahá'ís invited friends to their homes, offered them hospitality and answered their questions about the Faith. This technique created Bahá'ís and Bahá'í communities that were far more independent of travelling teachers.[30]

The other technique to be used extensively for the first time was the *pioneer*, someone who intentionally moves to a new place, finds housing and employment, puts down roots and teaches the Faith to acquaintances. Pioneers were essential for the Latin American goals, in particular, because they acquired the languages and cultural sensitivity to reach local people. They were also able to visit each other and thus serve as travelling teachers as well. Most pioneers went to capital cities and reached out to the better educated and the inquiring; Esperantists, Spiritualists and Theosophists were three particularly receptive groups.

The National Spiritual Assembly appointed committees to help Bahá'ís with the logistics of moving and settling, and sometimes subsidized them temporarily until they could support themselves. World War Two was a major impediment; gas rationing made the movement of teachers difficult and housing shortages made it hard to settle in new places. Materials to complete the exterior of the House of Worship were in short supply. But every goal was achieved. Not only was every Latin American nation opened to the Faith; by 1944, ten had local Spiritual Assemblies. At Shoghi Effendi's urging, in 1945 Puntas Arenas, Chile, the southernmost city in the world, elected a local Spiritual Assembly.

Shoghi Effendi gave the North American Bahá'ís 2 years to recover from the effort, then launched a second Seven Year Plan (1946–53). It called on the North American Bahá'ís to elect a separate National Spiritual Assembly for Canada, a single National Spiritual Assembly for all of South America and another for all of Central America and the Caribbean, to complete the interior and the gardens of the Bahá'í House of Worship and to re-establish the Bahá'í Faith in war-ravaged western Europe. American Bahá'í energy now turned east. Committees settled pioneers all across Europe. The German and Austrian Bahá'ís were found, brought back together and assisted to re-elect their local Spiritual Assemblies. Their National Spiritual Assembly was re-established in 1946. There was great receptivity in Europe to new ideas after the War, especially those promoted by Americans, so the teaching work proceeded well.

Shoghi Effendi stimulated specific efforts to reach American Indians with the Faith as well, based on 'Abdu'l-Bahá's encouragement in the Tablets of the Divine Plan. A local Spiritual Assembly was elected on the Omaha Indian reservation in Macy, Nebraska, in 1948. In Canada, efforts to reach the First Nations (Indians and Inuit) began in 1949 when two native Bahá'ís, Melba and Alfred Loft, pioneered to the Tyendinaga Mohawk reserve (reservation) of Mr Loft's tribe. The first indigenous native in Latin America to become a Bahá'í lived in Panama in 1947. The plan ended victoriously at the Bahá'í House of Worship on 1 May 1953, when that structure was formally dedicated and opened to public worship, 41 years to the day after 'Abdu'l-Bahá laid the cornerstone in a hole cut in prairie sod.

FIGURE 9.2 *Bahá'í House of Worship in the United States (© Bahá'í International Community).*

The successes of the North American Bahá'ís inspired other communities to create their own plans. When the Canadian Bahá'ís elected their own National Spiritual Assembly in 1948, Shoghi Effendi gave them a five year plan. In 1944, the British Bahá'ís devised their own four year plan, which ended successfully in July 1950. In 1947, the Iraqi Bahá'ís adopted a three year plan; in 1947 the Egyptian Bahá'ís defined aims they wanted to achieve by 1953; the National Spiritual Assembly Australia and New Zealand devised a plan for 1947–53; the German and Austrian Bahá'ís created a plan for 1947–52. In spite of the turbulence leading up to the independence of the subcontinent, the Bahá'ís of India and Burma (and Pakistan, after 1948) decided to open a small private school, New Era, in the town of Panchgani in 1945, which eventually evolved into a top-notch private elementary and high school. They also set for themselves a four and a half year plan, 1946–50. Iran adopted a four year plan, 1946–50.[31] Most of the plans set goals to take the Faith to smaller cities, towns, villages and minority groups within their own national jurisdictions. The plans constituted preparation for the time when Shoghi Effendi would give goals to the entire Bahá'í world.

Development of Bahá'í institutions, 1944–53

The accelerating growth of the Bahá'í Faith after World War Two kept Shoghi Effendi very busy. According to his wife, Rúhíyyih Khánum (nee Mary Maxwell, whom he married in 1938), that was the reason he no longer wrote lengthy letters or translated works of Bahá'u'lláh into English.[32] He began to build up a secretarial staff in Haifa to assist him in his work. One early focus of their efforts was to coordinate work on the Shrine of the Báb, a simple square building of yellow sandstone with a flat roof onto which Shoghi Effendi added a superstructure of granite and marble, surmounted by a dome of golden tiles. The design was completed in 1944 and plans initiated in 1947, during the chaos and terrorism that preceded the establishment of the state of Israel. Arranging the importation of Carrara marble from Italy and other necessities in the early days of the state of Israel was immensely difficult, but the

FIGURE 9.3 *Shrine of the Báb (© Bahá'í International Community).*

building was completed in 1953. It was followed by construction of the Parthenon-like International Archives Building from 1954 to 1958. The period also saw the purchase of several historic properties in or near Acre and beautification of the area around the Shrine of Bahá'u'lláh.

In January 1951, Shoghi Effendi appointed an International Bahá'í Council. Some members were already living in Haifa; others were distinguished Bahá'ís he invited to reside there. He said that in the future the Council would be elected. He described it as the precursor body of the Universal House of Justice. He appointed the Council's officers. Its principal tasks were forging links with government officials, assisting him with the construction of the Shrine of the Báb and negotiating with the state of Israel regarding personal status matters (such as Bahá'í marriages and divorces). Most of the work was done by the individuals to whom Shoghi Effendi assigned numerous tasks; the body rarely met.[33]

The appointment of the Bahá'í International Council was followed, in December 1951, by the appointment of 12 Hands of the Cause of God; three in the Holy Land, three in Iran, three in the United States and three in Europe. While Bahá'u'lláh had appointed four Hands and given them tasks to accomplish, 'Abdu'l-Bahá had not appointed any living Hands (though he did refer to a few individuals posthumously as Hands). Shoghi Effendi had also named several individuals as Hands upon their decease, and had privately informed one Bahá'í, Amelia Collins, that she was a Hand of the Cause in 1947, but this was the first time he had made a public appointment of living, active Bahá'ís. On 29 February 1952, he appointed seven more Hands, raising the total to nineteen. Australasia, Africa and Canada had one each.[34]

In addition to the developments at the international centre of the Faith, the Bahá'í Faith began to develop a relationship with the United Nations. A Bahá'í Bureau in Geneva had earlier developed a relationship with the League of Nations during the interwar period. In 1947, the National Spiritual Assembly of the Bahá'ís of the United States was accredited as 'a national non-governmental organization qualified to be represented at United Nations through an observer'. In 1948 the 'Bahá'í International Community' (BIC) was created as an umbrella organization for all National Spiritual Assemblies and was also granted observer status. Shoghi Effendi (and later the Universal House of Justice) directed all BIC efforts. Both the BIC and the American Bahá'í representations at the UN continue to this day. In the intervening years, the staff have grown in numbers and have acquired an excellent reputation.[35]

We can obtain a glimpse of what Shoghi Effendi was like in February 1953 when Dr Marcus Bach, a professor of religious studies at the University of Iowa, visited him in Haifa. Bach described him as

a small, dark-complexioned man, dressed in Western attire but wearing a fez. His clean-shaven face and slender figure registered indomitable strength. He walked with head up as though an entourage of the faithful might be following him. He strode in, bowed to me with an almost imperceptible nod, and held out his hand. As we exchanged greetings there was a smile on his lips, though this did not entirely destroy my impression of a certain aloofness in his bearing. He welcomed me with a sensitivity that seemed to feel, rather than hear, my words.

The expression of his dark eyes, too, gave a hint of inner judgment based not on what was said but, rather, on what was sensed. He was self-possessed, self-sufficient, purposeful. I had been told he was a man of fifty-seven, but, judging from his unlined, youthful face, he might have been only forty. And though I stood head and shoulders above him, I felt diminutive. I envied him the sense of security and holy mission in life that filled his whole soul with confidence, beyond doubt and beyond question. . . .

He had no other purpose than to see his mission accomplished. Build the Faith! Complete the Shrines! Guard and guide the people! Resist the enemies of the Cause! Trust in God! The divan on which he sat might have been a throne, his words, the words of a king.

But the thing that struck me the most as our meeting progressed was his unquestioned devotion to the Galilean. He was fully as faithful to Jesus as he was to Bahá'u'lláh. . . . The knowledge, love, and commitment which Shoghi Effendi held for Jesus were a startling revelation. . . . The moments went by. The hour grew late. I had a notebook in my pocket but I did not open it that night. It might have helped me to remember his words, but not his faith. That was something to be felt and cherished.[36]

The Ten Year Crusade

In 1953 there were 12 National Spiritual Assemblies worldwide: one in Italy and Switzerland, one in Germany and Austria, one in Egypt and Sudan, one in Australia and New Zealand, one in India and Burma, one in Central America and the Caribbean, the United States, Canada, South America, the British Isles, Iran and Iraq. Shoghi Effendi gave plans to all twelve of them, rather than just to the North Americans; the capacities of all the communities had increased significantly. The Ten Year Crusade was to run from 1953 to 1963. The goals included increasing the number of countries, islands and significant territories in which the Bahá'í Faith was established – essentially every nation and major island group on the Earth – from 128 to 259, and increasing the number of National Spiritual Assemblies to 57. The effort required the Assemblies to appoint many committees, recruit Bahá'ís willing to learn new languages and move thousands of kilometres, then assist them with their difficulties. Sometimes Assemblies had to cooperate to help each other with goals.

In many cases, the old techniques of lectures and firesides given by travelling teachers and pioneers were not adequate, because the populations being reached often were not urban and educated. A good example of the new situation is given by the story of Ray Fernie and Elena Marsella Fernie. Elena Marsella was the first person to become a Bahá'í in Providence, Rhode Island, when pioneers arrived there in 1939, during the First Seven Year Plan.[37] In 1945 she pioneered to the Caribbean; in April 1951, when the first National Spiritual Assembly of the Bahá'ís of Central America and the Antilles was formed, she was elected to its membership, and then was elected secretary (which was the executive position). In 1953 she married Ray Fernie. When the goals of the Ten Year Crusade were announced, the National Spiritual Assembly of Central America and the Antilles was given the goal of establishing the Faith in Tuamotu Archipelago, the Marshall Islands and the Gilbert and Ellis Islands, all in the western and central Pacific Ocean. The Fernies decided to go to the Gilbert and Ellis Island Colony, even though they did not know where it was at first and could not figure out how to get there from Panama, where they lived.

After a lengthy journey and numerous government hurtles, in March 1954 they arrived on the coral atoll of Abaiang in the Gilbert Islands (modern Kiribati), inhabited by a few thousand fishermen and copra harvesters. The boat was greeted by a crowd – it did not arrive often – and the Fernies were carried ashore on the shoulders of natives, there being no dock. They knew only a word or two of Gilbertese, but a native kindly offered them an egg and Ray, an amateur magician, made it disappear. The people laughed 'for about half an hour'.[38] That night an English speaker showed up to translate the peoples' request for a magic show, which Ray offered under a series of lanterns, Elena adding a 'recital' on an old piano that was available. Because they were roughing it in a native hut – no 'European' accommodation being available on the island – and because they treated the natives respectfully as equals, they quickly had an audience. Their message that God had sent another Manifestation, that Jesus had promised him, and that the new teachings included the oneness and equality of all peoples created quite a stir on Abaiang.

The Protestant and Catholic missionaries on the island preached against them, which spread the news of the Bahá'í Faith further. Ray helped to open a non-sectarian school on the island, further angering them. By the end of 1955, 230 people had become Bahá'ís and three 'practice Assemblies' had formed. The fact that the Gilbertese were in charge of their own communities was attractive. In November 1955, the missionaries convinced the British colonial officials to order Ray's deportation. They assumed Elena would go with her husband, but since the order did not require her to leave, she remained until mid-1957 to solidify the community. One active local Bahá'í was deported to his native island, which spread the Faith there. The treatment of the Fernies caused a change in British colonial policy and Bahá'í pioneers were no longer turned away. The Bahá'í Faith became well-established and continued to grow. In 2000, the Kiribati government census reported that the country had 2,052 Bahá'ís, 2.6 per cent of the total population of 84,494.[39]

The Bahá'í Faith began to reach large rural populations in several other places during the Ten Year Crusade. In 1956, a Bolivian Aymara Indian returned to his village with the Bahá'í Faith. Members of an indigenous movement for Indian empowerment and nationalism, the 'Alcaldes Mayores Particulares', who worshipped the earth goddess Pachamama and the gods of the mountains, were intrigued by the Bahá'í emphasis on the oneness of humanity and equality of all peoples and by the claim that Bahá'u'lláh was the return of Wiracocha, whom they were expecting. Two thousand ultimately were attracted to the Faith. By 1960 Bolivia had 1,000 Bahá'ís, 95 per cent of whom were indigenous; the number increased to 6,000 by 1963. A Bolivian Indian initiated mass teaching of Indians in Argentina in 1962. In 1962, mass teaching of Quechuas began in Peru; efforts to reach the Mapuches in Chile were inaugurated in 1963. An all-Quechua local Spiritual Assembly formed in Ecuador in 1960, and Guaymi Indians became Bahá'ís in Panama and Colombia.[40]

Efforts to reach rural people in central India began about the same time. The Indian Bahá'í community, mostly of Parsee and Muslim background, urban, and educated, had not previously made efforts to reach the Hindu villages. In 1959 a Parsee Bahá'í woman and her brother began to visit villages in the district of Malwa, explain the Bahá'í Faith and invite the people to become

Bahá'ís. To their astonishment, hundreds responded. The Bahá'í teaching of equality and oneness, its emphasis on education, its acceptance of Krishna as a Manifestation of God, its claim that Bahá'u'lláh was the appearance of the Kalkin Avatar and its positive approach to Hinduism – in sharp contrast to Christian, Buddhist and Muslim teachers – were particularly appealing. In 2 years the official membership of the Indian Bahá'í community went from less than a 1,000 to 89,217.[41]

Uganda saw thousands of natives embrace the Bahá'í Faith in the 1950s; one of them, Enoch Olinga, even moved to Cameroon to help establish the Bahá'í Faith on Africa's western shores. The Kenyan Bahá'í community grew rapidly as well. Sub-Saharan Africa went from a handful of Bahá'ís to nearly 30,000 by 1963. Teaching on the remote Mentawai Islands of Indonesia by an Iranian Bahá'í physician and his wife, Rahmatu'lláh and Iran Muhajir, brought 5,000 people into the Faith between 1954 and 1958 and resulted in the establishment of seven schools to educate children.[42]

Except in areas where the Bahá'í Faith was persecuted or legally excluded – such as most Communist countries – virtually all the expansion goals were achieved by 1963. Of the 131 new places the Bahá'í Faith was to be established, 127 received Bahá'í pioneers. Approximately 1,300 pioneers settled in new places. All the National Spiritual Assemblies were established except one, in Afghanistan. The number of local Spiritual Assemblies worldwide increased from 611 to 3,551; the number of localities with Bahá'ís increased from 2,425 to 11,210. The United States sent out about a third of the pioneers, while expanding the number of Bahá'ís at home from 7,000 to 10,000. The total number of Bahá'ís in the world at least doubled, to about 408,000.[43] A notable aspect of the Crusade was the establishment of schools and projects to improve rural health, precursor efforts to the focus on social and economic development that came in the 1960s and 1970s.

Persecution

The growth of the Bahá'í community was accompanied by a certain amount of persecution from missionaries and established churches, but most of the trouble was concentrated in the Islamic areas of the globe. The arrival of Persian and American pioneers in

Morocco brought about the conversion of native Moroccans, and in 1962 14 Moroccan Bahá'ís were arrested and jailed, and three were sentenced to death. An international outcry resulted and all were released in 1963. The banning of Bahá'í institutions and confiscation of Bahá'í community property in Egypt in 1960, however, could not be reversed and persists to this day.

The worst outbreak of persecution in Iran in half a century began in late April 1955. It was triggered partly by the political situation; a CIA-sponsored coup had removed the Prime Minister in 1953 and the Shah was weak. A prominent Shi'ite cleric began a series of daily anti-Bahá'í sermons in his mosque and the government radio station carried them to the entire country. In early May, the Bahá'í administrative headquarters in Tehran – an impressive building with a prominent dome – was seized by the police, then turned over to the army, which began to demolish the dome, accompanied by widespread publicity. This seemed to give permission to 'an orgy of senseless murder, rape, pillage and destruction'. The House of the Báb, the place where the Báb declared his mission in May 1844 and a centre of Bahá'í pilgrimage worldwide, was twice attacked, desecrated and severely damaged; Bahá'u'lláh's house in Takur was occupied. In addition,

> shops and farms were plundered; crops burned; livestock destroyed; bodies of Bahá'ís disinterred in the cemeteries and mutilated; private homes broken into, damaged and looted; adults execrated and beaten; young women abducted and forced to marry Muslims; children mocked, reviled, beaten and expelled from schools; boycott by butchers and bakers was imposed on hapless villagers; young girls raped; families murdered; Government employees dismissed and all manner of pressure brought upon the believers to recant their Faith.[44]

The Bahá'í community responded to the assault with remarkable discipline. In Iran, Bahá'ís neither recanted their Faith, nor fought back; they proclaimed their innocence whenever they could and corrected slander and misinformation in conversations with friends and neighbours. Outside Iran, Shoghi Effendi coordinated a massive response. Bahá'í local and National Spiritual Assemblies were instructed to cable protests to the Shah, Prime Minister and the Iranian Parliament. The flood of cables from places utterly obscure to the officials produced a 'deep impression' because they had not realized the Bahá'í Faith had spread way beyond Iran's borders. A worldwide publicity campaign, including an appeal to the United Nations – the Bahá'í International Community had been an observer for some years – deeply embarrassed the Shah's government. In August it began to curb the violence, which continued into 1956. The government could not curb the hatred for the Bahá'ís, however, which remained particularly intense among the clerical establishment.

Construction of new edifices

The persecution of Iran's Bahá'ís underlined one fact: the construction of a House of Worship in Tehran, which Shoghi Effendi had made a goal of the Ten Year Crusade, was impossible. He replaced it with the goal to build two Houses of Worship, in Sydney, Australia, and Kampala, Uganda, where an indigenous Bahá'í community was rapidly forming. Both were completed in 1961. He had already set a goal to build a Temple in Frankfurt, Germany, in the heart

FIGURE 9.4 *Bahá'í House of Worship in Uganda (© Bahá'í International Community).*

of Europe; that building was finished in 1964. The Crusade also included the goal of creating the first Mashriqu'l-Adhkár dependency in Wilmette, Illinois; a Home for the Aged opened in 1959.

The chief stewards

Part of the success of the Ten Year Crusade can be attributed to the efforts of the Hands of the Cause of God. In addition to providing general guidance about their responsibilities to guide, encourage and advise the Bahá'ís and their Spiritual Assemblies, Shoghi Effendi put them to work, assisting with the formation of certain National Spiritual Assemblies, representing him at their inaugural election and serving as his representative at various international Bahá'í conferences. In 1954 he asked the Hands outside the Holy Land to appoint Auxiliary Board members to serve as their 'deputies, assistants and advisors' in their work, thereby multiplying further their effectiveness and reach. When a Hand of the Cause died, Shoghi Effendi appointed a replacement, maintaining the number at 19. In October 1957 Shoghi Effendi raised the number of Hands to 27 and referred to them as 'Chief Stewards of Bahá'u'lláh's embryonic World Commonwealth, who have been invested by the unerring Pen of the Center of His Covenant ['Abdu'l-Bahá] with the dual function of guarding over the security, and of insuring the propagation, of His Father's Faith'.[45]

The description of the role of the Hands of the Cause proved portentous. In early November, 1957, while visiting London, Shoghi Effendi caught the Asiatic flu. He was recovering on the morning of 4 November when a coronary thrombosis stopped his heart, causing an instant and painless death at age 60.

The Guardian's passing plunged the Bahá'í world into profound grief and shock. He had been their source of inspiration for 36 years and was deeply loved. Rúhíyyih Khánum was nearly overcome with grief. The Hands of the Cause of God and representatives of many National Spiritual Assemblies gathered in London for his funeral, then the Hands flew to Haifa to meet. One of their first acts was to search his rooms thoroughly for a will. Both Bahá'u'lláh and 'Abdu'l-Bahá had left wills detailing the next steps the Bahá'í world was to take and the Bahá'í sacred writings enjoined the writing of a will on all believers. But Shoghi Effendi had not left one, a decision that was both difficult to understand and a severe test of faith.

Most Bahá'ís had expected Shoghi Effendi to appoint a Guardian to succeed him. The Will and Testament of 'Abdu'l-Bahá was quite specific about the mechanism Shoghi Effendi was to follow: the successor had to be an Aghsán or male descendant of Bahá'u'lláh; once Shoghi Effendi had selected his successor, he was to inform the Hands of the Cause; they were to elect a committee of nine to ratify the choice. But there were no male descendants of Bahá'u'lláh still within the Bahá'í community. All of Shoghi Effendi's cousins had rebelled against his authority and had married into the Covenant breaking families of 'Abdu'l-Bahá's half-brothers, so Shoghi Effendi had declared them Covenant breakers as well. Some Bahá'ís had even imagined that Shoghi Effendi and Rúhíyyih Khánum had had a child but were keeping him a secret to protect the child from excessive and inappropriate attention, but this was untrue; their marriage had been childless.

Not only was the Bahá'í Faith without a head, for the first time in its history, but there was no way to determine why it was without a head, because only the head of the Faith could interpret or elucidate the authoritative texts about the situation. The Bahá'ís were left to speculate. Fortunately, temporary leadership seemed possible because Shoghi Effendi had referred to the Hands of the Cause as the 'chief stewards'. The Will and Testament of 'Abdu'l-Bahá gave them the authority to expel Covenant breakers, if necessary, so they could maintain the Faith's unity. Shoghi Effendi had left them with a Ten Year Crusade, of which only four and a half years had elapsed; and he had defined detailed goals for the next five and a half years. He had also said that the global plans after the Ten Year Crusade were to be under the auspices of the Universal House of Justice. The Hands, therefore, had a kind of road map laid out for them to follow: they were to complete the Ten Year Crusade and call for the election of the Universal House of Justice. The road map did not include a day-to-day role for the International Bahá'í Council.

The Hands' deliberations in Haifa were long and slow, partly because of their grief, partly because they did not all speak a common language, so everything had to be translated between English and Persian. Some sought a mechanism whereby they could select another Guardian, for it seemed inconceivable that the provisions of

'Abdu'l-Bahá's will would come to an end after only one Guardian. One Hand, Charles Mason Remey (1874–1974) even insisted that the Hands choose a Guardian.[46] The consensus of the group, however, was that they had to be scrupulous in following the existing guidance in the writings of Bahá'u'lláh, 'Abdu'l-Bahá and Shoghi Effendi, and not exceed it at all, for they had no sphere of authority to do so. Only the Universal House of Justice could resolve their dilemmas about the Guardianship.

Their initial concerns were to maintain unity and continuity. All 27 Hands gathered except one who was 96 years old and unable to travel; but even she assented to their decisions via notarized documents. They chose from among themselves nine Custodians to reside in Haifa and direct the affairs of the Bahá'í Faith on a day-to-day basis; the entire body of the Hands met annually. At their first conclave they made it clear that they would decide when to call for the election of the Universal House of Justice. Through the able legal assistance of Shoghi Effendi's attorney, they were able to gain control over all the Bahá'í assets in Israel, thereby depriving the Covenant breakers of any possible claim to the holy places and ensuring that all bills were paid. Shoghi Effendi had called for a series of international conferences in 1958 and had appointed Hands to represent him; the conferences were held and they helped to rally the Bahá'ís.

The Claim of charles Mason Remey

Unity, thus, was maintained. In November 1959 the Hands announced that the election of the Universal House of Justice would occur in April 1963, when the Ten Year Crusade came to an end. That upset Remey, who came to believe that Shoghi Effendi had in fact appointed him the next Guardian. He withdrew from activity and was replaced as one of the nine Custodians administering activities in Haifa. Before he left Israel, two Hands who were old friends spoke to him about his feelings.

In April 1960, Remey sent a letter to all National Spiritual Assemblies announcing his claim to be the second Guardian of the Bahá'í Faith. His claim assumed that the Guardianship was an institution meant to endure forever, therefore the Will and Testament had to be reinterpreted creatively to make that possible. Shoghi

Effendi had appointed Remey the President of the International Bahá'í Council, had stated that the International Bahá'í Council was the precursor of the Universal House of Justice and 'Abdu'l-Bahá's Will and Testament made the Guardian the head of the Universal House of Justice; therefore, Remey said, he was the next Guardian. Of course, if Remey were correct that only the Guardian could be the head of the International Bahá'í Council, only Shoghi Effendi could have occupied that position; otherwise, he had created a situation where the Bahá'í Faith had two Guardians at once.[47] Remey also reinterpreted the term 'aghsán' in reply to the objection that 'Abdu'l-Bahá's Will specified that the Guardian had to be a descendant of Bahá'u'lláh; he claimed it only referred to the sons of Bahá'u'lláh, all of whom had died, and therefore was inapplicable. Many Remeyites have argued that 'Abdu'l-Bahá had called Remey a 'spiritual son' but the phrase is probably found in tablets to other Bahá'ís and is of uncertain significance. Remey had no reply to the requirement in the Will that the Hands had to ratify the Guardian's choice, nor did he explain satisfactorily why he signed statements by the Conclave of Hands for 3 years that contradicted his claim, including one that said Shoghi Effendi had not appointed a successor.

Remey's belief that he was the Guardian roughly coincided with the Hands' decision to replace the Bahá'í International Council appointed by Shoghi Effendi with an elected body in April 1961, in order for the Bahá'í world to gain experience with an international election. The Hands of the Cause of God had announced that they considered themselves ineligible to serve on either the elected Bahá'í International Council or the Universal House of Justice.[48] The decision terminated Remey's position as President of the Council.

The Hands described Remey's claim in a cable to the Bahá'í world as 'PREPOSTEROUS' and 'CLEARLY CONTRARY SACRED TEXTS'; it 'CAN ONLY BE REGARDED AS EVIDENCE CONDITION PROFOUND EMOTIONAL DISTURBANCE'. The only organized acceptance of his claim was by five members of the National Spiritual Assembly of France, prompting the Hands to dissolve that Assembly and call for a new election. On 26 July 1960, they declared Remey and the Bahá'ís who accepted him Covenant breakers.[49] His group numbered a few hundred at most, but at a time of grief and confusion in the Bahá'í world, they created considerable anguish and doubt.

Cut off from the mainstream Bahá'ís, Remey organized his followers as the 'Orthodox Bahá'ís Under the Hereditary Guardianship'. On 5 December 1961 he sent one follower, Joel Marangella, a sealed envelope with a note on it telling him to open it when he felt the time was right. In September 1964 Remey appointed a second International Bahá'í Council and designated Joel Marangella its President, a clear sign that Marangella would be his successor. At that point Marangella opened the envelope and discovered Remey had indeed appointed him the next Guardian. In February 1966 Remey wrote Marangella again, according to Marangella, and turned over all authority for the 'affairs of the Faith' to him.[50]

In 1962, Remey directed his American followers to organize a National Spiritual Assembly Under the Hereditary Guardianship (NSAUHG). In 1964, he told the body to sue the National Spiritual Assembly of the Bahá'ís of the United States for all Bahá'í property and the right to use the word 'Bahá'í'. The National Spiritual Assembly countersued. In October 1966, Remey told his Assembly to drop the matter and disbanded the NSAUHG. As a result, his group failed to show up when the countersuit came up before the court, resulting in a ruling in favour of the countersuit and an order that they cease calling themselves Bahá'ís.[51]

In late 1966, Remey wrote Marangella and told him to turn all International Bahá'í Council records over to Remey, because the Council no longer existed. Subsequently, Remey provided his followers little guidance. His writings became increasing condemnatory of Shoghi Effendi's ministry and contradicted his own earlier statements. In 1967 Remey announced that Donald Harvey (d. 1991), who had never been a member of the second International Bahá'í Council, was designated the third Guardian. Marangella was shocked and sent Remey a photo static copy of the original appointment, which Remey had not annulled. Marangella concluded that Remey was now senile and had forgotten the earlier appointment, which had become active once the second International Bahá'í Council was established and Marangella had unsealed the envelope.[52] Harvey replied that Remey was still Guardian and had annulled his earlier appointment. A split among Remey's followers began to form, which Remey did not attempt to heal. In 1969 Marangella issued a public proclamation that he was the third Guardian and provided a detailed explanation how he arrived at the claim.[53]

Remey lived another 5 years, dying in Florence, Italy in 1974, 3 months short of his hundredth birthday. He was buried without religious rites. A few of his followers accepted Harvey, but most followed Marangella, whose group took the name the Orthodox Bahá'í Faith. Another man, Leland Jensen (1914–96) claimed that Remey's adopted son, Joseph Pepe, was actually the third Guardian – a claim Pepe denied – and as the most prominent 'teacher' of Pepe's movement, Jensen established the Bahá'ís Under the Provision of the Covenant (BUPC). His teachings included pyramidology and interpretation of biblical prophecies, as well as Bahá'í concepts. At peak, both the Orthodox Bahá'ís and the BUPC had only a hundred or so members. The BUPC has been subject to considerable sociological research because Jensen made many dramatic predictions (such as a Soviet nuclear attack on the United States) that were unfulfilled.[54] The group split into two factions in 2001.

Ultimately, Remey's claims and his followers had virtually no impact on the Bahá'í Faith. At peak, his followers numbered less than a two-thousandth of the Bahá'ís. Because their primary message has remained an unrelenting attack against the Universal House of Justice and the Hands of the Cause, non-Bahá'ís have never been attracted in any significant numbers. Because Bahá'ís were told to ignore them, the attacks have been ineffective in recruiting from the mainstream community.

Shoghi Effendi's legacy of 36 years of guardianship was a dramatic and enormous expansion of the Bahá'í community worldwide, a remarkable diversification of its membership, an impressive enrichment of its literature, an extraordinary enlargement and beautification of its sacred places in the Holy Land and the construction of a highly effective and innovative Administrative Order to ensure its future. With the completion of the Ten Year Crusade, the Bahá'í community's continued development and progress became the responsibility of the Universal House of Justice.

CHAPTER TEN

Developments under the Universal House of Justice, 1963–96

On 21 April 1963 – the centenary of Bahá'u'lláh's declaration of his mission to his close followers in Baghdad – 288 members of National Spiritual Assemblies worldwide gathered in the house of 'Abdu'l-Bahá and Shoghi Effendi in Haifa for the election of the Universal House of Justice. They represented 51 of the 56 National Spiritual Assemblies in existence; those unable to attend in person voted by mail. It may have been the first international election in human history involving delegates being elected indirectly by a worldwide population.[1]

The resulting body was the supreme governing council of the Bahá'í Faith. Of the nine members, four were American (one of whom was African American, with some American Indian ancestry), three were Iranian and two were British. The institution of the Hands of the Cause of God was still intact to assist the new supreme body, because the Hands had insisted that they not be voted for, hence none of the members of the Universal House of Justice were Hands. For Bahá'ís the world over, the election filled a hole in their religion's organization and was viewed with immense relief and a sense of accomplishment. A week later, over 6,000 Bahá'ís gathered for the first Bahá'í World Congress in Royal Albert Hall, London, where they were introduced to the Universal House of Justice and celebrated the successful conclusion of the Ten Year Crusade.[2]

The House spent its first year organizing itself. A very early decision was that all nine members had to reside permanently in Haifa, so that the body could meet regularly. It took time for the members to wrap up their affairs on four continents and relocate. After lengthy consultations with the Hands of the Cause, on

6 October 1963, the House announced that it 'finds that there is no way to appoint or to legislate to make it possible to appoint a second Guardian to succeed Shoghi Effendi'.[3] This was a matter the Hands of the Cause had no authority to resolve.

The House of Justice also began consideration of several other matters. One was its procedures. The Will and Testament of 'Abdu'l-Bahá specified that the Guardian was the head of the Universal House of Justice; consequently, the House decided to choose no permanent officers, but to rotate chairing and other tasks among its members. It began an extensive and lengthy study of the writings of Bahá'u'lláh, 'Abdu'l-Bahá and Shoghi Effendi that pertained to the House's duties and functions, an effort that culminated in the Constitution of the Universal House of Justice in November 1972. The Constitution specified such details as the nature of membership in the Bahá'í community, the method of formation of local and National Spiritual Assemblies, the obligations of Assembly members, the manner and frequency of election of the House, the nature of Bahá'í elections, the House's right to review any decision of a local or National Spiritual Assembly, the appeal of Assembly decisions by individuals or institutions, the appointment of Counsellors and Auxiliary Board members and amendment of the House's Constitution.

The House also began to explore the problem of continuing the responsibilities and duties of the Hands of the Cause of God. The Will and Testament of 'Abdu'l-Bahá gave the authority to appoint Hands to the Guardian, consequently in November 1964 the House announced that 'there is no way to appoint, or legislate to make it possible to appoint, Hands of the Cause of God'. In 1968 it established a new institution, the Counsellors, who worked with the Hands and gradually assumed their responsibilities, such as appointing and overseeing the work of the Auxiliary Board members. Unlike the lifetime appointment of the Hands, Counsellors are appointed for a specific term, now 5 years.[4]

Developments during the nine year plan and beyond

The Universal House of Justice also consulted extensively with the Hands of the Cause about a plan to follow up on the accomplishments of the Ten Year Crusade. On the first day of Ridván (21 April) 1964 they launched a Nine Year Plan with 'twin objectives': 'expansion and universal participation.' It called for the opening of 70 new territories to the Faith and the reestablishment of the Faith in 24 others; an increase in the number of National Spiritual Assemblies to 108, roughly double the total in 1963; an increase in local Spiritual Assemblies to 13,700; an increase in localities with at least one Bahá'í to over 54,000; completion of two more Bahá'í Houses of Worship, in Asia and Latin America and translation of Bahá'í literature into an additional 143 languages. Every National Spiritual Assembly was given a complete set of goals; the United States, for example, was to raise the number of local Spiritual Assemblies from 331 to 596. The Universal House of Justice aimed to enrich Bahá'í literature, develop the properties of the Bahá'í World Centre, draft its Constitution and continue the functions of the Hands of the Cause into the future.[5]

Most of its goals were exceeded and supplemental goals were added. Propelling the Bahá'í community forward were the cultural changes and tensions of the tumultuous 1960s. Membership data is fairly complete for the United States and shows the growth rate, which ran about 4 or 5 per cent a year in the 1950s, accelerating to 9 or 10 per cent per year about 1963, when the number of Bahá'ís in the United States first exceeded 10,000. Coinciding with the acceleration in growth was a relaxation of some of the procedures for enrolling new believers. Previously, they were expected to study several books and be able to explain their contents before being admitted to community membership, but in 1964 the House of Justice said that all the new believers needed, in addition to the spark of faith, was to 'become basically informed about the Central Figures of the Faith, as well as the existence of laws they must follow and an administration they must obey'.[6] By 1969 the community had doubled to 20,000.

By 1971 the numbers in the United States had doubled again, to 40,000; in 1972 the number of American Bahá'ís rose to 60,000. Two developments were about equally responsible for the sudden explosion in the number of American Bahá'ís. The first was the radical turn of the youth movement following the Tet Offensive in Vietnam and the assassinations of Martin Luther King and Robert Kennedy. Millions of young people began to search for a solution to the seeming collapse of societal values and purpose; a small fraction of them became Bahá'ís.

This great increase in what might be termed the 'Bahá'í middle class' (in an economic sense; there was also an increase in minority membership, to be discussed next) was not confined to the United States, but was a phenomenon throughout the developed world. Youth were disillusioned with the status quo in many countries, as the Paris riots of 1968 demonstrated. The Danish Bahá'í community had 62 members in 1962, about 114 in March 1971, and about 194 in March 1974; a 70 per cent increase in 3 years. The Swedish, Dutch, German and English communities repeated the same pattern. Almost all of the new members were young and single.[7] Anecdotal reports indicate the same pattern of growth occurred in Canada, Australia and New Zealand as well.

For the Bahá'ís it was both exciting and worrisome, for the influx of young people brought concerns about more than long hair and dirty blue jeans. Drinking alcohol, smoking marijuana and free love were incompatible with Bahá'í membership, but it was not easy to enforce standards that had been taken for granted by the older generation of Bahá'ís.

Firesides – gatherings in a home to discuss the Faith and share hospitality – sometimes went most of the night as excited young people asked dozens of questions and studied Bahá'í texts together. Many Bahá'ís who joined in that era remember the excitement created when someone declared their faith at almost every weekly fireside. To attract new people, enthusiastic new believers went to parks to play Bahá'í songs on their guitars. American Bahá'ís drafted into the military service taught their fellow soldiers and sailors. Universities were centres of very active Bahá'í clubs. Annual youth conferences brought youth together for talks, workshops and goal setting. In Europe, they were usually international gatherings.

Short-lived musical groups formed and travelled to sing about the Bahá'í Faith. Some American groups even travelled to Europe or Latin America to perform. Reinforcing the momentum in the United States was a very popular musical group, Seals and Crofts, who produced a series of hit albums in the late 1960s and early 1970s. After every concert, they invited their fans to a midnight fireside in a nearby rented space. The local Bahá'í community turned out in force and followed up with interested people.

The very rapid increase created huge problems with consolidation, for most of the new believers were enthusiastic, but knew little. Their demand for Bahá'í literature caused an enormous increase in publishing. In the United Sates, the Bahá'í Publishing Trust was able to buy a new building with cash. Perhaps a third of the new American Bahá'ís drifted away from the Faith in the next decade, and another third in the two decades after that. But enrolment of new members had increased so much that the number of American Bahá'ís never decreased, at least on paper. The community was permanently enlarged, its capacity permanently increased.

Thousands of the new Bahá'ís, as youth or adults, eventually pioneered outside their countries for a time and strengthened Bahá'í communities all over the globe. Their maturing literary capacities caused the number of Bahá'í books published every year to triple or quadruple in the 1980s. Their desire to study the Bahá'í Faith fostered an explosion in Bahá'í scholarship, starting in the late 1970s. Their artistic interests led to the composition of dozens of popular new Bahá'í songs, production of a series of Bahá'í promotional films and enrichment of the arts in the Bahá'í community.

Reaching minority populations

The youth provided human resources for reaching minority groups. The Universal House of Justice set Nine Year Plan goals in Europe to reach Basques, Swedish Finns, Sami (Lapps) and Roma (Gypsies). The US Bahá'ís were to reach Chinese Americans, Japanese Americans, American Indian tribes, African Americans and Spanish speakers.[8] Efforts by youth to reach American Indians achieved its first major success a year before the Nine Year Plan began. In 1962 when two young Navajos, Franklin and Chester Kahn, became Bahá'ís and decided to bring the Faith to their home on the Navajo reservation of northern Arizona. They called a meeting, to which 400 Navajos and 800 Bahá'ís from off the reservation showed up; 200 of the Navajos chose to identify themselves with the Bahá'í Faith. Franklin and Chester Kahn were eventually elected to the National Spiritual Assembly. In 1983 the National Spiritual Assembly opened the Native American Bahá'í Institute on the Navajo Reservation to provide services to the local Bahá'ís. The number of Navajo Bahá'ís reached 400 by 1985.[9]

A major reason the Navajo were attracted to the Bahá'í Faith was because it affirmed their traditional culture and religion. The Kahn family (all of whom became Bahá'ís) included many medicine men, and as Bahá'ís they felt they had to continue their study and practice of Navajo spiritual ways. Some Navajo Bahá'ís told an interviewer that the Bahá'í Faith gave them a positive appreciation of Christianity, which otherwise had been opposed to Navajo ways. They expressed the belief that the Hero Twins, figures central to Navajo religion, were Manifestations, and that the Báb and Bahá'u'lláh had been prophesied in their tribal traditions.[10]

The Navajo were not the only tribe attracted to the Bahá'í Faith. The National Spiritual Assembly established a list of 19 reservations on which to settle pioneers. By 1967, 15 Bahá'ís had settled on reservations in order to serve the local population and teach the Bahá'í Faith. By 1968 the number had grown to 25. In 1969, the American National Spiritual Assembly appointed a 'Bahá'í Indian Council' to coordinate the reservation efforts. Bahá'í communities on reservations sponsored 'Council Fires' to which everyone was invited.[11] American Indian Bahá'ís visited each other's reservations and travelled to Latin America to meet native believers there. Local Spiritual Assemblies were elected on the reservations as soon as the number of Bahá'ís reached nine.

Efforts to reach African Americans accelerated in the early 1960s, with African American Bahá'ís leading the effort. In 1969 the National Spiritual Assembly appointed a 'Deep South Committee' to focus on large-scale expansion of the Bahá'í Faith in the south, a very traditional part of the country where Bahá'í growth had lagged. Shoghi Effendi had advised the American Bahá'ís in 1957 to concentrate on reaching African Americans, rather than pursuing a strategy of 'placating' and 'enrolling' whites while also enrolling blacks at the same time. A teaching conference in Frogmore, South Carolina, was a great success and laid the ground work for new efforts.[12]

The new approach used the techniques of mass teaching, developed in India and other developing countries, to reach rural African American populations. A team of Bahá'ís began to go door to door in South Carolina in 1970, offering anyone who would listen a quick review of basic Bahá'í teachings, proclaiming Bahá'u'lláh as the return of Christ, and asking people whether they believed in him. They were surprised to find that hundreds would say 'yes'. Within months the technique was being used in Florida as well:

> The basic teaching methods for mass teaching were outlined to sixty-eight Bahá'ís present at the Mass Teaching Conference held in Gainesville, Florida, August 22–23 [1970] . . . The Florida State Goals Committee selected twelve target areas and then twelve teams were selected . . . Three and a half hours later the victories were recorded: Sixty new believers, two (possible) assemblies, seven new groups, and nine new towns opened to the Faith.[13]

On 30 January 1971, the Universal House of Justice sent a cable (in 'telegraphese') announcing 'PROCESS ENTRY BY TROOPS RAPIDLY ACCELERATING UNITED STATES EVIDENCED BY ENROLLMENT 8000 NEW BELIEVERS SOUTH CAROLINA COURSE SIX WEEKS CAMPAIGN RAISING NUMBER NEW BELIEVERS ENTIRE COUNTRY 13,000 SINCE RIDVÁN [21 April 1970] PROCESS GATHERING MOMENTUM'.[14] By the mid-1980s, the number of new Bahá'ís in South Carolina had exceeded 20,000, making it the most populous state, for Bahá'ís, in the United States. Mass teaching techniques were used to reach Spanish-speaking farm workers in California and Oregon and Haitian farmer workers in Florida. Door to door teaching was even used in northern cities and middle class suburbs.

The technique was controversial. It was one thing to mention the Faith to people one knew, when it was in a social context; quite another to announce it to strangers who might be offended. In the past, people were enrolled as Bahá'ís when they had acquired more than a little basic knowledge, but now the criterion for membership was possession of the spark of faith; it was assumed that knowledge would follow later. But teams of visiting Bahá'í teachers were not present long enough to follow up, and it was difficult for later teams to find newly declared believers who lived in houses that lacked street numbers (which was often the case in the rural south). Sometimes the new believers in a town could be brought together to elect a local Spiritual Assembly, but with no knowledge of Bahá'í administration or motivation to learn, few of the assemblies functioned.

Many Bahá'ís moved to the rural South to build communities out of the new believers. The South Carolina Bahá'í community, over decades, had acquired experience in functioning interracially, and that helped. But some of the arrivals had difficulty overcoming cultural differences. The Bahá'í communities did not have clergy and thus could not assume the organization or the social role of rural black churches. Some of the new Bahá'ís had limited reading skills and thus could not read the Bahá'í authoritative texts. As a result, 35 years later, less than 10 per cent of the new Bahá'ís still had good addresses in the membership database, although many of them, if asked, might say they were Bahá'ís.[15]

In spite of these difficulties, mass teaching of minorities had an important impact on the Bahá'í community. The black proportion of the American Bahá'í membership increased far above its percentage in the general population. The membership of the National Spiritual Assembly gradually shifted to reflect the increased diversity of the Bahá'ís; two, sometimes three, African Americans served on the nine-member Assembly, and usually one American Indian as well. To consolidate the new believers, the Louis Gregory Institute was opened in Hemingway, South Carolina, in 1972 to host classes and social service projects. A radio station, WLGI, was inaugurated in 1984 to broadcast commercial free educational and musical programmes to the rural African American population.

A similar story can be told about the expansion of the Bahá'í Faith in Colombia, South America. Inspired by Hand of the Cause Muhajir, who brought 5,000 people into the Faith in the Mentawai Islands, in 1970 15 Bahá'ís in Colombia decided to set a goal for themselves of enrolling 100,000 Colombians into the Bahá'í Faith. They started in the rural villages around Cali in the department of Norte del Cauca in south-western Colombia, proclaimed the advent of Bahá'u'lláh as a new Manifestation of God, and spoke about the oneness of God, the oneness of religion and the oneness of humanity. In a few months they had brought in about 1,000 new Bahá'ís. The effort spread to other parts of Colombia as well and 2,000 more people became Bahá'ís.[16] The results led to passionate discussions among members of the National Spiritual Assembly of Colombia and the project leaders:

'Shouldn't we concentrate entirely on expansion and worry about consolidation later?' 'Shouldn't we stop expansion and immediately proceed to consolidate?' 'If the functioning of Local Spiritual Assemblies is the key to the establishment of the World Order of Bahá'u'lláh, shouldn't we concentrate all our efforts in that direction?' 'Three thousand Bahá'ís are too few; maybe we should accelerate the rate of expansion. The problem is that not enough numbers have entered the Faith yet; once they do, all the problems will take care of themselves.' 'What if we only concentrate on the nine members of the Local Spiritual Assemblies and deepen them first?'' 'The answer may be in the mass media, since the process of teaching one-on-one is proving inadequate.'[17]

These and other ideas were debated in Colombia. The Universal House of Justice guided their efforts and stated that expansion and consolidation had to go hand in hand and that neither should be stopped in favour of the other. Over time, the Colombian Bahá'ís reached various conclusions: that while they could inform a highly receptive population, faith was a gift that God bestowed; they had to work on their own faith and not judge the faith of others by their own personal standards; the best way to learn was through action; and that teaching efforts had to evolve based on new experiences and understandings. The nature of the teaching they had discovered was new and different from individual teaching of friends and relatives, but just as valid. They began to concentrate on prayer and memorization of passages from Bahá'u'lláh as preparation for teaching and held frequent reflection gatherings for the teachers to consult about the results of their efforts. They also began to create simple booklets that could be given to the new believers to deepen their understandings. With these developments, in another 2 years the Colombian Bahá'í community expanded to 10,000.[18]

At that point, new challenges became clear. While the number of Colombian Bahá'ís involved in the teaching effort rose to 200 – especially youth – most only participated occasionally, and many drifted away as the pressure that they should shoulder greater responsibility proved to be too much. There was a shortage of funds and of people who knew how to manage it. Personal differences sometimes weakened or broke up teaching teams. More far-reaching was the problem that the new believers had no idea how to create Bahá'í communities, hence the communities barely functioned. Local Spiritual Assemblies rarely met. As a result, the National Spiritual Assembly decided that additional teaching should occur in places where there already were Bahá'ís, and community building should be the new focus. In another 2 or 3 years, Colombia had 30,000 Bahá'ís, located in about 200 Bahá'í communities.[19]

A shortage of active teachers, however, remained the chief problem; the dedicated teachers still numbered only about 50, money was still short and the health of some was deteriorating. Consequently the focus shifted back to the individual. An institute, the Ruhi Institute, was opened in Puerto Tejado outside Cali, and it sought to develop a systematic educational process for the new Bahá'ís. They quickly realized it had to include, in many cases, literacy and a basic education, and a related project, the Rural University, was founded in 1974.[20]

The pattern seen in Colombia was common worldwide. The huge increase in membership was accompanied by a large decrease in the percentage of Bahá'ís who were active by various measures: contributing to the Bahá'í funds, voting in Bahá'í elections, participating in Nineteen Day Feasts and holy days and volunteering for teaching and service projects. Many of the new members were illiterate, had little or no access to schools or even to basic services like safe drinking water, and were not used to taking collective responsibility for organizing and developing their local religious community. Aware of this problem, the Universal House of Justice had made universal participation a goal of the Nine Year Plan. This launched the Bahá'í community on a process of finding ways to consolidate the new believers. Institutes – usually with their own buildings – were established to bring Bahá'ís together for classes and workshops. A variety of low-literacy training materials were published and refined. The Bahá'í authoritative texts were recorded on cassettes. Materials for children's classes were published, because in many rural areas the children were easy to reach with Bahá'í prayers, songs and teachings.

The teaching of rural peoples that began in the Nine Year Plan continued subsequently and greatly increased the number of Bahá'ís worldwide. By 1986, all-Bahá'í villages could be found in the Bolivian altiplano, the New Guinea Highlands, Korea, Bangladesh and the rural Philippines. Ten countries or territories were more than 1 per cent Bahá'í: Belize, the Marshall Islands, Kiribati, Samoa, Sikkim, Solomon Islands, St Lucia and Dominica, Swaziland,

Tonga and Tuvalu. India reported as many as 2 million Bahá'ís. The number of Bahá'ís worldwide stood at 1 million in 1968, 3.2 million in 1979, and 4.3 million in 1986.[21] Substantial Bahá'í communities – a 100,000 Bahá'ís or more – developed in Kenya, Zaire, Malaysia, Brazil, Bolivia, Uganda and Vietnam, though the Communist victory in Vietnam nearly destroyed the Vietnamese community and Idi Amin's ban of the Bahá'í Faith about 1977 severely damaged the Ugandan community. The Iranian Bahá'í community, whose 200,000 members had been over 90 per cent of the Bahá'ís in the world as late as World War Two, continued to grow to about 300,000 members, but its percentage of the Bahá'í world's membership dropped to less than 10 per cent.

The dedicated service of the Hands of the Cause was an important factor in the enormous expansion of membership, the acceptance of the new Bahá'ís by the existing community, and the consolidation that occurred. Freed of administrative work as a result of the election of the Universal House of Justice, they devoted themselves to near-constant travel. They consulted with Assemblies and committees to encourage projects and formulate bold plans, met with Presidents, Prime Ministers and tribal royalty, and spent most of their time travelling to and living with the Bahá'ís.

The travels of Shoghi Effendi's widow, Rúhíyyih Khánum (1910–2000), were perhaps the most impressive. Between 1963 and 1993 she travelled half a million miles by air, more than 100,000 miles by car and land rover and uncounted miles in trains, boats, canoes and animal-drawn carts, visiting 185 countries and territories. She spent 9 months of 1964 in India and 7 months of 1967 in Latin America. Much of August 1969 through February 1973 she travelled in Africa, visiting 34 countries and meeting 17 heads of state. Later in 1973 she visited Alaska; 1974 saw her in China, India, Sikkim and Nepal. In 1975 she completed the 7-month 'Green Light Expedition' travelling 8,000 miles by boat up the Amazon and its tributaries, and ending up in the Peruvian highlands. The year 1976 was devoted to East and South Asia and Australia; in 1978 she went to Europe, Japan and Taiwan. The 1980s were equally busy. At the age of 83, after the Iron Curtain fell, she visited Mongolia and 13 republics of the former Soviet Union. She spent as much of her time as possible with tribal and rural peoples.[22]

The impressive global expansion of the Bahá'í community caught the attention of many governments and made the proclamation of the basic Bahá'í teachings to government leaders urgent. In 1968, the hundredth anniversary of many of Bahá'u'lláh's epistles to the kings and rulers of the world, the Universal House of Justice published a volume of translations of those messages titled *The Proclamation of Bahá'u'lláh* and asked National Spiritual Assemblies to meet with heads of state to present it to them. A special limited edition of the book was presented to 140 heads of state, two or three by mail, 55 via the country's ambassadors and the rest in person. One head of state, the Malietoa (King) Tanumafili II of Western Samoa (1913–2007) was intrigued and requested more information. After reading Bahá'í scriptures and meeting with Bahá'ís to ask questions, he became a Bahá'í, the first reigning monarch to do so.[23]

The five year plan, 1974–9

The Nine Year Plan concluded in 1973 with accomplishments that far exceeded the expansion goals. National Spiritual Assemblies numbered 113 rather than 108; local Spiritual Assemblies 15,186 rather than 13,700; localities with Bahá'ís 69,541 rather than 54,000. A House of Worship was to be built in Asia, but that was postponed; however, the House of Worship in Panama was dedicated in 1972. After a year of respite, the Universal House of Justice gave the Bahá'í world the Five Year Plan in April 1974. It had three major objectives: 'preservation and consolidation of victories won; a vast and widespread expansion of the Bahá'í community; development of the distinctive character of Bahá'í life particularly in the local communities'.[24] The number of National Spiritual Assemblies was to increase to 131; the number reached 130 because all Bahá'í institutions in Iraq, Uganda, Congo-Brazzaville, Vietnam and Cambodia, including their National Spiritual Assemblies, were banned. Local spiritual assemblies and localities with Bahá'ís were to increase to 23,931 and 90,012 respectively; they reached 25,511 and 103,323 instead. Work began on Houses of Worship in India and Samoa.

While the Five Year Plan called for a 'vast and widespread expansion', the pace of growth distinctively slowed. The US community grew from 63,000 in 1974 to 77,000 in 1979, an increase of 14,000. The period saw 20,000 Americans become Bahá'ís, but also witnessed about 6,000 withdrawals of membership, resulting in an average increase in membership of 5 per cent per year; far lower than in the 1960s, probably because the social conditions of the country had changed. Some mass teaching was carried out, but because of the problems of consolidation, efforts were fewer, smaller and focused more on follow-up. Growth in Western Europe, Canada, Australia and New Zealand dropped similarly. In the developing world, mass teaching of rural populations continued, but consolidation – a goal of the Plan – remained a difficult problem. New Bahá'ís began to create many songs quoting Bahá'í texts or on Bahá'í subjects. Correspondence courses became a new approach to consolidation in India, Italy, Malaysia, Pakistan, Philippines and seven countries in Latin America. The Universal House of Justice gave 39 countries the goal of using radio for teaching and deepening, and asked 12 to initiate use of television.[25]

The Universal House of Justice also gave itself some important goals in the Five Year Plan. Shoghi Effendi had called for the construction of a series of monumental administrative buildings set on a 'far-flung arc' on Mount Carmel and the Universal House of Justice decided that the first one would be its own Seat, a magnificent domed edifice fronted by 20 Corinthian columns of Pentelikon marble – the same marble from which the Parthenon was built. Excavations began in 1975; the building was completed in 1982.[26] Beautification of Bahá'í holy places in and near Acre continued. Three new volumes of Bahá'í scripture were translated into English and published, one each for the writings of the Báb, Bahá'u'lláh and 'Abdu'l-Bahá.

The Expansion of Bahá'í scholarship, 1963–79

The expansion of the Bahá'í community in the Occident during the Nine Year Plan and developments in the Iranian Bahá'í community made possible a new emphasis on Bahá'í scholarship. During the ministry of Shoghi Effendi and during the Nine Year Plan, Iranian Bahá'ís published a stream of commentaries on Bahá'í sacred texts, community histories, memoirs, theological and philosophical treatises and dictionaries of specialized terms. Virtually none of the scholarship was translated into western languages. In the United States, an intellectual periodical, *World Order,* was published monthly from 1935 to 1949. It carried short articles on Bahá'í teachings, poetry and reminiscences.

With the advent of the Five Year Plan, Universal House of Justice gave Iran and Canada important scholarship goals. In Iran, an Institute for Advanced Bahá'í Studies was to be opened in Tehran. It offered a series of rigorous courses on Bahá'í scriptural works, various Bahá'í teachings and on Islam to dozens of young Bahá'ís, which stimulated further the scholarly research already going on in that country. When subsequent persecution of the Iranian Bahá'í community sent many of the trained young people abroad, it enriched Bahá'í studies worldwide and fostered a major effort to translate Persian and Arabic scholarship into English, French and German.

The Canadian Bahá'ís were asked to cultivate 'opportunities for formal presentations, courses, and lectureships on the Bahá'í Faith in Canadian universities and other institutions of higher learning' and in response the National Spiritual Assembly decided to inaugurate a scholarly organization, the Canadian Association for Studies on the Bahá'í Faith, thereby initiating the world's first formal Bahá'í scholarly organization. Americans were allowed to join as well and they soon equalled the Canadians in number; in 1980 the organization was renamed the Association for Bahá'í Studies (ABS). Other national Spiritual Assemblies followed Canada's example and organized their own affiliate ABS agencies. The North American ABS began annual scholarly meetings in 1976 that attracted hundreds of attendees. A monograph series inaugurated that year evolved into the *Journal of Bahá'í Studies* in 1988.[27]

A similar process unfolded more informally in Britain, where a group of graduate students in Middle Eastern studies and sociology, encouraged by Hand of the Cause of God Hasan Balyuzi – the author of several important scholarly works on the Faith in English and Persian – and with the sponsorship of their academic departments, began in April 1977 to hold annual Bahá'í Studies seminars.[28] Their efforts were encouraged and guided by the Universal House of Justice. Starting in 1982 they began to circulate papers in photocopied form as the *Bahá'í Studies Bulletin.* Eventually their efforts led to the formation of the Association of Bahá'í Studies for the United Kingdom, which began to publish *Bahá'í Studies Review.*

The United States already had an intellectual magazine – *World Order* – that published scholarly articles, poetry and some fiction, accompanied by artistic photography. It had been revived in 1966. Similar periodicals began in France (*Pensée Bahá'íe*) and Italy (*Opinioni Bahá'í*) in the 1970s. In Los Angeles, a group of Bahá'ís began to meet in the late 1970s as the 'Los Angeles Bahá'í Studies group' to give and circulate provocative papers on Bahá'í subjects. Some of them went on to found Kalimát Press, dedicated primarily to scholarly works on Bahá'í subjects. Others Los Angelinos started *dialogue* magazine in the mid-1980s, which had a similar goal.

The different scholarly efforts had very different outcomes. The relationship between scholarship and a religion's institutions is often tense because scholarship investigates basic beliefs and sacred events and can arrive at conclusions that shock or discomfit administrators and believers alike. Bahá'í scholarship stressed independent investigation of truth and the harmony of reason and revelation, but it could not develop without a relation to the Bahá'í Administrative Order; the principle of unity requires a degree of collaboration and consultation.

To give Bahá'í institutions a role in writing about the Faith, in 1906 'Abdu'l-Bahá had initiated the requirement that all works by Bahá'ís about the Bahá'í Faith be reviewed, because the Bahá'ís often had inaccurate notions of what the Faith stood for. Shoghi Effendi had developed the literature review process further, assigning it to the national Spiritual Assemblies. The Universal House of Justice had clarified its principal concerns to be accuracy, dignity and timeliness. Review had become reasonably effective at insuring the reliability of introductory pamphlets and books, but the reviewers often had no idea what to do with scholarly works on subjects about which nothing had been published before, some of which touched on historical or theological matters that could cause persecution of the Bahá'í community in countries where it was regarded with suspicion or enmity.

World Order, run by an editorial board of academics in the humanities appointed by the National Spiritual Assembly, struggled with poor quality manuscripts, but saw the range and quality of submissions gradually improve. The National Spiritual Assembly had given it the authority to conduct its own review, so literature review was not an issue for it. The Association for Bahá'í Studies, run by an executive committee appointed by the National Spiritual Assembly of Canada, also had literature review authority. Initially it tended to view Bahá'ís in Middle East studies and religious studies with ambivalence, and they in turn tended to regard the ABS, which sought to include the rank and file fully, as not a serious academic organization. It took decades to chip away at the mutual suspicion and overcome mutual hurt feelings.

The Bahá'í studies effort in Britain had a very difficult time in the early 1980s over literature review of a book that caused its author to leave the Bahá'í Faith and write against it, but gradually Bahá'í studies became well-established there. Much of the best scholarship in Bahá'í history, sociology, scripture study has been done in, or published in, Britain. The Los Angeles Bahá'í Studies group lasted only a few years and broke up partly over the requirement that the public distribution of its notes be put through literature review. *Dialogue* magazine was short lived and ceased publication after a dispute about the prepublication distribution of a controversial manuscript.

The Islamic revolution and systematic persecution of the Iranian Bahá'í community

The development of Bahá'í scholarship, the growing relationship with governments and the strengthened experience with use of radio and television all proved to be important capacities in the summer of 1978 when unrest began against the rule of Shah Muhammad Reza Pahlavi in Iran. The shah's secret police had been ruthless in controlling political dissent in Iran and had infiltrated or broken up many networks that could organize against him. But the secret police could not break up the Islamic clerical networks, and two anti-Bahá'í organizations that were particularly fanatical in their understanding of Islam had been tolerated. When the clerics and the anti-Bahá'í groups turned against the Shah, the unrest developed into a full-blown revolution.

The Bahá'ís remained neutral in the conflict. They provided millions of dollars of free medical care to the injured at their Mitháqíyyih Hospital in Tehran. The secret police organized a mob to attack the House of the Báb in Shiraz – the holiest Bahá'í shrine in the country – and the local clerics actually turned the mob away so that they would not be blamed for anti-Bahá'í fanaticism, which would complicate their efforts to take over the country. The government dismissed Bahá'ís from their jobs to placate the Islamists. The Islamists justified their hostility against the Bahá'ís on the grounds that a former Prime Minister had been a Bahá'í (which was not true, though his grandfather had been), that Bahá'ís were members of the secret police (also not true) and that the Shah's personal physician and cook had been Bahá'ís (which was true, but hardly a serious matter, considering how many Muslims worked for him).[29]

The Shah departed Iran in January 1979 and was succeeded by an unstable situation where Marxists and various Shi'ite factions and 'committees' fought for power. But most were united in their enmity against the Bahá'ís and persecution steadily increased, in spite of persistent efforts of local Spiritual Assemblies and the National Spiritual Assembly to meet with officials and clarify the nature of the Faith. The national Bahá'í headquarters was seized in February and with it the list of all of Iran's Bahá'ís. Mitháqíyyih Hospital was seized, all Bahá'í physicians and staff dismissed and all Bahá'í elderly in the attached Home for the Aged were expelled. The Children's Company, a six-decade old Bahá'í investment company, was seized and its millions of dollars of assets confiscated. The company holding all community property (because Bahá'í assemblies could not get legal incorporation) was seized and all Bahá'í community properties – including all holy places – were confiscated. Attacks on Bahá'ís included burning of houses and business, stealing of livestock and assaults on individuals. Two Bahá'í girls were kidnapped and forced to marry Muslim men. Bahá'í cemeteries were seized. Bahá'ís who died either of natural causes or because of violence directed against them were laid to rest in fields set aside for infidels. Prominent Bahá'ís were assassinated or disappeared. International journalists in Iran were pressured not to cover the persecution.[30]

In September 1979 the House of the Báb was attacked by a mob and desecrated. The Universal House of Justice directed Bahá'í local and National Spiritual Assemblies around the world to send cables of protest to Ayatollah Khomeini; over 10,000 were dispatched, but to no avail. The seizure of the American embassy in November 1979 distracted the world and allowed the Islamic 'committees', which were still under loose central control, to pursue their attacks on the Bahá'í Faith. A series of arrests of prominent Bahá'ís began in February 1980. In July, three members of the Spiritual Assembly of Tabriz, a major city in Iran's northwest, were arrested, and when they refused to sign a pledge promising not to participate in Bahá'í administration, two were tried and executed. Four Tehran Bahá'ís were tried and executed. An old Bahá'í shepherd was found clubbed to death. In Yazd a mob, whipped up by an anti-Bahá'í sermon at a mosque, attacked Bahá'í houses and other properties. Then in August the entire National Spiritual Assembly of the Bahá'ís of Iran was kidnapped and disappeared. It was not until December, when the bodies of five were found, that it was confirmed that they were murdered.[31]

Bahá'ís around the world publicized their deaths and held memorial services. A new National Spiritual Assembly of Iran was established because the results of the previous election had been retained; the next nine people, in order of voting, were automatically selected. Local Spiritual Assembly members, increasingly, were arrested, put on trial for various charges, their release was promised if they renounced the Bahá'í Faith and became Muslims, and they were executed when they refused. The Bahá'ís usually reconstituted their local Assemblies, however, because they were busy coordinating relief work for Bahá'ís rendered homeless or jobless, for Bahá'ís were being systematically expelled from government agencies and educational positions. Rural Bahá'í villagers were often being driven from their homes and were living in tents in refugee camps. Bahá'í youth carried messages, sometimes on intercity buses, to maintain secure communications between the National Spiritual Assembly and the local Assemblies. The Universal House of Justice coordinated an extensive diplomatic effort to convince governments to pressure Iran, and it called for efforts to publicize the horrendous persecution going on. The European Parliament and the United Nations Sub commission on the Protection of Minorities passed resolutions condemning the persecution. Many National Spiritual Assemblies established offices of External Affairs for the first time, usually in their national capital. The effort surprised some Bahá'ís, who had understood the Bahá'í avoidance of partisanship to mean avoidance of political matters altogether. The Universal House of Justice began to guide the

Bahá'í community towards a new relationship with governmental officials and agencies.[32]

In December 1981 eight members of the second National Spiritual Assembly of Iran were arrested and executed. A third National Spiritual Assembly was immediately constituted, but by then many of the remaining names on the list of voting results were of people who had been executed.[33] Bahá'í students were expelled from the universities; they have not yet been allowed back. Bahá'í children sometimes were dismissed from public schools. In some places, business licenses of Bahá'ís were invalidated. Pensions of Bahá'í retirees were cancelled and sometimes demands were placed on them to repay all the payments they had received. Bahá'í physicians were denied the right to practice in hospitals. Iranian embassies were instructed not to renew the passports of Bahá'ís living abroad. In some cases, the custody of Bahá'í children was taken from their parents. Two thousand Bahá'ís who constituted nearly the entire village of Saysan in north-western Iran were driven away and everything was bulldozed: houses, businesses, the Bahá'í Centre, even the cemetery. It was an act of ethnic cleansing that meets the definition of a crime against humanity. The Iranian government, when presented with the facts of persecution in diplomatic and journalistic contexts, simply denied them and replied that the Bahá'ís were spies of Israel and the United States and had been tools of colonial powers since the beginning. To back up the latter claim, two forged documents were adduced, one purporting to be a memoir of a Russian diplomat sent to Iran to start a religion to split Islam, the other a supposed resolution of a group of prominent Jews to do the same. Bahá'ís were also accused of prostitution, partly because Bahá'í marriages had always been illegal in Iran, and no legal form of civil marriage had ever been available to them in the country.[34]

By April 1983, 139 Bahá'ís had been killed in Iran. In June ten Bahá'í women in Shiraz, aged 17 to 57, were hanged after months of torture and imprisonment during which they were constantly pressured to recant their Faith. The youngest, Mona Mahmudnezhad, daughter of a martyr, was still in high school and had been arrested for teaching classes for Bahá'í children; her execution was widely publicized by a popular music video composed by Canadian Bahá'í musicians. The hangings provoked widespread outrage and revulsion around the world. But members of Bahá'í institutions were forced into hiding by the continuous pressure and their families were harassed for knowledge of their whereabouts.

On 29 August 1983 government officials signed an official order banning all Bahá'í institutions. Bahá'ís are obliged by their religion to obey the government, so after consultation with the Universal House of Justice, the Iranian Bahá'ís complied. The last act of the National Spiritual Assembly of the Bahá'ís of Iran was to compose a lengthy open letter to the Iranian government about the nature of the Bahá'í Faith and injustices perpetuated against the Iranian community. Copies were distributed to 2,000 prominent Iranians within the country.[35]

The dissolution of Bahá'í institutions did not end the persecutions; by 1986 another 60 Bahá'ís had been martyred. Four of the members of the third National Spiritual Assembly were eventually martyred. But gradually, the number of deaths, which had steadily increased, tapered off: 4 (1978), 8 (1979), 24 (1980), 48 (1981), 32 (1982), 29 (1983), 30 (1984), 7 (1985), 7 (1986), 6 (1987), 2 (1988), 1 (1989), 1 (1992).[36] Various factors may have been at work. The Islamic government had never taken the Bahá'í Faith very seriously and may have assumed that pressure would cause most Bahá'ís to recant. The Communists had recanted their Marxism – often publically on television – and ostensibly returned to the Islamic fold, thereby destroying the Communist party of Iran. Relatively few Bahá'ís – especially the prominent ones – gave up their faith in the face of death, thereby protecting the rest of the community from similar pressure. Furthermore, martyrdom has always held a place of honour in Shi'ism; having Shi'ites conferring what was perceived by many Iranians as martyrdom on innocents damaged public perceptions of the government and Islam.

The executions exacted high costs internationally for Iran. Parliaments around the world passed resolutions condemning it; the US Congress passed seven. Heads of state protested it. Iran's ambassadors were under constant pressure about human rights abuses. The UN General Assembly and its human rights agencies were constantly investigating and reporting about it. Nobel laureates, human rights organizations and church bodies condemned it. The *New York Times* editorialized against it. Hundreds of newspapers, and magazines, including *Le Monde* and *The Economist*, published articles about it. The outpouring of publicity about the Bahá'í Faith was so great that in 1985 the Universal House of Justice announced that the Bahá'í Faith was emerging from obscurity.[37] The Iranian government also had to consider the impact the persecutions had on the Bahá'í world. Between 1979 and 1983 about 30,000 Bahá'ís fled Iran. The vast majority of them were dedicated; persecution usually strengthens faith. Some European countries nearly doubled their Bahá'í populations as a result; Australia and Canada saw a significant increase in numbers; even the United States received about 12,000 refugees.[38] Generally, the refugees spoke some English or French already and had professional degrees or experience, allowing them to integrate into their new countries fairly quickly and with relatively few problems for the host Bahá'í community. African and Latin American countries received relatively few refugees, but they provided a badly needed pool of Bahá'í knowledge, administrative experience and – once the arrivals were established in businesses or professions – contributions to the local Bahá'í funds.

The persecution also had a major impact on the Bahá'ís themselves. Bahá'ís everywhere, from wealthy suburbs to tiny rural villages in the developing world, understood injustice and executions and were very impressed by the steadfast faith they witnessed, which strengthened their own commitments. Bahá'í institutions had to develop new skills with the press and government officials. Bahá'í authors were inspired to write about the situation; musicians composed songs and videos. Even though the Iranian Bahá'í community had been contributing the bulk of the income of the International Bahá'í Fund, the rest of the Bahá'í world arose and made up the difference.

Consequently, by the mid-1980s the Islamic Republic moved towards a new approach to its Bahá'í problem: force their children to attend public schools with powerful Islamic indoctrination, block all access to university education and keep the community impoverished. Islamic courts often did not honour the wills of deceased Bahá'ís. Sometimes they could not take Muslims to court or rely on the police to protect their property. If a Bahá'í father died, his life insurance policy might not be honoured. If a Bahá'í needed to be hospitalized, her Bahá'í physician might not be able to attend her in the hospital and Muslim physicians might provide inferior care. If a Bahá'í wanted to sell property, Muslims might refuse to purchase it for a fair price. Bahá'í businessmen faced boycotts.

Young Bahá'í men were drafted into the army and sent to the Iraq front. This new approach, sometimes termed 'pressing the felt' in Persian – referring to the constant pressure necessary to convert animal hair into felt – was designed to keep the Bahá'í community weak and small while minimizing international media attention.

The seven year plan

All these attacks, determined efforts to defend the Bahá'ís, and enormous burdens fell during the Seven Year Plan, which the Universal House of Justice gave the Bahá'í world in April 1979 immediately upon the end of the successful Five Year Plan. The Seat of the Universal House of Justice was to be completed and the remaining three buildings on the Arc were to be designed. The International Teaching Centre, the coordinating agency for the Hands of the Cause and Counsellors, was to be developed further. Ties with the United Nations, which date back to 1947, were to be strengthened.

FIGURE 10.1 *Bahá'í House of Worship in India (© Bahá'í International Community).*

The Bahá'í House of Worship in India was to be completed. Twenty-two new National Spiritual Assemblies were to be formed, raising the total to 147; the number actually reached 148. Many Assemblies that were dependent on support from the International Bahá'í Fund were to move towards financial self-sufficiency. The number of local Spiritual Assemblies was to be raised from 23,624 to 30,850; it actually increased to 32,854. Starting in 1980, National Spiritual Assemblies were asked to complete annual statistical reports reporting how many local Spiritual Assemblies were holding Nineteen Day Feasts, Holy Day observances, children's classes and contributing to the National Bahá'í Fund in order to measure the gradual maturation of their functioning and the impact of any training programmes. The number of localities with Bahá'ís was to increase to 115,457; it reached 116,707.[39]

Efforts to refine the consolidation process continued. Mobile teaching institutes – vehicles equipped with projection equipment and literature – were established in nine countries. Audiovisual materials were prepared in many tribal languages for use in consolidating the new Bahá'ís. Correspondence courses were to be developed by 39 more National Spiritual Assemblies, for a total of 65, because they were proving effective. In Colombia, the Ruhi Institute began to develop a series of training booklets about understanding the Bahá'í sacred texts, prayer, life after death and giving children's classes; nuclei of books 1 and 3 in their future training curriculum. At least three Bahá'í radio stations were to be established in areas of mass teaching; efforts were already underway in Bolivia, Chile, Peru, Panama and South Carolina, and all of them were successful.[40] The South American stations, located in Quechua and Aymara-speaking areas in the Andes, decided to broadcast indigenous music, which had been ignored by the dominant media or often treated as inferior. To record it, the stations organized musical competitions and concerts, thereby greatly stimulating local culture.

Two new aspects of the plan were creation of schools and the advancement of women. For decades, Bahá'í communities in the developing world had been opening schools for children where public education was unavailable; starting in 1983, the Seven Year Plan encouraged schools and other social and economic development projects such as reforestation efforts, community gardens to support the Bahá'í Fund and public health projects. Many

National Spiritual Assemblies were given the goal of advancing the status of women, which usually involved organizing women's conferences and establishing self-improvement groups for rural women.[41]

The year 1986 was declared the International Year of Peace by the United Nations, so the Universal House of Justice chose to release *The Promise of World Peace* that year. The 50-page statement, addressed to the 'peoples of the world', was distributed free to tens of thousands of people, including the Secretary-General of the United Nations and 167 world leaders. The effort was similar to the distribution of the *Proclamation of Bahá'u'lláh* almost 20 years earlier, but with two notable differences; because of the persecution in Iran, the Bahá'ís were much better known; and this time the Universal House of Justice chose to use their own words, rather than a translation of Bahá'í scripture.

The United States was given the goal of raising the number of local Spiritual Assemblies to 1,650, including at least 35 on Indian reservations, and increasing the number of localities with Bahá'ís to 7,200. These were achieved. The total number of Bahá'ís grew from 77,000 in 1979 to about 100,000 in 1986, representing about 12,000 Persian arrivals, 30,000 declarations and 19,000 withdrawals (of people who became Bahá'ís as far back as 1970). The overall growth rate dropped to about 3 per cent per year, a far cry from the rapid expansion of two decades earlier. Bahá'ís rarely initiated mass teaching efforts because so few of the declarants became active Bahá'ís. Furthermore, the old techniques of publicizing firesides in homes or meetings in public places were less effective in an era when people feared visiting strangers' houses, relied on television for much of their information, rarely attended public lectures and worked longer hours. The objective of doubling the number of Bahá'ís in New York, Illinois, California, and Washington, DC, proved totally out of reach.[42]

The six year plan

With the completion of the Seven Year Plan in April 1986, the Universal House of Justice announced a Six Year Plan, to conclude in 1992, the centenary of Bahá'u'lláh's passing, which they declared a Holy Year.

The Plan took on a different character than earlier ones because the Universal House of Justice announced that henceforth the National Spiritual Assemblies themselves would make their own plans and submit the goals to the Universal House of Justice; the House would provide the overall framework of the plan only. It identified seven major objectives for the progress of the Bahá'í world:

> carrying the healing Message of Bahá'u'lláh to the generality of mankind; greater involvement of the Faith in the life of human society; a worldwide increase in the translation, production, distribution and use of Bahá'í literature; further acceleration in the process of the maturation of national and local Bahá'í communities; greater attention to universal participation and the spiritual enrichment of individual believers; a wider extension of Bahá'í education to children and youth and the strengthening of Bahá'í family life; and the pursuit of projects of social and economic development in well-established Bahá'í communities.[43]

Each objective was accompanied by a list of suggestions for goals or approaches to take.

The House of Justice assigned itself several ambitious goals: it would complete the translation of the Kitáb-i-Aqdas and supplementary materials into English, thereby providing the Most Holy Book for the first time to the western believers; the law of Huqúqu'lláh* would become binding on all the Bahá'ís in the world in 1992, rather than just on the Iranians, which required a significant expansion of the Huqúqu'lláh boards of trustees and education of the Bahá'ís about the law; construction would commence on the three remaining monumental administrative buildings on the Arc; work on the nine terraces below the Shrine of the Báb and the nine above the Shrine of the Báb would begin, thereby creating monumental gardens from the foot of Mount Carmel to the top; and the international relations work would be further systematized.[44]

The situation in Iran remained a grave concern. Pressure on Iran was maintained, even though martyrdoms and imprisonments were

---

*The law of Huqúqu'lláh, a sort of tithe on surplus income after necessary costs are subtracted, was described in Chapter Five.

fewer. United Nations bodies passed seven resolutions about the persecution. The policy of impoverishing and discriminating against the Bahá'ís became official when the 'Golpaygani Memorandum' was promulgated in February 1991, signed by Supreme Leader Ali Khamenei himself. Ominously, the memorandum called for a plan to 'confront and destroy their [the Bahá'ís'] cultural roots outside the country'.[45]

The collapse of communism brought emancipation to Bahá'ís behind the Iron Curtain and triggered the largest geographical expansion of the Bahá'í community since the Ten Year Crusade. Four decades of experience in founding Bahá'í communities paid off, and the Bahá'í Faith was established in Eastern Europe, the republics of the former Soviet Union and Mongolia in just a few years. Pioneers settled, reached out first to English teachers and translators, then to the rank and file of the citizenry, who were extraordinarily receptive to anything new from the outside world. Believers who had been cut off for as much as 50 years were found and welcomed back into the community. Mass teaching brought 12,000 people into the Bahá'í Faith in the Eastern Bloc by 1992, creating the usual consolidation problems, though it helped that most new Bahá'ís were literate. Bahá'í literature was quickly published in their languages; often the translations had been ready for decades. National Spiritual Assemblies were formed in most of the Eastern bloc countries by the mid-1990s. As a result, the total number of National Spiritual Assemblies worldwide grew from 148 in 1986 to 165 in 1992.[46]

In the developing world, social and economic development projects and Bahá'í children's classes became major emphases of the plan. Mass teaching continued strongly; almost a million people became Bahá'ís, mainly between 1988 and 1990.[47] But consolidation remained a high priority. In the United States, the community grew from 100,000 to 120,000, a 20 per cent expansion in 6 years (3% per year). The worldwide growth statistics looked less impressive than they really were because in many countries the National Spiritual Assemblies redistricted their local communities. The Universal House of Justice had always wanted community boundaries to conform to those of the local civil jurisdictions (such as townships, incorporated towns and counties). Often a civil jurisdiction had several villages within it, and during the era of mass teaching a Spiritual Assembly had been formed in each. Now the

Bahá'í communities were consolidated together. When India redistricted, the number of local Spiritual Assemblies there dropped by 11,000.[48]

Worldwide, the number of local Spiritual Assemblies went from 25,330 to 20,435 (not bad, considering India's reduction). The number of localities with Bahá'ís increased from 114,988 to 120,046.[49]

The Holy Year and the three year plan

In 1992 the Bahá'ís commemorated the hundredth anniversary of Bahá'u'lláh's passing. The Universal House of Justice declared it a Holy Year and called for the convening of the second Bahá'í World Congress, in New York City. The 4-day event was attended by 27,000 people from around the world. Nine simultaneous subsidiary congresses were attended by thousands more and were linked to New York live via satellite. A 400-voice choir and a 70-piece orchestra performed a series of original works, including the first Bahá'í gospel music and an oratorio celebrating the coming of Bahá'u'lláh. Attendees also toured a special pavilion about 'Abdu'l-Bahá as the Centre of the Covenant. The events of the holy year generated considerable positive publicity for the Faith, including a 2-hour session of Brazil's Federal Chamber of Deputies (the lower house of the Brazilian Congress) devoted to Bahá'u'lláh.[50]

The Holy Year was followed by a Three Year Plan, April 1993 to April 1996. It focused on three major developments: 'enhancing the vitality of the faith of individual believers, greatly developing the human resources of the Cause, and fostering the proper functioning of local and national Bahá'í institutions'.[51] These developments were to support and contribute to the seven objectives previously stated in the Six Year Plan. While the plan called for a 'massive expansion of the Bahá'í community', the focus now was more on consolidation.

The 3-year period did see some expansion, with India reporting 44,000 new Bahá'ís, Bangladesh 56,000, the United States at least 13,000 (from 120,000 to 133,000; a growth of 3% per year), Haiti and the Philippines 7,000 each, Papua New

Guinea 6,500, Kenya 5,000 and Albania 4,000. The number of National Spiritual Assemblies increased to 174. The percentage of members of National Spiritual Assemblies who were women increased to 32 per cent, an impressive achievement considering the lack of opportunities for women in many parts of the world. But the number of local Spiritual Assemblies decreased, to 17,335.[52]

Sixty four communities broadcast programmes on the radio; 63 reported efforts to advance the status of women; 18 reported health care activities; and 46 reported educational efforts such as Bahá'í courses and lectures at universities or scholarly conferences on Bahá'í-related subjects. Many assemblies were able to report a significant increase in the number of local Spiritual Assemblies that organized their own annual election, held the Nineteen Day Feast, prepared teaching plans, met regularly or contributed to the Bahá'í funds. They also reported regular deepening programmes to enrich the believers' understanding of the Bahá'í authoritative texts, dawn prayers in many agricultural villages, numerous institute courses and programmes, efforts to encourage personal goal setting, plans to encourage regular family prayers and educational efforts in the law of Huqúqu'lláh. Social and economic projects advanced significantly, with 1,600 development activities reported.[53]

The effort to plan the development of the Bahá'í community was now 50 years old. Under Shoghi Effendi, most of the goals had focused on increasing the number of countries, territories and significant islands where the Bahá'í Faith was located. Under the Universal House of Justice, the goal of universal participation had been added; then in the Five Year Plan, development of local Spiritual Assemblies and milestones in community life such as observance of Feasts and Holy Days; then in the Seven Year Plan, involvement in the life of society and the pursuit of social and economic development projects. In the Six Year Plan, these various foci of activity were brought together into a list of seven overall objectives, to which Three Year Plan added three underlying developments.

The Bahá'í community had learned a lot about how to introduce a new religion to the world. National Spiritual Assemblies had been formed in most of the places they could be formed. But over the last decade, the number of Bahá'ís had plateaued at about 5 million. Partly because of redistricting, the number of local Spiritual Assemblies had dropped substantially (to 17,000, less than two-thirds the peak of 25,000). The number of localities had remained roughly constant in the range of 110,000 to 120,000. The time had come to take the various goals and the techniques for achieving them and organizing them in new, systematic ways so that they would be mutually supportive, allowing meaningful expansion and effective consolidation to continue.

CHAPTER ELEVEN

The current epoch, 1996–2012

When the Universal House of Justice inaugurated the Four Year Plan in April 1996, it described the plan as a 'turning point of epochal magnitude'. Its central aim was to 'advance the process of entry by troops', a term Shoghi Effendi had used to describe a phase in the growth of the Bahá'í Faith. He said it had started in a few places, such as India, Indonesia, Uganda and the Gilbert Islands, in the late 1950s, and the Universal House of Justice said it occurred in the southern United States in 1970. The plan called for 'marked progress in the activity and development' of the three principal actors in the plan: the individual, the Bahá'í institutions and the local community. The House noted that different communities were in different stages of entry by troops and that what was needed now was appropriate steps in each place 'to achieve a level of expansion and consolidation commensurate with their possibilities'.[1]

A key need was training, so that more Bahá'ís had the skills to teach the Faith to others and deepen the new believers more effectively. Therefore the Universal House of Justice called for the establishment of 'permanent institutes designed to provide well-organized, formally conducted programmes of training on a regular schedule'. The network of institutes was to be 'on a scale never before attempted' by Bahá'ís. No single curriculum was established; the institutes were to develop new materials or modify existing ones. The Universal House of Justice later called for the establishment of a 'culture of learning' in the Bahá'í community worldwide. Its goal was to overcome passivity, drilled into people over the centuries by ruling classes, bosses and clergy. The creation of the new civilization called for by Bahá'u'lláh required the

creation of an active populace that would organize itself through
a process of spiritual elections and determine its own development
through consultation. Because the Bahá'í Faith lacked clergy, an
active membership was essential.[2]

The Universal House of Justice also changed the date of formation of local Spiritual Assemblies. In 1977 it had allowed their
election any time in the 12-day Ridván festival (21`April–2 May).
Starting in Ridván 1997, the election could occur on the first day
only.[3] Previously, teams of Bahá'ís would travel to mass-taught communities and bring the Bahá'ís together for the Assembly election.
When all Assemblies had to be formed on the same day, this became
impossible; each community had to organize its own election. The
change caused a decrease in the total number of Assemblies, but
an increase in the number that began to function. The number of
local Spiritual Assemblies in the United States dropped to about
1,400, partly because many Assemblies in mass-taught areas of
the rural South ceased to form. The National Spiritual Assembly
also stopped publicizing situations when the number of Bahá'ís in
a civil jurisdiction dropped below nine (usually because someone
moved out). This made it less likely someone would move in and
return the community to the minimum required for the formation
of a Spiritual Assembly.

In May 1997 the Universal House of Justice announced
the establishment of a new institution, the Regional Council,
below the level of the National Spiritual Assembly but above
the level of the local Spiritual Assembly. Its five to nine members could be elected annually by all the members of the local
Spiritual Assemblies in the region, or they could be appointed by
the National Spiritual Assembly.[4] This was not totally new; India
had already had State Bahá'í Councils for over a decade because of
the difficulties of administering the affairs of a large Bahá'í community in a country with limited communication and transporta-
tion. Later, Zaire was allowed to form Councils. The United States
established four regional councils initially for the north-eastern,
central, southern and western states; later, the latter two split in
half, raising the number of Councils to six; in 2012, the number
was increased to ten. The United Kingdom established councils for
England, Northern Ireland, Scotland and Wales. By April 2011,
180 regional councils had been formed in 48 countries.[5] Nations
with relatively small Bahá'í populations did not establish any

regional councils, which existed to decentralize the administrative and teaching work. One responsibility they acquired was appointment of training institutes – committees to coordinate training (most institutes had no building). The institutes in turn began to create dozens, even hundreds of study circles across their region where Bahá'ís could come together face to face to study, thereby establishing a network of learners across the world.

Some institutes began to create materials for study circles, but more chose to adopt the Ruhi Institute materials, which had originated in Colombia in the 1970s and 1980s and which had undergone steady refinement. The Ruhi books provided knowledge and fostered memorization of passages from Bahá'í sacred texts, but they were not a catechism; their main focus was imparting skills for the path of service. Book 1 taught people to conduct devotional programmes in their houses (which consist of reciting or singing selections of prayers and scriptures) and emphasized use of music and the arts, Book 2 focused on visiting people in their homes to discuss spiritual subjects, Book 3 provided materials and advice for conducting spiritual education classes for children, Book 4 discussed the lives of the Báb and Bahá'u'lláh and ways to tell stories about them, Book 5 contained materials to teach classes for older children, Book 6 covered teaching the Bahá'í Faith to others and Book 7 offered training to be a Ruhi tutor. The Ruhi books were fairly simple and generic, easy to translate into many languages, and did not require special art materials or extra books. They were designed for groups to go through them together with the assistance of a tutor who did not need extensive training. They usually required literacy, so they were not as effective with illiterate populations, which many rural Bahá'ís in developing countries were. They were lengthy; on average, each required about 40 hours to complete. They were effective with non-Bahá'ís and Bahá'ís who knew almost nothing about the Faith. They quickly spread, especially once Counsellors and Auxiliary Board members began to encourage their use.

The Four Year Plan ended with only a modest expansion of the Bahá'í community: National Spiritual Assemblies went from 174 to 181; localities with Bahá'ís from 121,058 to 129,949. The number of local Spiritual Assemblies decreased from 17,148 to 12,591 because there could no longer be campaigns to elect Spiritual Assemblies during the Riḍván festival. Social and economic

projects, worldwide, increased from 1,600 to 1,900. The number
of Spiritual Assemblies in the United States dropped to about
1,200. The number of American Bahá'ís increased from 133,000
to 141,000, a growth rate of less than 2 per cent per year. But
the creation of over 300 national and regional training institutes
and uncounted study circles increased Bahá'í human resources
and capacities, with over 100,000 Bahá'ís participating in training courses. The Universal House of Justice was pleased: 'the culture of the Bahá'í community experienced a change. This change
is noticeable in the expanded capability, the methodical pattern of
functioning and the consequent depth of confidence of the three
constituent participants in the Plan – the individual, the institutions and the local community'.[6]

Education, scholarship and the arts, 1990–2000

The last decade of the twentieth century saw important developments in Bahá'í education and scholarship. Bahá'í private primary and secondary schools were founded or expanded in Brazil,
Canada, the Czech Republic, El Salvador, Haiti, India, Macao,
Nigeria, Swaziland, Thailand and Zambia. Núr University,
a Bahá'í-inspired institution of higher education in Bolivia,
expanded to several thousand students, as did Unity College in
Ethiopia. Landegg Academy started university-level programmes
in Switzerland. In Iran, the Bahá'í Institute for Higher Education
(BIHE) which had started modestly in 1987 to provide a college
education for Persian Bahá'ís (who were denied access to universities in that country) expanded its services and began to use the
world wide web to tap into educational talent outside Iran. In
1998, the Iranian government cracked down on BIHE, seizing its
local offices and classrooms, confiscating its computers and libraries, and arresting its faculty and administrators. Undaunted, the
Iranian Bahá'ís continued to develop their system for university
education. By shifting more of BIHE's operation to the internet,
it became harder to shut down. Even though the institution could
not be accredited, its graduates were accepted as masters and doctoral candidates in numerous prestigious western universities. The

government's opposition to BIHE was only one facet of its persecution of the Faith, which included the execution of one Bahá'í, the imprisonment of others and continued pressure and discrimination against all Bahá'ís.

Interest in academic study of the Bahá'í Faith led to establishment of the Bahá'í Chair for World Peace at the University of Maryland (1990) and Chairs for Bahá'í Studies at the Universities of Indore (1990) and Lucknow (1995) in India and the Hebrew University in Jerusalem (1999). An academic peer-reviewed journal published in Poland, *Dialogue and Universalism*, devoted an entire issue to Bahá'í studies in 1996. Growing interest in Bahá'í Studies in the 1980s and 1990s led to the establishment of Associations for Bahá'í Studies in Argentina, Australia, Brazil, Cameroon, English-speaking Europe, French-speaking Europe, German-speaking Europe, Italy, Japan, Malaysia, New Zealand, Papua-New Guinea and Singapore. The European Bahá'í Business Forum and the United States based Bahá'í Justice Society were established. The Bahá'í Academy in India, Yerrinbool Bahá'í School in Australia and the Wilmette Institute in the United States began to offer advanced courses on Bahá'í subjects, the latter two through the internet. The 'Irfán Colloquia, a series of privately funded and organized Bahá'í Studies conferences, began to hold as many as six meetings a year in venues as far-flung as California and Italy in both English and Persian and published a steady stream of proceedings.[7]

Study of the Bahá'í Faith continued to develop in the Persian language as well, thanks to the interest of the large expatriate community. An Institute for Bahá'í Studies in Persian opened in Ontario and published a series of scholarly works in the Persian language, supplementing other Persian-language Bahá'í periodicals such as *'Andalíb* and a press publishing Persian-language Bahá'í books in Germany. Bahá'ís in Iran took an active part in the effort, thanks to the internet.

The establishment of the internet created many new possibilities for collaboration and consultation of Bahá'ís about their religion. Many listservs were established, some to discuss contentious subjects, others to provide scholarly discussion via the web. Two listservs, Tarikh (for Bahá'í history) and Tarjuman (for translating Bahá'í texts), emerged as primary venues for providing professional, collegial collaboration on academic matters. Other listservs networked Bahá'ís interested in science and religion, architecture, English as a second language teaching and other subjects.

The arts continued to develop in the Bahá'í community as well. Radio Bahá'í Ecuador's annual Andean Music Festivals drew as many as 3,000 people to hear traditional music. Artistic exhibits by prominent Bahá'í artists, concerts by musicians and arts festivals sponsored by Bahá'í communities occurred all around the world. To encourage artists in the Bahá'í community, workshops and conferences were held in such diverse places as Southport, United Kingdom; Reno, Nevada; Santiago, Chile and Sri Lanka.[8]

Continued emergence from obscurity

The late 1990s also saw continued emergence of the Bahá'í community from the state of obscurity. Ninety-nine National Spiritual Assemblies established external affairs offices. External affairs work worldwide was coordinated through annual meetings of representatives of the leading national offices and of the Bahá'í World Centre. Four priorities shaped their efforts: human rights, the status of women, global prosperity and moral development. The principal representative of the Bahá'í International Community* at the United Nations represented all non-governmental organizations and spoke on their behalf at the Millennium Summit of heads of state in New York in early 2000. A Bahá'í was co-chair of the 1999 Parliament of the World's Religions in Cape Town, South Africa. Bahá'í representatives were invited to attend interfaith gatherings in Jordan, Germany, New Delhi and Vatican City. Bahá'í representatives attended interfaith events at both Westminster Palace and Lamberth Palace in London, the meeting place of the British Parliament and the residence of Archbishop of Canterbury, respectively.[9]

The completion of work on Mount Carmel brought considerable prestige and exposure to the Bahá'í Faith. The 19 garden terraces ascending a thousand feet from the base of Mount Carmel to its summit created a sacred place of Edenic beauty that could be

---

*Religions are represented as nongovernmental organizations of religious communities at the UN, not as religions per se.

compared to few other places on Earth. It soon emerged as one of Israel's leading tourist destinations. An artistic event held there on 1 January 2000 was one of hundreds of events telecast internationally to celebrate the new millennium. In May 2001 the terraces and the three new monumental administrative buildings on the Arc adjacent to the terraces were formally dedicated. The World Heritage Committee of UNESCO inscribed the shrines of the Báb and Bahá'u'lláh and their surrounding gardens on the World Heritage List in 2008.[10]

The twelve month plan, 2000–1, and five year plan, 2001–6

In November 1999, the Universal House of Justice announced that advancing the process of entry by troops would be the primary goal of the Bahá'í world until 2021, the end of the first century of the 'Formative Age' (which succeeded the 'Heroic Age' of the Faith upon 'Abdu'l-Bahá's passing in 1921).[11] The 21-year period, which they characterized as the 'Fifth Epoch'** of the Formative Age, would begin with a Twelve Month Plan, followed by a series of four Five Year Plans. It was the first time the Universal House of Justice had laid out a series of plans with a common goal covering such a long time period.

The Twelve Month Plan focused on continued development and strengthening of the network of training institutes and called for greater attention to classes for children, junior youth (ages 12–14) and youth. Thus it made education a priority for all ages. Twenty-five area growth programmes were established around the world to explore the relationship between sustainable growth and systematic training. Their experience shaped many elements of the Five Year Plan that the Universal House of Justice defined in 2001 and 2002.

**Shoghi Effendi divided Bahá'í history into a Heroic Age, during the lifetimes of the Báb, Bahá'u'lláh, and `Abdu'l-Bahá, a Formative Age, and a Golden Age that would occur many centuries in the future. He divided the Formative Age into the first and second epochs, 1921–53 and 1953–63 respectively. The Universal House of Justice defined the Third and Fourth Epochs as 1963–86 and 1986–2000 respectively.

The January 2001 message of the Universal House of Justice that laid out the Five Year Plan (April 2001–April 2006) continued the emphasis on classes for all ages and called for the institutes to use a sequence of courses that imparted skills and that built on each other. In addition to training programmes for children's and junior youth classes, the courses needed to provide skills for systematic programmes of growth.[12]

To facilitate the creation of systematic programmes of growth, the House of Justice called for the creation of *clusters:*

> Most of these will consist of a cluster of villages and towns, but, sometimes, a large city and its suburbs may constitute an area of this kind. Among the factors that determine the boundaries of a cluster are culture, language, patterns of transport, infrastructure, and the social and economic life of the inhabitants. The areas into which a region divides will fall into various categories of development. Some will not yet be open to the Faith, while others will contain a few isolated localities and groups; in some, established communities will be gaining strength through a vigorous institute process; in a few, strong communities of deepened believers will be in a position to take on the challenges of systematic and accelerated expansion and consolidation.[13]

The passage introduced sweeping changes in the way the Bahá'í Faith functioned at a local level. Shoghi Effendi had based the boundaries of local Bahá'í communities on the smallest civil unit locally: the city, incorporated village, township or county. As a result, metropolitan areas might have dozens of local Spiritual Assemblies, often administering the activities of only a few dozen people each. Coordination across a metropolitan area was often ad hoc; in some places one local Spiritual Assembly would sponsor a media committee, another children's classes and yet another the monthly newsletter. Teaching the Faith to others was loosely coordinated at best because each Assembly had its own teaching plan and often had a teaching committee.

The introduction of the cluster and its coordinating committees (appointed by the regional council or National Spiritual Assembly) overlaid on top of the existing network of local Spiritual Assemblies solved some of those problems, although it introduced new ones:

now cluster committees had to coordinate with local Spiritual Assemblies. The passage above also offered a way to classify clusters, and soon the letters A through D were used to do so; a D cluster had no Bahá'ís, while an A cluster was ready for the 'challenges of systematic and accelerated expansion and consolidation', which additional guidance from Haifa defined. Within a year, National Spiritual Assemblies around the world had divided their territories into clusters, over 16,000 altogether. The United States had over 900; India, 1,580.[14]

In December 2001, the Universal House of Justice introduced yet another important concept; the *two essential movements*: 'The first is the steady flow of believers through the sequence of courses offered by training institutes, for the purpose of developing the human resources of the Cause. The second, which receives its impetus from the first, is the movement of geographic clusters from one stage of growth to the next'.[15]

A few months later, Ridván 2002, as the Five Year Plan completed its first year, the Universal House of Justice added a new element: *core activities*. Initially there were three: study circles, devotional gatherings and children's classes. The latter two could be held by anyone, Bahá'í or not, at any time and place; study circles required someone with tutor training, but it was open to people of any religion or even any age. A fourth core activity, classes for junior youth (ages 12–14), developed gradually through the plan as it became clear the needs of that age group were different from those of younger children.[16] These four activities were seen both as means for strengthening Bahá'í community life and as portals for attracting new people. A friend of a Bahá'í might attend a devotional programme held by a Bahá'í in his or her home and then join a study circle. Bahá'í children and junior youth might invite friends to join the class as well, and the children's parents might then become involved. Some inquirers might plunge straight into the study circles; they could take the entire sequence and become a tutor without formally enrolling in the Bahá'í community.

Together with clusters, the creation of core activities brought about a change in community culture perhaps as great as Shoghi Effendi's launch of the Administrative Order in the early 1920s in a community that had become used to the lack of organization, and occasionally opposed its creation. Since the Ruhi sequence already included books on all the core activities, use of the materials spread even faster. The seven books were translated into scores of languages as diverse as Quechua and Mongolian and training accelerated. From April 1996 to February 2003, about 10,000 people had completed Book 3; by the fall of 2003, 9,000 more. In 2001, only 616 people worldwide had completed Book 7, which provided the skills to be a tutor. Some tutors travelled long distances to provide training; in other cases, local people partially trained themselves. By 2006, 36,000 people had completed Book 7.[17]

In many places, the Ruhi books and the core activities proved to be a powerful combination for developing human resources and local Bahá'í communities. But there were many uncertainties about the new system, and sometimes controversies. Some Bahá'ís were pressured to take the Ruhi books or were told they were obligatory for all Spiritual Assembly members or for all children's and youth class teachers. A few were told they should cease conducting the fireside they were holding regularly in their homes – sometimes for decades – because firesides had been replaced by the core activities or competed with them. Others were told to stop holding deepenings because they were now obsolete. In a few cases, Bahá'ís were encouraged to cease their involvement in interfaith activities or social and economic development projects because they were 'distractions' from the new priorities. Some Associations for Bahá'í Studies closed to focus resources on the core activities. Communities were sometimes advised not to purchase Bahá'í Centres because they were now unnecessary, or to stop holding annual conferences. None of this advice was correct, and the Universal House of Justice was busy correcting these and other misconceptions.

With the definition of clusters, the two essential movements, core activities and systematic programmes of growth, the Five Year Plan took its final shape. Clusters established study circles that imparted the skills to establish and multiply the other core activities (devotionals and children's classes). Bahá'ís thereby gained experience and the cluster moved up to A-cluster status, when it launched a systematic programme of growth. In order to refine the process, resources were given to the most capable clusters first, not the ones that needed the most help. The advanced clusters thus became laboratories and their experience produced insights that could then be shared with the B-clusters. By the end of the plan in Ridván 2006, some 200 clusters worldwide had reached A status and had launched systematic programmes of growth. Classes for children and junior youth had tripled in number, devotional meetings had increased six fold and the number of study circles had surpassed 11,000.[18]

To give a few specific examples, in the cluster of Norte del Cauca, Colombia, where the Ruhi Institute originated, the Bahá'í community grew from 2,700 to 4,300 (out of a population of about 235,000). Devotional gatherings increased from 52 to 129, children's classes from 66 to 99 (serving 1,263 and 1,358 children respectively) and junior youth groups from 24 to 44 (serving 236 and 429 junior youth, respectively). In Kiribati (where Roy and Elena Fernie had introduced the Bahá'í Faith in 1953) the Ruhi books were translated into I-Kiribati from 2001 to 2003 and by April 2004 the nation had 48 tutors. On South Tarawa where the country's capital was located and where 1,343 of the 45,000 people are Bahá'ís, the Bahá'ís soon had 27 children's classes serving 330 children, 11 junior youth groups in the local schools and 30 people were becoming Bahá'ís every 3 months. In the Murun cluster in rural northern Mongolia, the Bahá'í population grew from under 300 to over 1,900 in 2004–6.[19]

In the United States, the effort to establish the core activities and the Ruhi sequence required so many resources that enrolments actually decreased for a year or two. A few veteran Bahá'ís, disillusioned by the changes in the Bahá'í community, became inactive or withdrew from membership. During the Five Year Plan, the number of American Bahá'ís increased from 144,000 to 154,000; a growth rate of less than 2 per cent per year.[20] It is not known whether international growth followed a similar pattern, but certainly the groundwork was laid for a system that could accommodate many new Bahá'ís if receptivity increased, as it had during the Great Depression, after World War Two and during the 1960s.

The second five year plan, 2006–11

The Universal House of Justice provided a series of refinements to the advancement of the process of entry by troops for the next Five Year Plan (2006–11). As already noted, junior youth classes were added as a fourth core activity. The House of Justice made Ruhi the official curriculum of the training institutes and their study circles through 2021, noting that it had proved its effectiveness.

The Ruhi curriculum was also to undergo some modification to meet the Faith's needs better; a new Book 5 would provide training to animate junior youth groups and a Book 8 would focus on the Covenant. The House of Justice emphasized that the Ruhi curriculum could not meet all the needs of the Bahá'ís for study of the Faith; that deepenings, conferences, and other programmes of study were important and should continue; and that Bahá'ís were not under any obligation to take the Ruhi courses. Bahá'ís who preferred not to study the books, however, should not hamper the spread of the Ruhi curriculum.[21]

The House of Justice also provided a summary of what had been learned about systematic programmes of growth. It suggested that clusters engage on a 3-month cycle of activity, starting with 2 weeks of intense activity to find receptive souls, followed by a consolidation phase when those interested were introduced to the core activities. Finally, the cluster would hold a reflection meeting open to anyone who was involved in the core activities – registered Bahá'í or not – to plan the next cycle of activity. The House of Justice called for the establishment of intensive programmes of growth in no less than 1,500 clusters by 2011.[22]

Implementation was slow at first; in the first 2 years of the plan, only 300 new intensive programmes of growth were launched. Therefore the Universal House of Justice decided to hold a series of 41 conferences at the plan's midpoint (late 2008 and early 2009), where nearly 80,000 Bahá'ís gathered to study the goals and commit themselves to local implementation. Three thousand, three hundred Bahá'ís in 131 countries moved to new places as pioneers to provide essential human resources. The result was 900 more intensive programmes of growth initiated in the last 2 years of the plan. The goal of 1,500 was surpassed by April 2010, a year early; by December 2010 the number of intensive programmes of growth had increased to 1,600. Some 375,000 people had taken Book 1 and 140,000 had taken Book 3 about children's classes. Almost half a million people were engaged in core activities at any particular time, and half of them were not Bahá'ís; 70,000 had received enough training (usually 3 or 4 books) to serve as tutors of study circles. Core activities grew 60 per cent, junior youth groups more than doubled in number and children's classes increased by 40 per cent. The largest numerical and percentage increases came in Africa, a clear sign that the core activities were effective for many rural peoples.[23]

The plan thus brought about a substantial expansion in capacity. In Nepal, for example, a 20-year old woman moved to a rural area where a few of her relatives lived and where there were a few Bahá'ís, but no activity. Within 9 months, there were children's classes, eight people had completed Ruhi Books 1 through 7, and 115 people attended the cluster's first reflection meeting. Malta experienced an expansion in membership and an increase in core activities from three to seventeen. Grants Pass, Oregon, saw a 50 per cent increase in Bahá'ís. In the United States, experimentation with 2-week periods of expansion led to a renewed emphasis on the 'direct method' for teaching the Faith, but generally the number of people reached door to door was kept to a manageable number, so that new approaches to consolidate them could be tried. The membership of the American Bahá'í community increased from 154,000 to 169,000.[24]

The third five year plan, 2011–16

The inauguration of a new Five Year Plan (2011–16) marked a new phase in advancing the process of entry by troops. Based on the experience gained during the previous plan, it included a renewed focus on social action and a new emphasis on public discourse. In January 2009, in a letter to the National Spiritual Assembly of Australia about the development of its retreat and conference centre, the Yerrinbool Centre of Learning, the House of Justice suggested that Yerrinbool's programmes concentrate on preparing Bahá'ís to participate in public discourse. As the Bahá'í community grows, it 'will find itself being drawn further and further into the life of society'. Therefore,

> The House of Justice encourages you to begin to examine the work of your community in terms of three broad areas of action, which, though distinct from one another, each with its own methods and instruments, must achieve a high degree of coherence between them, if they are to reinforce one another and lend substantial impetus to the movement of the Australian

people towards the spiritually and materially prosperous civilization envisioned in the writings of the Faith. What will ensure this coherence is the process of systematic learning that characterizes them all.[25]

The three areas of action were expansion and consolidation, social action and public discourse. The desire for social action 'will accompany the collective change which begins to occur in a village or neighbourhood as acts of communal worship and home visits are woven together with activities for the spiritual education of its population to create a rich pattern of community life'. It could be simple, small, informal efforts or complex programmes of social and economic development by Bahá'í-inspired non-governmental organizations. Participation in the discourses of society can occur at all levels of society and involve Bahá'ís offering 'generously, unconditionally and with utmost humility the teachings of the Faith and their experience in applying them as a contribution to the betterment of society'.[26]

The Universal House of Justice's Ridván 2010 message to the Bahá'í world offered further clarification. The purpose of the core activities was 'to raise capacity within a population to take charge of its own spiritual, social and intellectual development'. They were designed to join together study and service, because through serv-ice 'knowledge is tested, questions arise out of practice, and new levels of understanding are achieved'. Their purpose is to overcome the passivity 'bred by the forces of society today'.[27]

The core activities, therefore, were supposed to lead naturally to social action and public discourse. But the value of social action and public discourse 'is not to be judged by the ability to bring enrolments' nor is conversion their purpose. The Bahá'í commu-nity exists to foster 'civilization building' and recognizes that the efforts by others to improve society may benefit from knowledge of the Bahá'í principles, whether they are moved to join the Bahá'í community or not. The House of Justice cautioned Bahá'ís not to seek 'involvement in society' prematurely; they had to build their capacity for the effort gradually. The House suggested that a clus-ter select a neighbourhood or village and concentrate its efforts there, thereby creating in one place a stronger devotional life, pro-grammes for the spiritual education of children, groups to chan-nel the junior youth into service, projects of social action and involvement in local public discourse. Later, the efforts could be extended to other places.[28]

In a 28 December 2010 letter to the conference of the Counsellors, the Universal House of Justice added that the Bahá'í community had to extend 'to other spheres of operation the mode of learning which has so undeniably come to characterize its teaching endeavours'. The number of clusters with programmes of growth, of whatever level of intensity, was to increase from 1,600 to 5,000.[29]

The new focus on social action and public discourse were exciting for Bahá'ís attracted to the Bahá'í principles of social reform, who often had not found the emphasis on teaching alone to be sufficient. In the past, there had been some tension between an approach favouring teaching the Faith to others and an approach that favoured involvement in social reform. The Universal House of Justice's messages of 2009 and 2010 sought to set both in a larger framework and emphasized the potential coherence between the two.

Scholarship, education and external affairs

The decade from 2001 to 2011 saw the continued development of scholarship. A letter written on behalf of the Universal House of Justice, dated 24 April 2008, emphasized the importance of Bahá'í scholarship 'to enrich the intellectual life of the Bahá'í community, to explore new insights into the Bahá'í teachings and their relevance to the needs of society, and to attract the investigation of the Faith by thoughtful people from all backgrounds'. In short, it had potential to assist teaching, consolidation, social action and public discourse. The letter expressed the hope that each national Bahá'í community would eventually be able to establish its own Association for Bahá'í Studies with its own journal.[30]

Interest in Bahá'í Studies continued to grow. Religious studies texts increasingly included the Bahá'í Faith in sidebars, sections of chapters or entire chapters. The University of California at Los Angeles inaugurated a chair for the study of the history of the Iranian Bahá'í community in its Middle East Studies programme in 2011. Research on the Iranian Bahá'í community became more common, thereby recognizing its role in the emergence of modern Iran and recognizing its continuous persecution as an important aspect of Iranian history. Non-Bahá'í Iranians, who often had ignored the Bahá'í Faith or participated in a conspiracy of silence about it, increasingly condemned its persecution and defended its rightful place in Iranian society. Their vocal defence of the Bahá'í Faith coincided with a recrudescence of persecution against it. Starting in 2006, the number of Bahá'ís in prison began to rise sharply. A group of Bahá'í and Muslim youth in Shiraz who were offering literacy classes to poor children were arrested, the Muslims were released, and the Bahá'ís were sentenced to prison. Many Bahá'í cemeteries and holy places that had escaped earlier demolition were destroyed. Attacks on the Bahá'í Faith in the Iranian media were unrelenting and included such ludicrous charges as the Bahá'ís control the BBC and the Voice of America.[31] But for the first time it was possible for Iranians to hear the Bahá'í responses through Bahá'í satellite radio and television broadcasts in Persian and numerous Bahá'í websites. Persian media outside Iran, also, increasingly provided accurate information about the Bahá'í Faith.

After the disbanding of all Bahá'í institutions in Iran in 1983, the Universal House of Justice had appointed a committee of seven, called the Yárán or 'the friends', to carry out very basic tasks such as registering Bahá'í marriages (civil marriage does not exist in Iran and Bahá'ís cannot have an Islamic, Christian, Jewish or Zoroastrian marriage in Iran without renouncing their Faith). The Yárán had informed the government of its existence and in some cases had even written the government or met with government officials about attacks on the Bahá'ís. In March and May 2008, the seven were arrested. The international outcry was vigorous, putting the Iranian government in an extremely difficult position; executing the Yárán would damage diplomatic and even economic relations with important countries, but releasing them was unthinkable. Nobel Peace Prize laureate Shirin Ebadi took their case; as a result she received death threats. Her office in Tehran was raided and all files confiscated. After 2 years of imprisonment, the Yárán were finally put on trial for espionage, propaganda against the Islamic republic, the establishment of an illegal administration and corruption on Earth. After six brief court sessions where virtually no evidence was presented and only brief meetings with attorneys were allowed, in 2010 the Yárán were sentenced to 20 years in prison. The sentence was later reduced to 10 years and then reinstated to 20 years.[32]

A renewed effort was also made to destroy the Bahá'í Institute for Higher Education (BIHE) in 2007 and 2011. Classrooms, computers and libraries were again confiscated and websites temporarily blocked. Faculty inside Iran were arrested and offered the choice of signing a pledge not to continue teaching for BIHE or imprisonment; most chose the latter. In 2011, seven administrators and teachers were arrested, and, after a show trial, were sentenced to 4 to 5 years in prison. The international response included a video condemnation by Nobel Peace Prize laureates Desmond Tutu and Jose Ramos-Horta, a call for action by movie stars, criticism by the Secretary-General of the United Nations, several protest letters signed by hundreds of academics, an open letter of condemnation signed by the heads of 48 medical schools in the United States, resolutions by academic organizations, condemnation by the European Parliament and other legislative bodies, an inquiry into the persecution of Iran's Bahá'ís in the Canadian Senate led by Canada's first Muslim Senator and a campaign to get them freed sponsored by Amnesty International.[33] BIHE continues to provide Iranian Bahá'í students access to a university education.

The Egyptian Bahá'í community faced renewed discrimination as well, but took bold action to defend themselves. All Egyptians are required to have government-issued identity cards, which are essential for opening a bank account, obtaining a driver's license, enrolling in a university, obtaining employment and dozens of other daily tasks. The identification card has a space for 'religion' and in the past some Bahá'ís were able to convince local issuers to put 'Bahá'í' there; others were able to get 'other' in the field or convinced officials to leave it blank. But when the Egyptian government began to computerize its records in the early 2000s, it decided that the religion field had to be filled with either Jew, Christian or Muslim; nothing else was allowable. At that point Bahá'ís were unable to get identity cards.

In response, the Bahá'ís sued the Egyptian government. Egyptian human rights organizations supported them. The controversy went public and Bahá'ís debated Islamic clerics about their rights on Egyptian television, in the newspapers and on international Arab-language channels such as al Jazeera. In April 2006 a lower administrative court upheld the right for the Bahá'ís to have 'Bahá'í' on their cards, but the Supreme Administrative Court reversed the decision. A second suit called for a dash or 'other' to be entered into the religion field and succeeded, even though two Muslim lawyers appealed it. In 2009 the Supreme Administrative Court upheld the right of the Bahá'ís to such cards and after several months of delay, they were finally issued. After the overthrow of the government in early 2011, the Bahá'ís of Egypt addressed a letter to their fellow countrymen about Egypt's future.[34]

Bahá'ís also had difficulties in some Central Asian countries, the Caucasus and Romania. In other parts of the world, however, the Bahá'í community achieved emancipation. Indonesia lifted its ban on Bahá'í institutions in 2000, allowing the election of local Spiritual Assemblies and a National Spiritual Assembly for the first time in four decades. Indonesia still does not recognize Bahá'í marriages, however, and it is difficult for Bahá'ís to obtain birth certificates for their children as a result. The fall of Saddam Hussein allowed the Bahá'í Faith to organize again in Iraq, and Bahá'í communities exist in Afghanistan again. The government of Vietnam gave the Bahá'í Faith full legal recognition in 2008, allowing its National Spiritual Assembly to be elected for the first time since 1975. After a long and slow recovery from genocide, the Bahá'ís of Burundi were able to re-elect their National Spiritual Assembly in 2011 after a lapse of 17 years.[35]

In 2011–13, the Bahá'ís of Europe and North America celebrated the hundredth anniversary of 'Abdu'l-Bahá's visit to their continents. With a century of learning about ways to take the Bahá'í Faith to others, they could look back at his many accomplishments with new eyes. He was a master of public discourse, tuning his presentations to the understandings and needs of his audience. He was an exemplar of social action in his meetings with children's classes, his encouragement of the education of women, his visits to settlement houses and summer camps for youth, his care for the sick and his generosity to the poor. He was a brilliant teacher of the Faith to high and low alike, attracting people through his personality as well as his uplifting spiritual insights and his penetrating humour. He could accompany seekers and new Bahá'ís on their spiritual journey in order to strengthen their faith and fire up their dedication to serve Bahá'u'lláh. In short, he was the perfect example of the holistic approach to fellow human beings that the House of Justice was calling on Bahá'ís to achieve. Above all, 'Abdu'l-Bahá could see the end in the beginning, the brilliant civilization that the Bahá'í Faith was capable of creating, in the halting and feeble steps the Bahá'ís of his day were able to accomplish. It gave Bahá'ís perspective on their own checkered efforts and the pressing purpose for which they had sacrificed.

CHAPTER TWELVE

An evolving faith

In its century and half, the Bahá'í Faith has developed a reciprocal, iterative learning process to oversee the expansion of its community and the development of its teachings. The head of the Faith – first Bahá'u'lláh, then 'Abdu'l-Bahá, then Shoghi Effendi and now the Universal House of Justice – issued guidance about a particular subject, which was gradually disseminated to the community. The believers studied the guidance, consulted about it, acted on it and reflected on the results so they could refine their application of it. The head of the Faith encouraged some results, discouraged others and offered additional guidance, which then triggered a second iteration of the process.

The reciprocal process was possible for several reasons. The community trusted the head of the Faith, so the guidance was listened to and implemented with minimal resistance or opposition. Trust was possible because the community not only believed in, but felt that it had experienced a divine promise of infallibility in the guidance of all the heads of the Faith.

In a sense, this reciprocal, iterative process was not new. The disciples of Jesus, Muhammad and Buddha all trusted their master to guide them, and to the extent the historical sources are reliable, they suggest that the same process of guidance, implementation and new guidance prevailed. Muhammad experienced new revelations to clarify earlier ones, and the Buddha modified his advice as the Buddhist community grew; for example, he agreed to the establishment of an order of nuns after initially refusing to sanction one. The Bahá'í experience was new, however, for both theological and technological reasons. Theologically, a strong claim to ongoing infallible guidance was made from the very beginning (as opposed to the claims made later by institutions in other religions), which helped to keep the community focused and unified.

Technologically, the Bahá'í Faith came along at a time when the steamship, the telegraph, the railroad and modern postal systems made effective central control of a worldwide movement practical. The reciprocal and iterative process can be seen throughout Bahá'í history. Almost every aspect of modern Bahá'í community life was refined this way. Bahá'u'lláh specified that his religion was not to have clergy and that Houses of Justice were to be formed in every place consisting of at least nine members. 'Abdu'l-Bahá, seeing that the name was causing confusion, changed it temporarily to 'Spiritual Assembly' and specified that the members were to be chosen by secret ballot. Shoghi Effendi, seeing how the secret ballot was used in different places, specified that there was to be no mentioning of names, nominations or campaigning before a vote, and fixed the number of Assembly members temporarily at nine. 'Abdu'l-Bahá defined the manner of election of the secondary House of Justice (which came to be known as the National Spiritual Assembly) to be by delegates elected locally in districts, and the election of the Universal House of Justice to be by all the members of the secondary Houses of Justice. Bahá'u'lláh, 'Abdu'l-Bahá, Shoghi Effendi and the Universal House of Justice all determined the responsibilities of the Spiritual Assemblies, and the Universal House of Justice still modifies them from time to time.

A similar process refined the institution of the Nineteen Day Feast. The Báb established the calendar of 19 months consisting of 19 days each (19 times 19 is 361) and gave each month its name. Bahá'u'lláh accepted the calendar and modified it slightly by specifying that the four intercalary days (necessary to raise the total number of days in the year from 361 to 365) would fall before the month of fasting (26 February to 1 March), as would the leap day every fourth year. The Báb exhorted his followers to gather once every 19 days for prayer and fellowship. Bahá'u'lláh, in the Kitáb-i-Aqdas, enjoined 'a feast, once in every month', thereby establishing the Bahá'í Nineteen Day Feast.[1] 'Abdu'l-Bahá emphasized the Feast and made it the central community gathering; no Sabbath observance was ever established for Bahá'ís.* To the devotional and social aspects of the Feast implied in the Aqdas, Shoghi Effendi added a

---

*The Bahá'í Faith has no day of the week on which work should be suspended. Its 'Sabbath' is Friday, but there are no required observances on that day.

period to discuss community business; in the west, Bahá'í communities had already been holding community business meetings, so this was a modification of an existing practice. More recently, the Universal House of Justice has explained that non-Bahá'ís could be present for the discussion of routine community business. In this way, the institution of Feast came into existence gradually, over more than a century. Its implementation continues to develop. Common Bahá'í activities and efforts often evolved in a similar fashion. By encouraging Bahá'ís to hold meetings for information and hospitality in their homes, everyone became involved in teaching the Faith and dependence on trained teachers was lessened. At some point in the 1930s someone coined the term 'fireside' for this activity. Shoghi Effendi even urged that the Bahá'ís hold a fireside in their homes every 19 days, thereby giving Bahá'u'lláh's exhortation for the holding of a monthly 'feast' a different potential meaning.

Bahá'ís had been moving to new localities to establish their Faith since the time of Bahá'u'lláh, but in Shoghi Effendi's ministry it became an organized and coordinated effort with specified goals, and the term 'pioneer' was coined for such a person. Bahá'ís had come together to study the authoritative texts of their Faith and implement its guidance in their lives since the time of Bahá'u'lláh. At some point the term 'deepening' was coined for the activity and it was then adopted by the Bahá'í institutions. As the need for training large numbers of Bahá'ís in community-building skills became urgent, a new educational activity, the 'study circle', developed alongside the older, more informal deepenings, sponsored and coordinated by training institutes and utilizing a systematic curriculum.

Efforts to improve the social and economic conditions of people have been a part of the Bahá'í community as far back as the nineteenth century, and were a part of many Bahá'í communities in the Occident before 1912. Shoghi Effendi, however, encouraged the American Bahá'ís to focus their energies on spreading the Bahá'í Faith, with the result that in his 36-year ministry the Faith was taken to most countries of the world and its membership doubled. The American Bahá'ís did little to bring about social or economic change during that time; they had no resources left to devote to it. Social and economic development projects – most of them simple – became a priority for Bahá'í communities in the developing

world starting in the 1940s and 1950s, because of the serious lack
of educational and health services there. They were added to the
priorities of the Bahá'í community worldwide by the Universal
House of Justice through two messages in 1983, one of which
noted the 'dynamic coherence' that had to exist 'between the spiritual and practical requirements of life on earth'.[2] The establishment of training institutes, study circles and core activities caused a
shift in human resources and a temporary de-emphasis on projects
to improve social and economic conditions, until the Universal
House of Justice added them to the current (2011–16) Five Year
Plan, reconceived and redefined under the rubric of 'social action'.
The House of Justice again stressed the importance of coherence
between social action and efforts to spread the Bahá'í Faith. Public
discourse, another endeavour with a long history in the Bahá'í
community, had never been a priority before 2011, and had been
little discussed. It will be interesting to see how social action and
public discourse develop as priorities of the Bahá'í community in
this plan and the next (2016–21). The House of Justice's call for the
process of systematic learning to be extended to a wider range of
human endeavours suggests that training courses in social action
and public discourse may be developed.

Particularly noteworthy has been the emphasis on planning.
Bahá'u'lláh coordinated efforts to spread the Bahá'í Faith as
closely as primitive communications between the Holy Land and
the Orient would allow. He appointed four Hands of the Cause
in Iran to coordinate the community there and sent some of them
on international trips to spread the Faith. 'Abdu'l-Bahá utilized
cables, postal systems, emissaries and personal travel to strengthen
Bahá'í communities and penned the Tablets of the Divine Plan to
define the Faith's long-term expansion goals. Shoghi Effendi used
the National Spiritual Assembly of the United States and Canada
to embark on a series of expansion plans (the first Seven Year Plan,
1937–44, and the second Seven Year Plan, 1946–53), then gave a
master plan to all the National Spiritual Assemblies (the Ten Year
Crusade, 1953–63) to take the Bahá'í Faith everywhere in the free
world. The Universal House of Justice has continued the process
through plans of nine (1964–73), five (1974–9), seven (1979–86),
six (1986–92), three (1993–6), four (1996–2000), five (2001–6),
five (2006–11) and five (2011–16) years duration. Each plan was
more sophisticated than its predecessor.

Since 1996, learning how to coordinate and balance numerous emphases (teaching the Faith, consolidation, classes for children, programmes for junior youth and youth, enriching Bahá'í literature, developing Bahá'í scholarship and social action projects) has been an explicit goal. The Bahá'í World Centre often ran pilot projects in selected areas, examined the results, announced guidelines to the Bahá'í world, oversaw their implementation and modified the guidelines as experience was gained. The Nineteen Day Feast and the cluster reflection meeting have become venues where plans are reflected on, modified and tried again, strengthening and routinizing the iterative process of goal setting at the local level.

The result of these efforts has been an impressive expansion of the Bahá'í community. The World Christian Encyclopedia lists Christianity as the most widespread religion in the world (238 countries), followed by the Bahá'í Faith (218), Islam (204), Buddhism (126) and Hinduism (114).[3] Considering that the Bahá'í Faith has less than a hundredth as many members as the other faiths, this is a remarkable achievement. It has been possible because of systematic goal setting to send pioneers to every country in the world and because of the training and deepening processes that strengthen individual initiative among the believers. As a result of the latter, nine Bahá'ís are often enough to establish an active Spiritual Assembly in a capital city of a country and begin a growth process that probably would not occur if only nine Muslims, Christians or Buddhists were located in that same place.

The vast geographical diffusion that has been achieved has also resulted in a considerable expansion of membership. In 1900, the Bahá'í world probably had about 100,000 members in Iran, a few thousand more in the rest of the Middle East and Central Asia, a few hundred in the United States, India and Burma, and a dozen or two in Europe. Culturally, it was heavily dependent on the Islamic world. By 1963 the membership had grown to 400,000 and half were located outside the Islamic world. By 1990 the membership had hit 5 million, with no more than 300,000 in Iran and perhaps 10,000 more elsewhere in the Middle East. The vast majority of the community was of Christian, Hindu or various indigenous cultural backgrounds, with substantial numbers from Buddhist and Jewish backgrounds as well. The Bahá'í community was beginning to sink deep cultural roots all around the world, expressed in local music, dance, art and other symbolism.

The potential for further expansion of the membership in the developing world remains enormous, but human resources are the bottleneck, which the new system of training institutes and core activities is designed to remove. Expansion in the developed world (North America, Europe, Japan, Australia, New Zealand), has considerably slowed since the 1980s, but in most of those areas all religions have struggled to maintain their membership numbers, and many have shrunk in size. The fifty-fold expansion in Bahá'í membership that occurred in the twentieth century is certainly possible in the twenty-first, but even if a more modest expansion occurs (say, from 5 million to 25 million), the Bahá'í Faith will be larger than Judaism, Jainism and Sikhism.

Because of their consultative approach to problems, their Faith's exhortation to consort with the followers of all religions, their emphasis on virtue and principle and their interests in education and development, Bahá'ís already play a significant role in interfaith organizations, international development efforts, and among the non-governmental organizations working at the United Nations. As the capacities of the Bahá'í community grow and its membership increases, these role can only expand.

Less predictable is the shape of the Bahá'í community as it advances towards the future. Like a tree, the Bahá'í Faith continuously adds growth rings in the form of new understandings of its teachings and new institutions and agencies to implement them. The older heartwood – consisting of the Feast, the Spiritual Assembly and other venerable institutions – recently have had added to them the core activities emphasizing prayer and education, and like the outer sapwood rings of a tree, the core activities have brought vitality to the whole. The core activities themselves may not be permanent – when the sapwood transitions to become heartwood, some of it dies, but it nevertheless contributes strength to the tree – but the emphasis on education is securely grounded in the authoritative texts of the Faith. A religion focusing on independent investigation of truth and the unity of humanity through spiritually elected institutions by spiritually transformed individuals, rather than hierarchy or clergy, must educate and develop its members. Consequently one can predict the development of new understandings, new capacities, new innovations and new institutions as the Bahá'í Faith expands and implements its vision of the unity of humankind.

NOTES

Chapter One

1 Research Department of the Universal House of Justice to the Universal House of Justice, 1 October 2010 (copy in author's personal papers), provides the latest statistics on the writings of Bahá'u'lláh, the Báb, 'Abdu'l-Bahá and Shoghi Effendi. The estimate of 8 per cent of Bahá'u'lláh's writings translated into English was arrived at by taking all the works of Bahá'u'lláh available in the Ocean programme (available at http://bahai-education.org/ocean/; it has all of Bahá'u'lláh's writings available in English) and pasting them into a Word document, which totalled 1,063 pages and 479,028 words.

2 The Universal House of Justice, *The Compilation of Compilations*, I, 228.

Chapter Two

1 Bahá'u'lláh, *Gleanings from the Writings of Bahá'u'lláh*, 64.

2 'Abdu'l-Bahá, in *Bahá'í Prayers*, 101.

3 Bahá'u'lláh, *The Arabic Hidden Words*, no. 68.

4 Shoghi Effendi, *The World Order of Bahá'u'lláh*, 42.

5 Shoghi Effendi, *Messages to America*, 27; Shoghi Effendi, *The World Order of Bahá'u'lláh*, 41.

6 'Abdu'l-Bahá, *Bahá'í World Faith*, 230.

7 'Abdu'l-Bahá, quoted in Shoghi Effendi, *The Lights of Divine Guidance*, vol. 2, 50.

8 'Abdu'l-Bahá, *Promulgation of Universal Peace*, 191–2.

9 Bahá'ís do not normally conduct worship on a weekly basis, as do mosques, churches and synagogues. The Nineteen Day Feast occurs once every Bahá'í month (a Bahá'í month lasts 19 days, there being

19 Bahá'í months in a solar year). It was initiated by Bahá'u'lláh, developed by 'Abdu'l-Bahá (who made it a Bahá'í community event every Bahá'í month involving worship and social portions) and refined by Shoghi Effendi (who added the portion for consultation on community business).

10 'Abdu'l-Bahá, in *Bahá'í Prayers*, 138.

11 Bahá'u'lláh, *Kitáb-i-Aqdas*, para. 58.

12 'Abdu'l-Bahá, in *Bahá'í World Faith*, 401.

13 Bahá'u'lláh, *Gleanings from the Writings of Bahá'u'lláh*, 259.

14 Ibid., 270.

15 Momen, 'Baha'i Schools in Iran', 101.

16 'Abdu'l-Bahá, *The Secret of Divine Civilization*, 32.

17 Bahá'u'lláh, *Kitáb-i-Aqdas*, 46.

18 Ibid., 30.

19 'Wisdom-Talks of 'Abdu'l-Bahá, given at Chicago, IL, 30 April–5 May 1912, 9, a supplement to *Star of the West*, 3(3) (28 April 1912).

20 Bahá'u'lláh, in *Consultation: A Compilation*, 3.

21 'Abdu'l-Bahá, in *Consultation: A Compilation*, 5.

22 Ibid.

23 Ibid.

24 Ibid., 7.

25 'Abdu'l-Bahá, *Tablets of the Divine Plan*, 53.

26 Shoghi Effendi, *Bahá'í Administration*, 88.

27 If a tie vote occurs in any Bahá'í election and one of the persons tied for the post is a member of a minority, the tie is broken in favour of the minority and a second round of voting is unnecessary.

28 Letter written on behalf of Shoghi Effendi, in *The Lights of Divine Guidance*, vol. 2, 67–8.

29 Ibid.

30 Shoghi Effendi, *The World Order of Bahá'u'lláh*, 145.

31 'Abdu'l-Bahá has also compared the Nineteen Day Feast to the 'Lord's Supper', that is, the Eucharist, presumably to compare the spiritual unity each is supposed to bring. Here I refer specifically to the term 'body of Christ', present in the believers during the Eucharist, and the Bahá'í Administrative Order brought about through the act of voting.

32 The author, in 28 years as a Bahá'í, has never heard of anyone attempting to influence a Bahá'í election and only once has heard an allusion as to whom someone was planning to vote for.

33 Shoghi Effendi, *Bahá'í Administration*, 64.

34 Bahá'u'lláh states of the House of Justice that 'God will verily inspire them with whatsoever He willeth' (*Tablets of Bahá'u'lláh Revealed after the Kitáb-i-Aqdas*, 68) and requires everyone to obey it (Ibid., 27). In 'Abdu'l-Bahá's Will and Testament, 14, 'Abdu'l-Bahá states the Universal House of Justice is 'the source of all good and freed from all error'; in *Some Answered Questions* 172, he says the House has 'conferred infallibility'.

35 David Smith, 'The Bahá'í Community and Group Identity', paper presented at the Canadian Association for Studies on the Bahá'í Faith, 1976. It should be noted that Bahá'ís completed the survey at Nineteen Day Feasts, which are not usually attended by less active Bahá'ís; hence the survey reflects the attitudes of more active Bahá'ís.

36 Only Bahá'ís in good administrative standing can make monetary contributions to the Bahá'í Faith; non-Bahá'ís and Bahá'ís under sanctions cannot.

37 Note that persons who oppose the Bahá'í Faith but who never have claimed to be Bahá'ís or who have resigned their membership are not considered Covenant breakers.

38 David B. Barrett, George T. Kurian and Todd M. Johnson, *World Christian Encyclopedia*, 18.

39 *The Federalist Papers by Alexander Hamilton, James Madison and John Jay*, 43.

40 Bahá'u'lláh, *Tablets of Bahá'u'lláh Revealed after the Kitáb-i-Aqdas*, 93; Shoghi Effendi, *World Order of Bahá'u'lláh*, 203.

41 Duane Herrmann, email communication, 15 November 2011; Herrmann, 'Theodore Russell Livingston Served His Community'.

42 This was Dorothy Nelson (1928–) who was appointed by President Jimmy Carter and served 1979–95; see www.fjc.gov/servlet/nGetInfo?jid=1742&cid=999&ctype=na&instate=na.

43 To give a few examples: when South Africa, under apartheid, passed a law forbidding blacks to enter through the front doors of houses owned by whites, some Bahá'ís boarded up their front doors and asked everyone to enter through the back door. When South Africa passed a law forbidding non-profit and religious organizations to have governing boards that were racially mixed, all the white Bahá'ís resigned from the local spiritual assemblies, which henceforth had only blacks as members. When, about 1980, a city in Iran ordered the heads of about 100 Bahá'í households to report to the police station, the women went, arguing that the Bahá'í principle of equality of the sexes meant that either the man or the woman could be the head. The police station, unprepared to arrest about 100 women, let them go.

44 Shoghi Effendi, *The World Order of Bahá'u'lláh*, 42.

45 'Abdu'l-Bahá, quoted in Shoghi Effendi, *God Passes By*, 238.

Chapter Three

1 Bahá'u'lláh, *Gleanings from the Writings of Bahá'u'lláh*, 46–7.

2 Ibid., 5.

3 'Abdu'l-Bahá, *Some Answered Questions*, 202.

4 Bahá'u'lláh, *Gleanings from the Writings of Bahá'u'lláh*, 261.

5 Ibid., 65.

6 Hatcher, *The Purpose of Physical Reality*, 78–83.

7 Brown, "Abdu'l-Bahá's Response to the Doctrine of the Unity of Existence', 1.

8 I am indebted to Dr Roland Faber for this and several other points in Chapter Three.

9 Bahá'u'lláh, *Gleanings from the Writings of Bahá'u'lláh*, 65.

10 Ibid., 50.

11 Ibid., 67–8.

12 'Abdu'l-Bahá, *Some Answered Questions*, 108–9, 114.

13 'Abdu'l-Bahá, *Promulgation of Universal Peace*, 463.

14 Bahá'u'lláh, *Gleanings from the Writings of Bahá'u'lláh*, 173.

15 While all the Manifestations identified in the Bahá'í authoritative texts have been male, there is no statement that women cannot be Manifestations.

16 Bahá'u'lláh, *Gleanings from the Writings of Bahá'u'lláh*, 174.

17 www.etymonline.com.

18 *The Compilation of Compilations*, vol. I, 19.

19 'Abdu'l-Bahá, *Some Answered Questions*, 164–5.

20 Bahá'u'lláh, *Tablets of Bahá'u'lláh Revealed after the Kitáb-i-Aqdas*, 146; 'Abdu'l-Bahá, *Tablets of Abdul-Baha Abbas*, vol. 2, 469; 'Abdu'l-Bahá, *Some Answered Questions*, 133; Bahá'u'lláh, *Epistle to the Son of the Wolf*, 157; Collins, 'Mormonism and the Bahá'í Faith', www.bahai-studies.ca/journal/files/jbs/3.2%20Collins.pdf (accessed 15 October 2011). The claim that Shoghi Effendi may have called Joseph Smith a 'seer' is not part of the Bahá'í authoritative texts, but the report of an oral statement.

21 Bahá'u'lláh, *Tablets of Bahá'u'lláh*, 149.

22 The Báb, *Selections from the Writings of the Báb*, 109.

23 Taherzadeh, *The Revelation of Bahá'u'lláh*, vol. 1, 35–6.

24 Bahá'u'lláh, quoted in Shoghi Effendi, *The Advent of Divine Justice*, 80.

25 Letter written on behalf of the Universal House of Justice, 14 September 1987, available in Ocean electronic library.

26 Bahá'u'lláh, Kitáb-i-Íqán, 89; also see Collins, 'Islám's Tahríf: Implications for the Bahá'í Faith'.

27 See for example Momen, *Hinduism and the Bahá'í Faith*, ix–x; Chew, 'The Great Tao', 17.

28 Bahá'u'lláh, *Synopsis and Codification of the Kitáb-i-Aqdas*, 25.

Chapter Four

1 Bahá'u'lláh, *Gleanings from the Writings of Bahá'u'lláh*, 67; Bahá'u'lláh, *The Arabic Hidden Words*, no. 13.

2 Bahá'u'lláh, *Gleanings from the Writings of Bahá'u'lláh*, 67–8; Bahá'u'lláh, *The Arabic Hidden Words*, no. 13; Shoghi Effendi, *Directives from the Guardian*, 86.

3 Bahá'u'lláh, *The Arabic Hidden Words*, no. 31.

4 Bahá'u'lláh, *Prayers and Meditations by Bahá'u'lláh*, selection 181.

5 Bahá'u'lláh, *Kitáb-i-Aqdas*, para. 10, 13.

6 Ibid., para. 18.

7 Bahá'u'lláh, *Kitáb-i-Íqán*, 40; 'The Importance of Obligatory Prayer and Fasting', selections xvii, xviii.

8 Bahá'u'lláh, *Kitáb-i-Aqdas*, para. 149.

9 See a description of the siege of Fort Shaykh Tabarsí in Chapter Six.

10 Bahá'u'lláh, *Kitáb-i-Aqdas*, para. 2, 3, 4, 5.

11 Ibid., para. 1.

12 *Bahá'í Prayers*, 105.

13 'Abdu'l-Bahá, *Selections from the Writings of 'Abdu'l-Bahá*, 117.

14 Ibid., 118.

15 Shoghi Effendi, quoted in Bahá'u'lláh, *Kitáb-i-Aqdas*, 207.

16 Universal House of Justice to an individual believer, 27 October 2010, quoted in National Spiritual Assembly of the Bahá'ís of the United

States to the American Bahá'í community, 3 January 2011, author's personal papers.

17 This and the next two paragraphs are a summary of Walbridge, 'Bahá'í Laws on the Status of Men', 28–9.

Chapter Five

1 Bahá'u'lláh, *Gleanings from the Writings of Bahá'u'lláh*, selections CVI, CIX.

2 Bahá'u'lláh, *Kitáb-i-Aqdas*, para. 33; *Tablets of Bahá'u'lláh Revealed after the Kitáb-i-Aqdas*, 34, 156.

3 Bahá'í International Community, *Turning Point for All Nations*, part IVA.

4 'Abdu'l-Bahá, quoted in Esslemont, *Bahá'u'lláh and the New Era*, 79.

5 Shoghi Effendi, quoted in *Kitáb-i-Aqdas*, 192.

6 Ibid., 193

7 Usually pronounced in English mash-rek-ool-az-kar.

8 *Kitáb-i-Aqdas*, note 53, 190–1.

9 Bahá'u'lláh, *Gleanings from the Writings of Bahá'u'lláh*, 289.

10 'Abdu'l-Bahá, *Tablets of the Divine Plan*, 54.

11 Universal House of Justice Ridván 2011 message to the Bahá'ís of the World, author's personal papers.

12 Shoghi Effendi, *The Promised Day is Come*, 118.

13 'Abdu'l-Bahá, *Foundations of World Unity*, 100.

14 Bahá'u'lláh, *The Summons of the Lord of Hosts*, para. 1.182.

15 *The Compilation of Compilations*, extracts 1569 and 1571.

16 Universal House of Justice, *The Promise of World Peace*, para. 29–34.

17 Ibid., para. 19.

18 Shoghi Effendi, *Directives from the Guardian*, 19.

19 'Abdu'l-Bahá to Agnes Parsons, in Mahmúd-i-Zarqání, *Mahmúd's Diary*, 207.

20 Universal House of Justice, quoted in the compilation 'Promoting Entry by Troops', 9.

21 Bahá'u'lláh, *Gleanings from the Writings of Bahá'u'lláh*, extract CIV.

22 Shoghi Effendi, *World Order of Bahá'u'lláh*, 203.

Chapter Six

1 Abbas Amanat, *Resurrection and Renewal*, 114–21.

2 'The Bab, "Journey towards God"', translated by Todd Lawson, accessible at www.h-net.org/~bahai/trans/vol2/suluk/suluktr.htm.

3 Shoghi Effendi, *God Passes By*, 23.

4 Saiedi, *Gate of the Heart*, 114.

5 Ibid., 49.

6 Amanat, *Resurrection and Renewal*, 215–16.

7 Ibid., 261.

8 Ibid., 370; Geula, *Iranian Bahá'ís from Jewish Backgrounds*, 79–81; Fereydun Vahman, 'The Conversion of Zoroastrians to the Baha'i Faith', in Brookshaw, *The Baha'is of Iran*, 35; Maneck, 'The Conversion of Religious Minorities to the Bahá'í Faith in Iran: Some Preliminary Observations', 37.

9 Momen, *Selection from the Writings of E. G. Browne on the Bábí and Bahá'í Religions*, 318.

10 Saiedi, *Gate of the Heart*, 357–71.

11 Afnan, 'The Báb's Bayán: An Analytical Summary', 8. This work provides an excellent summary of the contents of the Persian and Arabic Bayáns.

12 MacEoin, *Sources of Early Bab Doctrine and History*, 85.

13 Nabíl, *The Dawn-breakers*, 297.

14 Ruhe, *The Robe of Light*, 86–7.

15 Zabihi-Moghaddam, 'The Babi-State Conflict at Shaykh Tabarsi', 97.

16 Ruhe, *The Robe of Light*, 109.

17 Rabbani, *The Bábís of Nayriz: History and Documents*, Vol. 2: *Witnesses to Bábí and Bahá'í History*, 120.

18 Nabil, *The Dawn-breakers*, 465–99.

19 Walbridge, 'Babi Uprising in Zanjan, The', in *Iranian Studies* 29: 3–4, 339–62; accessible at http://bahai-library.com/walbridge_babi_uprising_zanjan (accessed 14 October 2011); Shoghi Effendi, *God Passes By*, 44–7.

20 Firuz Kazemzadeh, Kazem Kazemzadeh and Howard Garey, 'The Báb: Accounts of His Martyrdom', *World Order*, 8(1) (Fall 1973), 32.

21 Shoghi Effendi, *God Passes By*, 24.

Chapter Seven

1 Bahá'u'lláh, *Epistle to the Son of the Wolf*, 22.

2 Bahá'u'lláh, *The Summons of the Lord of Hosts*, para. 1.6–1.7.

3 Bahá'u'lláh, *The Arabic Hidden Words* no. 14; Persian Hidden Words, no. 54.

4 Bahá'u'lláh, Seven Valleys, 4; Shoghi Effendi, *God Passes By*, 140.

5 Saiedi, *Logos and Civilization*, 82.

6 Rabbani, 'The Conversation of the Great-Uncle of the Báb', 34–5.

7 Shoghi Effendi, *God Passes By*, 139.

8 Buck, *Symbol and Secret*, 4–5; Saiedi, *Logos and Civilization*, 119–26.

9 Firuz Kazemzadeh, personal communication.

10 Bahá'u'lláh, quoted in Saiedi, *Logos and Civilization*, 242.

11 Bahá'u'lláh, quoted in Shoghi Effendi, *The World Order of Bahá'u'lláh*, 198.

12 Ibid., 135; Hatcher, *The Ocean of His Words*, 154–6.

13 Bahá'u'lláh, Tablet to Pope Pius IX, in *The Summons of the Lord of Hosts*, para. 121, 122, 138.

14 Bahá'u'lláh, Kitáb-i-Aqdas, para. 121. The reference to 'Abdu'l-Bahá as the one who had 'branched' from Bahá'u'lláh was vague, as Bahá'u'lláh referred to all his sons as 'branches', but in a later work Bahá'u'lláh clarified that this passage referred specifically to 'Abdu'l-Bahá.

15 Bahá'u'lláh, Kitáb-i-Aqdas, para. 90, 91, 93.

16 Moojan Momen, email communication, 4 December 2011.

17 Buck, 'An Introduction to Bahá'u'lláh's Book of Certitude with Two Digital Reprints of Early Lithographs'.

18 Moojan Momen, email to the Tarikh listserv, 14 November 2011, copy in author's personal papers.

19 Harper, *Lights of Fortitude*, 3–18.

20 Amanat, 'Messianic Expectation and Evolving Identities: The Conversion of Iranian Jews to the Baha'i Faith', 7–9; Vahman, 'The Conversion of Zoroastrians to the Baha'i Faith', 31–3.

21 Lee, 'The Rise of the Bahá'í Community of 'Ishqábád', 4–9.

22 Vahman, 'The Conversion of Zoroastrians to the Baha'i Faith', 31–3.

23 Momen, 'Jamál Effendi and the early spread of the Bahá'í Faith in South Asia', 49–53. All the information in the next few paragraphs about Jamál Effendi is summarized from this article.

24 Harper, *Lights of Fortitude*, 125–7.

25 Brown, 'Introduction', in ['Abdu'l-Bahá], *Traveller's Narrative*, II, xxxix–xl.

26 Balyuzi, *Bahá'u'lláh: The King of Glory*, 420–8.

Chapter Eight

1 Brown, 'Introduction', in ['Abdu'l-Bahá], *Traveller's Narrative*, II, xxxvi.

2 Taherzadeh, *The Covenant of Bahá'u'lláh*, 117.

3 Stockman, *The Bahá'í Faith in America*, vol. 1, 13–16, 163.

4 Ella Goodall, quoted on Stockman, *The Bahá'í Faith in America*, vol. 1, 151, 152.

5 Banani, 'The Writings of 'Abdu'l-Bahá', 69–70.

6 Stockman, *The Bahá'í Faith in America*, vol. 1, 158–62, 173–7.

7 Taherzadeh, *The Revelation of Bahá'u'lláh: Mazra'ih and Bahjí, 1877–92*, 290–1.

8 Momen, 'Baha'i Schools in Iran', 98, 100.

9 Rastigár. *Kitáb-i-Táríkh-i-Hazrat-i-Sadru's-Sudúr*, 42; Iraj Ayman, personal communication, 13 January 2012; Moojan Momen, personal email communication, 18 January 2012.

10 Fazel and Foadi, 'Bahá'í Health Initiatives in Iran: A Preliminary Survey', 128; Stockman, *The Bahá'í Faith and American Protestantism*, 172.

11 Ibid., 168.

12 Ibid.

13 Ibid., 180–2.

14 Stockman, *The Bahá'í Faith in America, 1900–1912: Early Expansion, Vol. 2*, 185; Nakhjavani, *The Maxwells of Montreal*, 320.

15 Stendardo, *Leo Tolstoy and the Bahá'í Faith*, 26–31.

16 Ma'ani, 'The Interdependence of Bahá'í Communities: Services of North American Bahá'í Women in Iran', 23–33; 'Adelaide Sharp', in *The Bahá'í World: An International Record, Vol. XVII, 1976–1979*, 419.

17 Stockman, *The Bahá'í Faith in America*, vol. 2, 290.

18 Ibid., 275–88, 306–14.

19 Stockman, *The Bahá'í Faith and American Protestantism*, 173; *Bahá'í News*, 1(8) (1 August 1910), 10; Momen, 'Baha'i Schools in Iran', 101.

20 Stockman, *The Bahá'í Faith in America*, vol. 2, 28, 59–60, 109.

21 Stockman, *The Bahá'í Faith and American Protestantism*, 173; Stockman, *The Bahá'í Faith in America*, vol. 2, 118, 249–52.

22 Ibid., 245.

23 Rabbani, "Abdu'l-Bahá's Proclamation on the Persecution of Bahá'ís in 1903', which provides a new translation for a treatise by 'Abdu'l-Bahá, originally published as Hadji Mirza Heider Ali, *Bahäi Martyrdoms in Persia in the Year 1903*, A.D. (Chicago: Bahá'í Publishing Society, 1904 and 1917). It is not clear why the authorship was attributed to Heider Alí, a prominent contemporary Bahá'í; possibly 'Abdu'l-Bahá did not want his authorship known.

24 Milani, 'Bahá'í Discourses on the Constitutional Revolution', 141–53.

25 Bushrui and Jenkins, *Kahlil Gibran: Man and Poet*, 9, 125; Ives, *Portals to Freedom*, 29.

26 Stockman, *'Abdu'l-Bahá in America*, 354.

27 For information about Dubois's view of 'Abdu'l-Bahá, see Stockman, *'Abdu'l-Bahá in America*, 110, 114; Tussing, 'FINISHING THE WORK: 'Abdu'l-Bahá in Dublin, 1912', 11.

28 Balyuzi, *'Abdu'l-Bahá*, 414–19.

29 Ibid., 420–5.

30 Garis, *Martha Root*, 88.

31 Hassall, 'Dunn, Clara (1869–1960) and Dunn, John Henry Hyde (1855–1941); Dunbar, 'Leonora Stirling Armstrong', 734; Sims, *Raising the Banner in Korea: An Early Bahá'í History*, 2.

32 Rabbání, *The Priceless Pearl*, 30–1.

33 Balyuzi, *'Abdu'l-Bahá*, 436–40; Vader, *For the Good of Mankind*, 70–80.

Chapter Nine

1 Malouf, *Unveiling the Hidden Words*, 13–14.

2 Khadem, *Shoghi Effendi in Oxford*, 7–15.

3 'Abdu'l-Bahá, *Will and Testament of 'Abdu'l-Bahá*, 11.

4 Shoghi Effendi to 'Dearly beloved brethren and sisters in 'Abdu'l-Bahá', 21 January 1922, in *Bahá'í Administration*, 15–17.

5 Weinberg, *Ethel Jenner Rosenberg*, 206–9.

6 Rabbání, *The Priceless Pearl*, 250.

7 Shoghi Effendi, *Bahá'í Administration*, 20.

8 Shoghi Effendi, *God Passes By*, 48.

9 Shoghi Effendi, *Messages to America*, 29.

10 Shoghi Effendi, *Messages to the Bahá'í World*, 1950–57, 63; Bahá'u'lláh, *Tablets of Bahá'u'lláh Revealed after the Kitáb-i-Aqdas*, 5.

11 Shoghi Effendi, *Messages to the Bahá'í World*, 84.

12 Weinberg, *Ethel Jenner Rosenberg*, 211–24.

13 Ibid., 227–8.

14 Bramson-Lerche, 'Some Aspects of the Development of the Bahá'í Administrative Order in America, 1922–36', 260–5.

15 Stockman, *The Bahá'í Faith in America*, volume 2, 45–6, 178–9; Braun, *From Strength to Strength*, 7.

16 For additional analysis of demographic data, see Stockman, *The Bahá'í Faith and American Protestantism*, chapter 2.

17 Hassall, 'Notes on the Bábí and Bahá'í Religions in Russia and Its Territories', 60–8; *The Bahá'í World: An International Record*, vol. 14, 1963–8, 479–80.

18 Heller, *Lidia*, 153–4, 239–41; *The Bahá'í World: A Biennial International Record*, vol. X, 1944–1946, 20–5. Zamenhof was a Polish citizen and a resident of the Warsaw ghetto.

19 Shoghi Effendi, *Bahá'í Administration*, 66.

20 Shoghi Effendi, *The Advent of Divine Justice*, 22.

21 Ibid., 29.

22 Ibid., 33–4.

23 Shoghi Effendi, *The Promised Day is Come*, 113, 115, 123, 124.

24 Bahá'u'lláh, *Gleanings from the Writings of Bahá'u'lláh*, 185, 326. The various Qur'án translations were found online.

25 Rabbání, *The Priceless Pearl*, 217.

26 Ibid., 91.

27 Shoghi Effendi, *Messages to the Bahá'í World*, 74.

28 Morrison, *To Move the World*, 246; Smith, 'The Global Distribution of Bahá'ís in the 1930s', 122–6, 131.

29 Braun, *From Strength to Strength*, 25–6.

30 Dahl, 'Three Teaching Methods Used during North America's First Seven Year Plan', 2–10.

31 *The Bahá'í World: A Biennial International Record, Vol. XI, 1946–1950*, 20–36.

32 Rabbání, *The Priceless Pearl*, 225.

33 Ibid., 252.

34 Shoghi Effendi, *Messages to the Bahá'í World*, 18–21.

35 *The Bahá'í World: An International Record, Vol. XIII, 1954–1963*, 785.

36 Bach, *A Meeting with Shoghi Effendi*, 30–41.

37 Stockman, *A History of the Bahá'í Faith in Rhode Island, 1866–1979*, 28.

38 Hassall, 'The Origins of the Bahá'í Faith in the Pacific Islands: The Case of the Gilbert and Ellice Islands', 43.

39 The entire story of Ray and Elena Fernie is taken from Hassall, 'The Origins of the Bahá'í Faith in the Pacific Islands: The Case of the Gilbert and Ellice Islands'.

40 Stockman, 'Americas', 8–9. For background information on the Alcaldes Mayores Particulares, see Waskar Ari-Chachaki (2008–10), 'Between Indian Law and Qullasuyu Nationalism: Gregorio Titiriku and the Making of AMP Indigenous Activists, 1921–1964', *Bolivian Studies Journal*, 15–17, 91–113, available at http://bsj.pitt.edu/ojs/index.php/bsj/article/view/11/136.

41 Garlington, 'Bahá'í Conversions in Malwa, Central India', 164–7.

42 Bahá'í World Centre, *Ministry of the Custodians*, 140, 270, 344.

43 Hassall, 'Bahá'í History in the Formative Age: The World Crusade, 1953–1963', 9, 11; *The Bahá'í World, 1994–95: An International Record*, 9.

44 *The Bahá'í World, vol. XIII, 1954–1963*, 292.

45 Shoghi Effendi, *Messages to the Bahá'í World*, 58–9, 127.

46 Harper, *Lights of Fortitude*, 302.

47 Bahá'í World Centre, *Ministry of the Custodians*, 234.

48 Ibid., 168.

49 Ibid., 196, 225.

50 'The Proclamation of Joel Bray Marangella', 12 November 1969, available at http://bahai-guardian.com.

51 Ibid.

52 Ibid.

53 Ibid.

54 See, for example, Robert Balch, Gwen Farnsworth, and Sue Wilkins, *When the Bombs Drop: Reactions to Disconfirmed Prophecy in a Millennial Sect* (Missoula, MN: University of Montana, 1982).

Chapter Ten

1 *The Bahá'í World: An International Record, Vol. XIV, 1963–1968,* 427.

2 Ibid., 59.

3 Universal House of Justice, *Messages from the Universal House of Justice: 1963–1986,* 5.1.

4 Ibid., 20.4a, 59.2, 59.5.

5 *The Bahá'í World: An International Record, Vol. XIV, 1963–1968,* 102–4.

6 Universal House of Justice, *Messages of the Universal House of Justice, 1963–1986,* 18.4.

7 Warburg, *Citizens of the World,* 246–9.

8 Universal House of Justice, *1964–1973 Analysis of the Nine Year International Teaching Plan of the Bahá'í Faith,* 14.

9 Weixelman, 'The Traditional Navajo Religion and the Bahá'í Faith', 31–51.

10 Ibid., 40–50.

11 'Only Six Indian Reservation Goals Still Unopened', *National Bahá'í Review,* July 1968, 4; 'Makah Reservation Council Fire Announced', *National Bahá'í Review,* July 1968, 12; 'Bahá'í Indian Council Formed', *National Bahá'í Review,* October 1969, 7; 'A New Day in Indian Teaching', *National Bahá'í Review,* 12.

12 'Southern Teaching Conference: The Challenge of Chattanooga' *National Bahá'í Review,* November 1969, 1–4; 'Frogmore Conference a Success', Ibid., 13.

13 *National Bahá'í Review,* October 1970, 7.

14 *Bahá'í News,* no. 480 (March 1971): 1.

15 The per cent of mass-taught believers from the early 1970s who still had good addresses was calculated by the author in 2008 because he

had access to the American national Bahá'í database, as an employee at the Bahá'í National Centre.

16 Ruhi Institute, *Learning About Growth*, 1–2.

17 Ibid., 2–3 (italics in the original).

18 Ibid., 3–17.

19 Ibid., 17–19.

20 Ibid., 18–24.

21 *The Bahá'í World: An International Record*, Vol. *XVIII, 1979–1983*, 127; *The Bahá'í World: An International Record*, Vol. *XIX, 1983–1986*, 67.

22 Harper, *Lights of Fortitude*, 177–9.

23 *The Bahá'í World: An International Record*, Vol. *XIV, 1963–1969*, 204–6; *The Bahá'í World: An International Record*, Vol. *XV, 1973–1976*, 279.

24 *Messages from the Universal House of Justice: 1963–1986, The Third Epoch*, 141.4.

25 Stockman, 'United States Membership and Enrollment Statistics, 1894–2005'; *The Bahá'í World: An International Record*, Vol. *XVII, 1976–1979*, 93, 215.

26 *The Bahá'í World: An International Record*, Vol. *XVIII, 1979–1983*, 465–72.

27 *The Bahá'í World: An International Record*, Vol. *XVII, 1976–1979*, 197–201.

28 Peter Smith, 'Bahá'í Studies Seminars at the University of Lancaster, 1977–1980', in *The Bahá'í World: An International Record*, Vol. *XVIII, 1979–1983*, 204–5.

29 Geoffrey Nash, 'The Persecution of the Bahá'í Community of Írán, Riḍván 1979–Riḍván 1983', *The Bahá'í World: An International Record*, Vol. *XVIII, 1979–1983*, 251–2.

30 Ibid., 252–5.

31 Ibid., 254–6, 338.

32 Ibid., 259.

33 In the mid-1980s, the author and a group of Bahá'ís was told by Guity Vahidi, the surviving member of the second National Spiritual Assembly, that the resulting third National Spiritual Assembly was often made up of Bahá'ís who had received only two or three votes at the 1978 national Bahá'í convention, because everyone with more votes had already been martyred.

34 Momen, 'Social and Economic Development in an Iranian Village: The Bahá'í Community of Saysan', 80–1; Ibid., 262–7.

35 *The Bahá'í World: An International Record*, Vol. XIX, 1983–1986, 188–94.

36 *The Bahá'í World: An International Record*, Vol. XX, 1986–1992, 390–7.

37 *The Bahá'í World: An International Record*, Vol. XIX, 1983–1986, 130.

38 Puran Stevens, former head of Refugee Services, Bahá'í National Centre, Wilmette, IL, personal communication, 8 January 2011.

39 *The Bahá'í World: An International Record*, Vol. XIX, 1983–1986, 62–6, 81.

40 Ruhi Institute, *Learning About Growth*, 28–38; *The Bahá'í World: An International Record*, Vol. XVIII, 1979–1983, 92, 111, 114–19.

41 *The Bahá'í World: An International Record*, Vol. XVIII, 1979–1983, 117–19, 123.

42 Stockman, 'United States Membership and Enrollment Statistics, 1894–2005'; 'The Seven Year Plan', 12–13. Since deaths and Bahá'ís moving out of the country have not been factored in (both would have been small), the withdrawal number should be considered very approximate.

43 *Messages of the Universal House of Justice, 1963–1986: The Third Epoch of the Formative Age*, 453.1–453.10.

44 *The Bahá'í World: An International Record*, Vol. XX, 1986–1992, 115–31.

45 http://news.bahai.org/human-rights/iran/education/feature-articles/secret-blueprint.

46 *The Bahá'í World: An International Record*, Vol. XX, 1986–1992, 192.

47 Universal House of Justice, *A Wider Horizon*, 79.

48 Stockman, 'United States Membership and Enrollment Statistics, 1894–2011'; *The Bahá'í World: An International Record*, Vol. XX, 1986–1992, 192.

49 Ibid.

50 *The Bahá'í World, 1992–93: An International Record*, 98–102.

51 *The Bahá'í World, 1993–94: An International Record*, 42.

52 *The Three Year Plan, 1993–1996: Summary of Achievements*, 25, 33, 35, 40, 159, 164–5.

53 Ibid., 28–67, 82–112, 132.

Chapter Eleven

1   Shoghi Effendi, *Citadel of Faith*, 117; *Turning Point*, 4.17–4.19.

2   Ibid., 4.27, 4.29, 30.1.

3   Ibid., 1.28.

4   Ibid., 14.1–14.13.

5   Bahá'í World Centre, *The Five Year Plan, 2006–2011: Summary of Achievements and Learning*, 41.

6   *The Bahá'í World, 1995–96: An International Record*, 317; *The Bahá'í World, 1999–2000: An International Record*, 313; *Turning Point*, 19.2, 21.2, 21.14, 22.2.

7   *The Bahá'í World, 1995–96: An International Record*, 117–21.

8   Ibid., 121–3.

9   *Turning Point*, 21.17–21.20.

10 Bahá'í World Centre, *The Five Year Plan, 2006–2011: Summary of Achievements and Learning*, 66.

11 *Turning Point*, 19.5.

12 Ibid., 22.4–22.7.

13 Ibid., 22.10.

14 Ibid., 30.2.

15 Ibid., 27.2.

16 Ibid., 29.4, 35.26.

17 Bahá'í World Centre, *The Five Year Plan, 2001–2006: Summary of Achievements and Learning*, 5; Lample, *Revelation and Social Reality*, 87.

18 *Turning Point*, 35.21, 35.31.

19 Bahá'í World Centre, *Attaining the dynamic of growth*, 21–2, 45–6, 53–4; Lample, *Revelation and Social Reality*, 90–1.

20 The misunderstandings about the nature of the core activities and the Ruhi sequence are drawn from personal experience or reports by friends. 'United States Bahá'í Membership and Enrollment Statistics, 1895–2011'.

21 *Turning Point*, 35.26, 36.4–36.6.

22 Ibid., 35.21–35.25.

23 Bahá'í World Centre, *The Five Year Plan, 2006–2011: Summary of Achievements and Learning*, 1–3, 7, 22.

24 Ibid., 8–9, 11–12; Stockman, 'United States Bahá'í Membership and Enrollment Statistics, 1894–2011'.

25 Universal House of Justice to the National Spiritual Assembly of the Bahá'ís of Australia, 4 January 2009, para. 3.

26 Ibid., para. 4–5.

27 Universal House of Justice, *The Five Year Plan, 2011–2016: Messages of the Universal House of Justice*, 1.5, 1.9, 1.10.

28 Ibid., 1.31–1.32, 1.5.

29 Ibid., 3.1, 3.11.

30 Department of the Secretariat of the Universal House of Justice to an individual, 24 April 2008, available at http://bahai-epistolary.blogspot.com/2009/01/dear-all-i-share-following-letter-on.html.

31 http://news.bahai.org/story/861.

32 http://news.bahai.org/human-rights/iran/yaran-special-report/.

33 http://news.bahai.org/story/864; www.iranpresswatch.org/.

34 http://news.bahai.org/story/726.

35 http://news.bahai.org/story/647; http://news.bahai.org/story/822.

Chapter Twelve

1 Bahá'u'lláh, *Kitáb-i-Aqdas*, para. 57.

2 Universal House of Justice, *Messages From the Universal House of Justice, 1963–1986: The Third Epoch*, 358.6, 379.1–379.10a.

3 David B. Barrett, George T. Kurian and Todd M. Johnson, *World Christian Encyclopedia: A Comparative Survey of Churches and Religions in the Modern World*, vol. 1, 4.

BIBLIOGRAPHY

(Note: All Bahá'í authoritative texts are available online at the Bahá'í Reference Library, http://reference.bahai.org/en/, where they can be downloaded in searchable form) 'Abdu'l-Bahá. *A Traveller's Narrative Written to Illustrate the Episode of the Báb*. Translated by Edward G. Browne. 2 vols. Cambridge: Cambridge University Press, 1891.

'Abdu'l-Bahá. *Some Answered Questions*. Wilmette, IL: Bahá'í Distribution Service, 1981.

Afnan, Muhammad. 'The Báb's Bayán: An Analytical Summary'. *World Order*, 31.4: 7–16.

Amanat, Mehrdad. 'Messianic Expectation and Evolving Identities: The Conversion of Iranian Jews to the Baha'i Faith'. In Brookshaw, Dominic Parviz and Seena B. Fazel (eds), *The Baha'is of Iran: Socio-historical Studies*. London: Routledge, 2008, pp. 6–29.

The Báb. *Selections from the Writings of the Bab*. Haifa: Bahá'í World Centre, 1978.

Bach, Marcus. *A Meeting with Shoghi Effendi*. Oxford: Oneworld, 1993.

Bahá'í International Community. *Turning Point for all Nations: A Statement of the Bahá'í International Community on the Occasion of the 50th Anniversary of the United Nations*. New York: Office of Public Information, 1995.

Bahá'í World Centre. *Attaining the Dynamic of Growth: Glimpses from five continents*. Haifa: Bahá'í World Centre, 2008.

—. *The Five Year Plan, 2001–2006: Summary of Achievements and Learning*. Haifa: Bahá'í World Centre, 2006.

—. *The Five Year Plan, 2006–2011: Summary of Achievements and Learning*. Haifa: Bahá'í World Centre, 2011.

—. *The Ministry of the Custodians, 1957–1963: An Account of the Stewardship of the Hands of the Cause*. Haifa: Bahá'í World Centre, 1992.

—. *The Three Year Plan, 1993–1996: Summary of Achievements*. Haifa: Bahá'í World Centre, 1997.

Bahá'u'lláh. *Writings of Bahá'u'lláh: A Compilation*. New Delhi: Bahá'í Publishing Trust, 1986.

Balyuzi, H. B. 'Abdu'l-Bahá: The Centre of the Covenant of Bahá'u'lláh. Oxford: George Ronald, 1971.
—. Bahá'u'lláh: The King of Glory. Oxford: George Ronald, 1980.
Banani, Amin. 'The Writings of 'Abdu'l-Bahá'. World Order, 6.1: 67–74.
Barrett, David B., George T. Kurian and Todd M. Johnson. World Christian Encyclopedia: A Comparative Survey of Churches and Religions in the Modern World. 2 vols. 2nd edn. Oxford: Oxford University Press, 2001.
Bramson-Lerche, Loni. 'Some Aspects of the Development of the Bahá'í Administrative Order in America, 1922–36'. In Moojan Momen (ed.), Studies in Bábí and Bahá'í History, Volume One. Los Angeles: Kalimát Press, 1982, pp. 255–300.
Braun, Eunice. From Strength to Strength: The First Half Century of the Formative Age of the Bahá'í Era. Wilmette, IL: Bahá'í Publishing Trust, 1978.
Brookshaw, Dominic Parviz and Seena B. Fazel. The Baha'is of Iran: Socio-historical Studies. London: Routledge, 2008.
Brown, Keven. 'Abdu'l-Bahá's Response to the Doctrine of the Unity of Existence'. The Journal of Bahá'í Studies, 11.3/4: 1–24.
—. 'A Bahá'í Perspective on the Origin of Matter'. The Journal of Bahá'í Studies, 2.3: 15–42.
Buck, Christopher. 'An Introduction to Bahá'u'lláh's Book of Certitude with Two Digital Reprints of Early Lithographs'. At www.h-net. org/~bahai/bhpapers/vol2/iqan&sn.htm. Accessed 14 November 2011.
—. Symbol and Secret: Qur'an Commentary in Bahá'u'lláh's Kitáb-i Íqán. Los Angeles: Kalimát Press, 1995.
Bushrui, Suheil and Joe Jenkins. Kahlil Gibran: Man and Poet. Oxford: Oneworld, 1998.
Chew, Phyllis Ghim Lian. 'The Great Tao'. The Journal of Bahá'í Studies, 4.2: 11–39.
Collins, William P. Bibliography of English-language Works on the Bábí and Bahá'í Faith, 1845–1985. Wilmette, IL: Bahá'í Publishing Trust, 1991.
—. 'Islám's Tahríf: Implications for the Bahá'í Faith'. World Order, 11.1: 22–31.
Dahl, Roger. 'Three Teaching Methods Used during North America's First Seven Year Plan'. The Journal of Bahá'í Studies, 5.3: 1–15.
Dunbar, Hooper. 'Leonora Stirling Armstrong'. In The Bahá'í World: An International Record, Vol. XVIII, 1979–83. Haifa: Bahá'í World Centre, 1986, pp. 733–38.
Fazel Seena and Minou Foadi. 'Bahá'í Health Initiatives in Iran: A Preliminary Survey'. In Dominic Parviz Brookshaw and Seena B. Fazel

(eds), *The Baha'is of Iran: Socio-historical Studies*. London: Routledge, 2008, pp. 122–40.

Gail, Marzieh. *Six Lessons on Islam*. Wilmette, IL: Bahá'í Publishing Trust, 1953.

Garis, M. R. *Martha Root: Lioness at the Threshold*. Wilmette, IL: Bahá'í Publishing Trust, 1983.

Garlington, William. 'Bahá'í Conversions in Malwa, Central India'. In Juan R. Cole and Moojan Momen (eds), *Studies in Bábí and Bahá'í History, Volume Two: From Iran East and West*. Los Angeles: Kalimát Press, 1984, pp. 156–85.

Geula, Arsalan. *Iranian Bahá'ís from Jewish Background: A Portrait of an Emerging Bahá'í Community*. Claremont, CA: Arsalan Geula, 2007.

Harper, Barron Deems. *Lights of Fortitude: Glimpses into the Lives of the Hands of the Cause of God*. Oxford: George Ronald, 1997.

Hassall, Graham. 'Bahá'í History in the Formative Age: The World Crusade, 1953–1963'. *The Journal of Bahá'í Studies*, 6.4: 1–21.

—. 'Dunn, Clara (1869–1960) and Dunn, John Henry Hyde (1855–1941)'. At http://www.bahai-encyclopedia-project.org/index. php?option=com_content&view=article&id=62:dunn-clara-and-j-hyde&catid=37:biography.

—. 'Notes on the Bábí and Bahá'í Religions in Russia and Its Territories'. *The Journal of Bahá'í Studies*, 5.2: 41–80.

—. 'The Origins of the Bahá'í Faith in the Pacific Islands: The Case of the Gilbert and Ellice Islands'. *The Journal of Bahá'í Studies*, 16.1/4: 33–59.

Hatcher, John S. *The Ocean of His Words: A Reader's Guide to the Art of Bahá'u'lláh*. Wilmette, IL: Bahá'í Publishing Trust, 1997.

—. *The Purpose of Physical Reality: The Kingdom of Names*. Wilmette, IL: Bahá'í Publishing Trust, 1978.

Heider Ali, Hadji Mirza ['Abdu'l-Bahá]. *Bahäi Martyrdoms in Persia in the Year 1903, A.D.* Chicago: Bahai Publishing Society, 1904 and 1917.

Hein, Kurt John. *Radio Bahá'í, Ecuador: A Bahá'í Development Project*. Oxford: George Ronald, 1988.

Heller, Wendy. *Lidia: The Life of Lidia Zamenhof, the Daughter of Esperanto*. Oxford: George Ronald, 1985.

Herrmann, Duane L. *Theodore Russell Livingston Served His Community*. Typescript, author's personal papers.

Ives, Howard Colby. *Portals to Freedom*. Birmingham, UK: George Ronald, 1948.

Khadem, Riaz. *Shoghi Effendi in Oxford*. Oxford: George Ronald, 1999.

Lample, Paul. *Revelation and Social Reality: Learning to Translate What Is Written into Reality.* West Palm Beach, FL: Palabra Publications, 2009.

Lee, Anthony A. 'The Rise of the Bahá'í Community of 'Ishqábád'. *Bahá'í Studies*, 5: 1–13.

Ma'ani, Baharieh Rouhani. 'The Interdependence of Bahá'í Communities: Services of North American Bahá'í Women in Iran'. *The Journal of Bahá'í Studies*, 4.1: 19–46.

Malouf, Diana Lorice. *Unveiling the Hidden Words: The Norms Used by Shoghi Effendi In His Translation of the Hidden Words.* Oxford: George Ronald, 1997.

Maneck, Susan Stiles. 'The Conversion of Religious Minorities to the Bahá'í Faith in Iran: Some Preliminary Observations'. *The Journal of Bahá'í Studies*, 3.3: 33–48.

Milani, Kavian. 'Baha'i Discourses on the Constitutional Revolution'. In Dominic Parviz Brookshaw and Seena B. Fazel (eds), *The Baha'is of Iran: Socio-historical Studies*. London: Routledge, 2008, pp. 141–55.

Momen, Moojan. 'Baha'i Schools in Iran'. In Dominic Parviz Brookshaw and Seena B. Fazel (eds), *The Baha'is of Iran: Socio-historical Studies*. London: Routledge, 2008, pp. 94–121.

—. 'Jamál Effendi and the early spread of the Bahá'í Faith in South Asia'. *Bahá'í Studies Review*, 9: 47–80.

—. *Selection from the Writings of E. G. Browne on the Babi and Baha'i Religions.* Oxford: George Ronald, 1987.

—. 'Social and Economic Development in an Iranian Village: The Bahá'í Community of Saysan'. *Bahá'í Studies Review*, 15: 67–81.

Morrison, Gayle. *To Move the World: Louis Gregory and the Advancement of Racial Unity in America.* Wilmette, IL: Bahá'í Publishing Trust, 1982.

Muhájir, Írán. 'Rahmatu'lláh Muhájir'. In *The Bahá'í World: An International Record, Vol. XVIII, 1979–1983.* Haifa: Bahá'í World Centre, 1986, pp. 651–59.

Nakhjavani, Violette. *The Maxwells of Montreal: Early Years, 1870–1922.* Oxford: George Ronald, 2011.

'A New Day in Indian Teaching'. *National Bahá'í Review*, April 1968, 12.

Rabbani, Ahang. 'Abdu'l-Baha's Proclamation on the Persecution of Baha'is in 1903'. *Bahá'í Studies Review*, 14.1: 53–67.

—. 'The Conversion of the Great-Uncle of the Báb'. *World Order*, 30.3: 19–38.

Rabbaní, Rúhíyyih. *The Priceless Pearl.* London: Bahá'í Publishing Trust, 1969.

Raman, S. P. 'My Quest for the Fulfillment of Hinduism'. *World Order*, 3.3: 20–28.

Rastigár, Nasr'lláh. *Kitáb-i-Táríkh-i-Hazrat-i-Sadru's-Sudúr*. Tehran: Lajnih-yi-Millí-i-Nashr-i-Áthár-i-Amrí, 104 BE/1947–8.

Ruhi Institute. *Learning About Growth: The Story of the Ruhi Institute and Large-scale Expansion of the Bahá'í Faith in Colombia*. Riviera Beach, FL: Palabra Publications, 1991.

Ruth J. Moffett. In *The Bahá'í World: An International Record, Vol. XVII, 1976–79*. Haifa: Bahá'í World Centre, 1981, 463–65.

Saiedi, Nader. *Gate of the Heart: Understanding the Writings of the Báb*. Waterloo, ON: Wilfrid Laurier Press, 2008.

—. *Logos and Civilization: Spirit, History, and Order in the Writings of Bahá'u'lláh*. Bethesda, MD: University Press of Maryland, 2000.

Shoghi Effendi. *The Advent of Divine Justice*. Wilmette, IL: Bahá'í Publishing Trust, 1966.

—. *Bahá'í Administration*. Wilmette, IL: Bahá'í Publishing Trust, 1968.

—. *The Promised Day Is Come*. Wilmette, IL: Bahá'í Publishing Trust, 1980.

—. *The World Order of Bahá'u'lláh*. Wilmette, IL: Bahá'í Publishing Trust, 1991.

Sims, Barbara R. *Raising the Banner in Korea: An Early Bahá'í History*. Tokyo: Bahá'í Publishing Trust of Japan, 1966.

Smith, Peter. *An Introduction to the Baha'i Faith*. Cambridge: Cambridge University Press, 2008.

—. 'The Global Distribution of Bahá'ís in the 1930s'. *Bahá'í Studies Review*, 15: 115–32.

Stendardo, Luigi. *Leo Tolstoy and the Bahá'í Faith*. Oxford: George Ronald, 1985.

Stockman, Robert H. *'Abdu'l-Bahá in America*. Wilmette, IL: Bahá'í Publishing Trust, 2012.

—. *A History of the Bahá'í Faith in Rhode Island, 1866–1979*. Typescript, 1980, author's personal papers.

—. *Americas*. Unpublished article for the Bahá'í Encyclopedia.

—. *The Bahá'í Faith and American Protestantism*. PhD dissertation, Harvard Divinity School, 1990.

—. *The Bahá'í Faith in America: Origins, 1892–1900, vol. 1*. Wilmette, IL: Bahá'í Publishing Trust, 1985.

—. *The Bahá'í Faith in America: Early Expansion, 1900–1912, vol. 2*. Oxford: George Ronald, 1995.

—. *United States Membership and Enrollment Statistics, 1894–2011*. Typescript, author's personal papers.

Taherzadeh, Adib. *The Covenant of Bahá'u'lláh*. Oxford: George Ronald, 1992.

—. *The Revelation of Bahá'u'lláh: Mazra'ih and Bahjí, 1877–92*. Oxford: George Ronald, 1987.

The Bahá'í World: A Biennial International Record, vol. X, 1944–1946. Wilmette, IL: Bahá'í Publishing Trust, 1949.

The Bahá'í World: A Biennial International Record, Vol. XI, 1946–1950. Wilmette, IL: Bahá'í Publishing Trust, 1952.

The Bahá'í World: An International Record, Vol. XIII, 1954–1963. Haifa, Israel: Universal House of Justice, 1970.

The Bahá'í World: An International Record, Vol. XIV, 1963–1968. Haifa, Israel: Universal House of Justice, 1974.

The Bahá'í World: An International Record, Vol. XV, 1973–1976. Haifa, Israel: Bahá'í World Centre, 1978.

The Bahá'í World: An International Record, Vol. XVII, 1976–1979. Haifa: Bahá'í World Centre, 1981.

The Bahá'í World: An International Record, Vol. XVIII, 1979–1983. Haifa: Bahá'í World Centre, 1986.

The Bahá'í World: An International Record, Vol. XIX, 1983–1986. Haifa: Bahá'í World Centre, 1994.

The Bahá'í World: An International Record, Vol. XX, 1986–1992. Haifa: Bahá'í World Centre, 1998.

The Bahá'í World, 1992–93: An International Record. Haifa: Bahá'í World Centre, 1993.

The Bahá'í World, 1993–94: An International Record. Haifa: Bahá'í World Centre, 1994.

The Bahá'í World, 1994–95: An International Record. Haifa: Bahá'í World Centre, 1996.

The Bahá'í World, 1995–96: An International Record. Haifa: Bahá'í World Centre, 1997.

The Bahá'í World, 1999–2000: An International Record. Haifa: Bahá'í World Centre, 2001.

The Seven Year Plan: Messages from the Universal House of Justice to the Bahá'ís of the World and of the United States, Naw-Rúz 1979, Announcing the Objectives of the Fourth Global Teaching Campaign. Wilmette, IL: Bahá'í Publishing Trust, 1980.

The Six Year Plan: Messages of the Universal House of Justice. Wilmette, IL: Bahá'í Publishing Trust, 1986.

Tussing, Phillip, *FINISHING THE WORK: 'Abdu'l-Bahá in Dublin, 1912.* Unpublished Typescript.

Universal House of Justice. *1964–1973 Analysis of the Nine Year International Teaching Plan of the Bahá'í Faith.* Wilmette, IL: Bahá'í Publishing Trust, 1964.

—. *Messages from the Universal House of Justice: 1963–1986, The Third Epoch.* Wilmette, IL: Bahá'í Publishing Trust, 1996.

—. *The Five Year Plan, 2011–2016: Messages of the Universal House of Justice.* West Palm Beach, FL: Palabra Publications, 2011.

—. *The Promise of World Peace*. Haifa, Israel: Bahá'í World Centre, 1985.

—. *Turning Point: Selected Messages of the Universal House of Justice and Supplementary Material, 1996–2006*. West Palm Beach, FL: Palabra Publications, 2006.

—. *A Wider Horizon: Selected Messages of the Universal House of Justice, 1983–1992*. Riviera Beach, FL: Palabra Publications, 1992.

Vader, John Paul. *For the Good of Mankind: August Forel and the Bahá'í Faith*. Oxford: George Ronald, 1984.

Vahman, Fereydun. 'The Conversion of Zoroastrians to the Baha'i Faith'. In Brookshaw, Dominic Parviz and Seena B. Fazel (eds), *The Baha'is of Iran: Socio-historical Studies*. London: Routledge, 2008, pp. 30–48.

Walbridge, Linda and John Walbridge. 'Bahá'í Laws on the Status of Men'. *World Order*, 19.1/2: 25–36.

Warburg, Margit. *Citizens of the World: A History and Sociology of the Baha'is from a Globalisation Perspective*. Leiden: Brill, 2006.

Weinberg, Robert. *Ethel Jenner Rosenberg: The Life and Times of England's Outstanding Bahá'í Pioneer Worker*. Oxford: George Ronald, 1995.

Weixelman, Joseph O. 'The Traditional Navajo Religion and the Bahá'í Faith'. *World Order*, 20.1: 31–51.

Whitehead, O. Z. *Some Early Bahá'ís of the West*. Oxford: George Ronald, 1976.

—. *Some Bahá'ís to Remember*. Oxford: George Ronald, 1983.

Zarandí, Nabíl. *The Dawn-breakers: Nabíl's Narrative of the Early Days of the Bahá'í Revelation*. Translated and edited by Shoghi Effendi. New York: Bahá'í Publishing Committee, 1932.

INDEX